TIME HAS COME

Other Books by Jim Bakker

The Prison Years: I Was Wrong

Prosperity and the Coming Apocalypse

The Refuge

More Than I Could Ever Ask
By Lori Graham Bakker

How to Prepare *Now* for Epic Events Ahead

TIME HAS COME

JIM BAKKER
with Ken Abraham

Published by Worthy Books, an imprint of Worthy Publishing Group, a division of Worthy Media, Inc., One Franklin Park, 6100 Tower Circle, Suite 210, Franklin, TN 37067.

HELPING PEOPLE EXPERIENCE THE HEART OF GOD

ebook available at www.worthypublishing.com

Audio distributed through Oasis Audio; visit www.oasisaudio.com

---

Library of Congress Control Number: 2012947227

ISBN: 978-1-61795-085-8 (hardcover w/jacket)

ISBN: 978-1-61795-365-1 (trade paper)

Published in association with Ted Squires Agency, Nashville, Tennessee

Cover Design: Mary Hooper, Milkglass Creative

Cover Image: iStock Photography

Printed in the United States of America

15 16 17 18 19 20 VPI 9 8 7 6 5 4 3

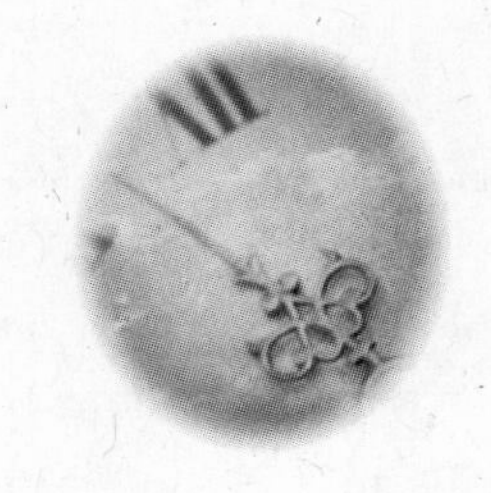

Dedication

We are now entering the days I write about in this book, days of betrayal and sorrow when the love of many is growing cold. More than ever I am so thankful for those who have faithfully walked by my side. I dedicate this book to them, men and women like Ben, Andrew, Mondo, and Maricela, who work every day to produce and edit our programs, doing whatever it takes to broadcast around the world. I wish I could tell you about every member of our ministry team and all the guests on our television show, and my wonderful board of directors, but it would fill another book. Without them and my faithful friends who pray for me, watch my program, and support my ministry, I would still be in a prison cell and not back in public ministry. I dedicate this book to them.

I also dedicate this book to my wonderful family. God has blessed me with children—Ricky, Marie, Claire, Lil' Lori, Maricela, Jamie, and Tammy Sue, my kids—who are the joy of my life and make my journey so worth traveling, even though bumpy at times. Moreover, I could not find a better wife or mother to care for this amazing family and to work by my side and minister with me every day around the world than my beautiful wife, Lori. God does restore.

God has beautifully and completely restored Lori's life as well. Pressured to abort her own babies in her youth, Lori now wants to help young women and girls make the right choice to give life to their unborn babies. The ministry of Lori's House will provide a place of safety and respite for girls who, like her, have had untimely pregnancies, but this time with a different outcome. It is a safe place that offers a different option to abortion. All of the proceeds from this book will go toward building Lori's House, and there is no greater cause anywhere, for her or me, than to help save innocent lives.

Lori's mom, Char Graham, is the best mother-in-law any man could have, and she has been by our side helping to guide and direct our ministry through calm and troubled waters. Having my sister Donna, who has been looking out for me for more than seventy-two years, living here in the Ozarks, and Lori's brother Mark, my grandson James, and just recently my cousin Pat, editor extraordinaire, also working with our ministry is, as Lori says, "more than I could ask."

It is not possible to name everyone to whom I want to acknowledge my debt of thanks, but you know I appreciate you more than I can possibly express.

I want to dedicate this book especially to all the interns in our broadcast ministry school who are building the "Generation NOW" network to reach this generation. My legacy!

This book would not be possible without my dear friend and co-writer, Ken Abraham.

Most of all I dedicate this book to Jesus, the One who never, never, never left me; nor will He you!

Contents

Contents

TIME HAS COME

1

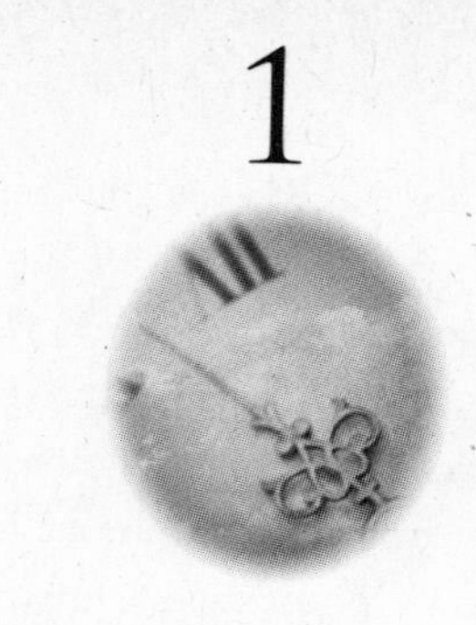

The Dawning

Sunday morning dawned unusually quiet on the rocky, sparsely populated island. Not that the burly Roman guards cared one way or the other. One day was the same as the next to them, another opportunity to badger and abuse the prisoners under their domination, as the overlords mercilessly extracted every bit of work possible from their wards.

The mineral mines and rock quarries were the only reason Rome cared about the isolated, barren turtle of terrain stuck out in the Aegean Sea. That and the fact the rugged island—thirty-five nautical miles from the tiny island of Miletus, the closest dry land, and approximately fifty-five miles from the major seaport at Ephesus on the southern coastline of Asia Minor—made for an ideal penal colony.

The deep and rough waters surrounding Patmos limited access to ferry boats and frigates. It was a virtually inescapable island where the forced labor crews had but two alternatives: work or die. The guards needed no weapons to corral and control the criminals in their charge, but they kept an iron boot on the throats of the prisoners. Few men banished to the dreaded isle ever left alive.

The grueling, arduous life on Patmos might drive young men insane, but for older men—such as John bar Zebedee who had lived for nearly a century—it was meant to be unbearable. Sometimes the torturous punishment perversely meted out on Patmos caused even conscience-seared, jaded soldiers to grimace.

John bar Zebedee was not dangerous. What was his crime? He hadn't killed anyone. He was no threat to anyone. He certainly was no thief. Even on this godforsaken rock, the old man gave away more of the foul, bug-infested food grudgingly dished up to prisoners than he ate himself.

So he'd written a record of a so-called Christ, a Messiah—Jesus, they called Him—a man the Romans had crucified half a century ago. John was convinced this criminal had risen from the dead and was still alive. Was that cause for him to be banished? Apparently, the emperor deemed the old man's public statements as seditious, even treasonous.

Since Domitian had come to the throne in AD 81, the emperor had become increasingly obsessed with power. Now almost fifteen years later, he referred to himself as a god and demanded worship from everyone in his domain. Anyone who refused to acknowledge Caesar as Lord was severely beaten, tortured, or banished to a work camp until he or she recanted or dropped dead.

John had refused to bow to the emperor, and he had steadfastly proclaimed absolute allegiance to only one Lord, the one to whom he had committed his life—this Jesus. In addition to his writings about the life of Christ, John's defiance of the emperor's egomaniacal edict had landed the aged apostle on the desolate rock known as Patmos. For nearly eighteen months, he had existed here on meager allotments of bread and brackish water. His simple linen and wool robes had long ago become a patchwork of rags that barely shielded his body from the scorching sun during the day or the fierce cold of the sea air at night.

Old John trudged over mounds of stone, lugging heavy loads of mineral rock. Accustomed to rigorous work, his strength rivaled that of men thirty years his junior. He was much stronger than he appeared, not simply because of good genes and good living, but because he seemed to draw on an inner reserve the other prisoners lacked. Once, though, he tripped, lost his footing, and fell onto some sharp-edged rocks, slicing open his leg. Pain rippled through his leg as blood coursed from the open wound.

"Come on, old man," a guard roared, unsheathing his sword and clanking it against a wagon filled with stones. "Get up! It's not time to rest yet." The sentinel roughly kicked John in the back, jolting the old man onto the sharp rocks again. More blood. John knew better than to remain on all fours. The guard's next kick would be to his head. The gray-haired elder stumbled to his feet, doubled over from the pain in his back and leg, but lurching forward, away from the guard and back toward the mine shaft where he had been excavating with the makeshift tools so generously provided by the Romans.

"May God forgive you," John said, his voice raspy, as he gasped for breath and swept a strand of long, matted hair away from his face.

Earlier, John might have responded much differently. Even the peace-loving Jesus had referred to John and his brother, James, as "Sons of Thunder," descriptive no doubt of their fiery dispositions. Over the years John's volatile side had mellowed, not with age, but with the knowledge that vengeance belonged to God. John refused to carry a grudge or to allow resentment toward the deviate emperor or his guards.

When Jesus was crucified in Jerusalem, even as He hung on the cross, He had asked John to care for His mother, Mary, and John had done so until she passed away. After Mary's burial, John began his own itinerant ministry, traveling from Jerusalem to various parts of Judea and as far away as Ephesus, telling the story of what he had experienced with Jesus.

By then the long-smoldering, latent revolutionary elements within Judea had ignited, the flames fanned by those obsessed with the delusion that the tiny province could throw off the heavy yoke of Rome, fomenting uprising after uprising against the occupiers. The zealous Jewish people became so odious to the emperor, he finally authorized the Roman general Titus to lay siege to Jerusalem until the Jews capitulated.

Titus spared no evil effort, leading his army to the city's walls during the height of Passover, the most sacred celebration in the Jewish religion. As hundreds of thousands of pilgrims clogged the city, Titus launched a vicious attack. The Jews responded by sequestering themselves behind the thick city walls. But within five months, in AD 70, Jerusalem's walls were breached and the city laid waste. On Mount Moriah, just inside the Eastern Gate, the Temple of God—rebuilt by the Jews after their return from exile in Babylon—was a mere shadow of the ornate beauty of Solomon's Temple before it, though nonetheless, a magnificent structure. As Titus's troops stormed the city, the temple was torn down stone by stone so each legionnaire would have a nugget of inlaid gold from the walls. The Romans slaughtered more than a million Jews, and a hundred thousand more were captured. Titus's troops crucified so many Jews during the campaign that the area around Jerusalem was left bereft of trees. Subsequent persecutions and dispersions of the Jews made moving northward an easy decision for John.

At first John traveled throughout Asia Minor in relative safety, headquartering his missionary efforts out of a small hillside house overlooking Ephesus. But then the persecutions spilled over onto the followers of Jesus during the reign of Nero, becoming more overt during the reign of horror spawned by Domitian. As each of Jesus' original disciples was martyred rather than renounce what he had seen, heard, and knew—that Jesus Christ was alive, that He was no longer entombed in Jerusalem, that His body had not been stolen, that He had risen from the dead and had appeared to them and to more than five hundred other people—John anticipated that he, too, faced a martyr's death.

Ironically, John was now something of a celebrity, albeit an unwitting one. He was the youngest of the Twelve, and he had outlived the others. As the last living eyewitness to so many secrets of Jesus' inner circle, John recounted incidents about the Lord's life, death, and resurrection to which he had been privy. There were always people who wanted to hear his version of the "good news." Recognizing that he was growing older and the personal witnesses were becoming fewer and fewer was motivation for John to write an account of what he knew about Jesus. But his primary reason for writing was, as he stated at the conclusion of his gospel, "that you may believe that Jesus is the Christ, the Son of God; and that believing you may have life in His name."[1] Consequently, John's Gospel was well received almost everywhere, that is, except Rome. There it had evoked the wrath of Domitian upon the aging apostle.

The Vision

As John toiled in a cave-like shaft on a Sunday morning, his mind drifted to the many times he had joined with fellow followers of the Way to worship on the Lord's day, the designation believers applied to Sunday as a weekly reminder of the resurrection of Jesus Christ. John had served the church in Ephesus for a number of years before his arrest, so sweet memories of men, women, and children of that church often flooded his thoughts. Sometimes, when he had been assigned to cart rock from one of Patmos's treacherous ridges, if the sky were clear, John could look across the Aegean and see the silhouette of the bustling seaport that had once been his home. He had also worshipped with the Way in Antioch, on the borders of Syria, where the believers were first called Christians, and he had visited a number of churches in Asia Minor. He had taught about Jesus the Christ in many fledgling churches in the lands north of Israel—at least until the day the soldiers seized him and sent him to Rome to stand trial.

Now, even in the midst of the awful circumstances on Patmos, the elderly saint kept his faith strong by recalling the words of Jesus as well as the Old Testament scriptures he had learned as a child. It was not uncommon for John to become immersed in the presence while he worked in the mines or the quarry. He sometimes slipped into a sublime awareness of God's majesty and was oblivious to all else around him. Without saying a word he was in the Spirit, in a state of praise and worship and exaltation of God that seemed to allow the Spirit to permeate his entire being. Despite the din of clanging picks and shovels and the obscene curses of the guards around him, John could be enveloped in the presence of God.

Thus he was on the Lord's Day when he heard a loud voice, crystal clear like the sound of a trumpet. Startled but not fearful, John understood the words, "Write in a book what you see, and send it to the seven churches: to Ephesus and to Smyrna and to Pergamum and to Thyatira and to Sardis and to Philadelphia and to Laodicea" (Revelation 1:11). John knew those churches. He had visited them, encouraging the believers in each congregation to hold fast to their faith, even in the face of Caesar's persecution and oppression.

More important, John recognized something familiar about the voice. He'd heard it a thousand times before, but never like this. It was *His* voice—the voice of Jesus!

John whirled to see the source, but to his surprise, he did not see Jesus. Instead, he saw seven golden lampstands. But wait! In the midst of the lampstands was a majestic figure like no human John had ever seen before. The figure was clothed in a garment down to his feet, the sort of robe a Jewish high priest might wear, with a golden belt of some kind around his chest. His head and hair looked like white wool, only brighter, like snow. His eyes were like fire. John dared not look at those eyes, yet he found it impossible to avoid them and not be attracted to them. The figure's penetrating eyes seemed to sear right through him, seeing his innermost being. The man's feet looked as though they were finely polished brass, as if refined in a furnace. But the voice sounded as powerful as a waterfall. The figure held in the right hand seven stars, and from his mouth was a two-edged sword. Yet his face was not contorted. Far from it. His countenance was radiant, like the sun on a bright day, shining in all its strength.

John's mind raced. His heart beat frantically. His mouth was suddenly dry. Yet for all of the figure's awesome majesty, John knew Him immediately. This was Jesus! Not the lowly Jesus whom John had known in Galilee, not the Jesus who was pummeled by Roman soldiers as He dragged His cross through the Jerusalem streets on His way to Golgotha, the place of the skull. This person was not like the close friend whom John had leaned against the last time he and the disciples had eaten together before the soldiers came that fateful night. He didn't look like the person who had appeared to the two believers on their way to Emmaus or the Jesus who had appeared to the disciples as they had hunkered down in fear three days after the crucifixion. No, this Jesus was regal in a sense John did not know was possible. Yet it was Jesus nonetheless.

As much as John loved Him, there was only one reaction that made any sense at this moment. Overwhelmed, somewhere between terror and awe, John fell at Jesus' feet as though he were a dead man.

John had anticipated the Lord's return for many years. Immediately after Jesus had ascended into heaven, John and the other followers expected Him to return within days, weeks, or months. As the years passed, they recognized that although Jesus had promised to come back for them and take them to the place He was preparing for them, they must have misunderstood the schedule. That did not dim their faith or deter His returning, however. Jesus had never lied to them, and everything He had ever predicted had come true, specifically and completely. John never doubted he would see Jesus again, but he never imagined he would meet Him like this!

John had often considered what it might be like to see Jesus again. He'd even wondered how he might greet Jesus on His return. Would he kiss His cheek in the traditional Jewish greeting? hug Him? shake His hand? Would he gush about his lost friend or inquire if now was the time for the fulfillment of all things? None of those gestures, heartfelt as they might be, seemed appropriate now.

Still lying prostrate, not certain that he was alive, much less conscious, John felt a hand on his shoulder. He raised his gaze to find Jesus standing next to him, His right hand on John.

"Do not be afraid," Jesus said to the aged apostle (v. 17).

As John stared up at Him in awe, the words somehow made sense. He felt his heart calm, his mind clear. Jesus said, "I am the first and the last, and the living One" (vv. 17, 18).

John gulped. Jesus was all that. In fact, He was more alive than John had ever seen Him. The old apostle dared not speak; he could only listen.

"I was dead," said Jesus (v. 18), as John tried to nod in understanding, recalling the crown of thorns on Jesus' head, the spear through His side, His body wrapped for burial and placed in the tomb offered by Joseph of Arimathea. There was no question that Jesus had been dead. John well knew that.

"Behold, I am alive forevermore," Jesus said, allowing John to scan His features again. "And I have the keys of death and of Hades" (v. 18).

Still in the Spirit, John's heart leaped nonetheless at the reminder that Jesus had conquered the hellish netherworld. Mesmerized by Jesus' voice and presence, John listened intently as He looked him in the eyes and said, "Write the things which you have seen, and the things which are, and the things which will take place after these things" (v. 19).

Whether Jesus noticed the look of amazement on John's face as he beheld Him standing among the seven lampstands, the old man couldn't be sure. But as if Jesus could read his mind, He explained, "The mystery of the seven stars which you saw in My right hand, and the seven golden lampstands: the seven stars are the angels of the seven churches, and the seven lampstands are the seven churches" (v. 20).

It was obvious that Jesus did not expect a reply, so John remained silent as He dictated specific messages for the seven churches in Asia Minor. But there was more—much more.

Time seemed to stand still as John continued in the Spirit and Jesus opened his heart and mind to see amazing events in heaven as well as astounding and staggering wonders that were soon to happen on earth. It was as though sights and sounds joined to produce a theater in John's mind. But this was no three-act play. The images kept coming. Some scenes John saw and heard were difficult to comprehend, images of things for which he had no context, but they were obviously real. Visions of heaven overwhelmed him, filling his heart with unutterable praises and worship. Some scenes John saw were disconcerting: portions of the world experiencing pressure-packed times of floods, famines, diseases, wars, earthquakes, signs in the skies and in the seas. Yet the overriding message that Jesus continually impressed on him both surprised and reassured him. Simply put, the prevailing message was, "Do not fear."

It was as though God Himself was speaking to John's heart and mind, saying, "I know you have had a difficult time, dear friend, and there are increasingly tumultuous times ahead. But I have never left you alone, nor will I ever. I understand the pain and loneliness you are experiencing, and I want you to know, in the end, it will have been worth it."

The visions continued to come. They were as powerful as a volcano yet as fresh as a waterfall, flowing at John faster than he could comprehend. To his amazement, his mind absorbed and processed the information easily, as though his mind had been enlightened in some way to understand things of the Spirit. At times Jesus Himself revealed specific events to John; at other times an angel transmitted the messages. Never, however, did John have any doubt that the words he was to record came from anywhere but the heart of God.

What Lies Ahead

John had no idea how long he was in the Spirit that Lord's Day, immersed in the power of God, oblivious to everything around him. The visions ran the gamut from the letters to the churches, to prophecies regarding the rise of a satanically inspired Antichrist, to the return of Christ, how Jesus would ultimately conquer all evil, and to the glories of the future existence of God's people when He initiates a new heaven and a new earth. Throughout every message was the inexorable declaration that Jesus Christ is King of kings and Lord of lords.

Finally, after what seemed like weeks but might have been only minutes, the elderly apostle awakened and saw that he was alone, lying on his back in a cool area of the mine. He slowly roused and sat up. His body felt like that of a teenager, robust and vigorous, ready to take on the world. John ran his hand through his matted hair. He looked down at the disheveled rags on his body. None of that mattered now. He must write exactly what had been indelibly etched on the photographic plates of his mind and what he could still see and hear so vividly.

"Hey, old man," another prisoner called out. "Are you all right? You were sleeping for a while."

"Yes, yes," John answered. "I'm fine. I can't recall when I've ever felt better."

"Good, because the guards will be coming back soon. They were ready to toss you on the scrap heap awhile ago. But just as they were ordering us to pitch you into the fire, a thunderstorm blew up outside. I've never seen lightning like that, and apparently neither had the guards. They took off for their barracks and left you right where you were. You are one lucky fellow, that's for sure."

"Far more than you know," John replied with a confident smile. He nodded and stood to his feet. There was much work to do. "Blessed, indeed," he said. John glanced at the bleak conditions around him. The oppressors were still there. The eyes of so many were still clouded by hopelessness. Nothing had changed, and yet everything had changed. John looked heavenward and whispered quietly, "Even so, Lord Jesus, come."[2]

This is the untold story of Revelation. This drama is the most fascinating and uplifting story ever told. It is the exciting conclusion to the mystery of the gospel. And the message for you and me is the same as it was for John: *Do not fear.* Yes, you will encounter a dangerous dragon stalking the earth for a season, but the Son is in a safe place. He is in the same safe place for you that He was for John. Granted, the Dragon is roaring and breathing fire, but he eventually will be destroyed, as will all who align themselves with him. The Son is absolute Lord today, and He will reign victoriously forever.

Now here's the really good news: He has promised that where He is, you can also live. He will never leave you or forsake you, and beyond that, He will soon return to earth to deal once and for all with evil. Your future with Him is secure, and the retirement plan is out of this world!

2

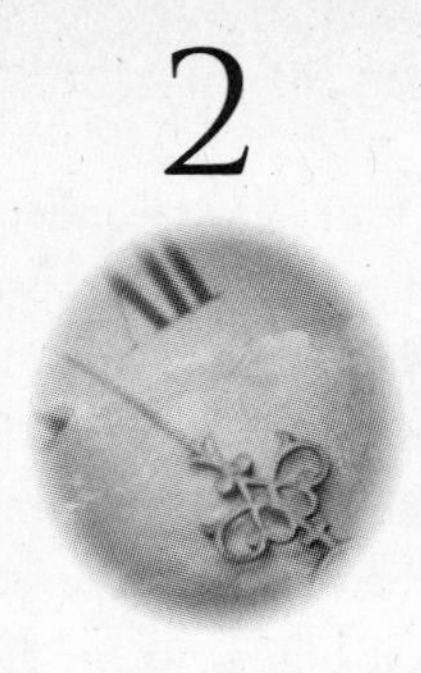

Don't Hit the Rocks!

W*hat am I supposed to do with this message?* The aged apostle pondered this question as he rolled up the scroll on which he was writing. *Certainly, there is hope in these times. Real hope, not some illusory hope built on lies and spiritual-sounding fabrications with less substance than fog. The hope is that the Christ child now reigns as king. But some of the other things I have seen cause my heart to shudder. Some teachers say that everything is getting better, that peace and prosperity are at hand. But I have seen and heard much that reveals even more difficult times will precede the Lord's return. I must warn my friends and family. I must let the church know that the Dragon is trying to lull us into complacency.*

In January 2012, all the charts were readily available. The sea lanes were clearly marked and warnings prominently posted. The information had been common knowledge for years. Yet the captain and crew of the cruise ship *Costa Concordia* ignored the truth of their charts and allowed the luxury liner to venture too close to the dangerous rocks off the coast of Giglio, an island near Tuscany. The ship slammed into a large rock formation, ripping a gash in the hull, capsizing the huge vessel. More than forty-two hundred terrorized passengers and crew scrambled to reach lifeboats, some of which were already under water. Dozens of people were severely injured, and thirty-two died.

As the world watched in horror, we wondered, How could this happen? How could the crew have missed the obvious, well-marked dangers?

Ironically, many churches in America are doing something similar. They are ignoring the clearly marked warning signs. The information has been readily available for years in the book of Revelation, yet our captains are content to perpetuate a party atmosphere that keeps everyone happy while leading us ever closer to danger and possible destruction.

Revelation is one of the most maligned and misunderstood books in the Bible. Martin Luther, the hero of the sixteenth-century Protestant Reformation, refused to preach from it and barely acknowledged it as part of the Bible. He claimed, "Christ is neither taught or recognized in it."[3] Some Christians are reluctant to read it for fear they won't understand it—or fear they will. Most contemporary congregations do not want to hear about Revelation. Many pastors are reticent to preach about it, and they do not want anyone else to discuss the book from their pulpits. As I have traveled across the United States in recent years, I have been shocked at the number of pastors who say things such as, "Jim, you can preach anything you feel led to preach here in our church, but please, please don't preach about the book of Revelation. You will scare our people."

Can you imagine that? Preach anything but the information we need to know if we are going to safely navigate the treacherous waters into which we are heading in the days to come.

Whether our leaders are willing to speak of these matters or not, we need to get ready now! When the prophecies of Revelation begin to happen, there will be little time to prepare, because cataclysmic events will happen so rapidly the world will still be reeling from one calamity when the next will hit. Revelation opens with the announcement that the things God has shown John will "shortly come to pass" (1:1, KJV) and warns "the time is at hand (1:3)."

In the Greek in which John wrote, the word *shortly* does not necessarily mean soon or immediately. It means suddenly, within a fixed place in time, a space or period in which something takes place. It can also mean swiftly, quickly. In other words, when it all starts to happen, watch out! Once started, all these things will happen suddenly; the events of Revelation will roll out quickly, the fulfillment of the prophecies will proceed on an irrevocable, inexorable, unstoppable course. When these things begin to happen, we will feel as though we are riding a wildly out-of-control roller coaster.

Many first-century believers—including, no doubt, the apostle John—expected Jesus to return within their lifetime. When He didn't, some people became disillusioned and discouraged. They did not understand that certain things had to happen in history before Christ's return. For instance, according to Jesus' own words, Jerusalem had to be under Jewish control before the end-times events begin to happen. That did not occur until 1948, when the nation of Israel was reestablished and Jerusalem once again came under the governance of the Jewish people, although both Christianity and Islam have sacred sites there. Consequently, most, if not all, of the prophecies recorded in Revelation can easily be fulfilled in our generation. Now, when the prophetic mysteries begin to unfold, they will occur in rapid succession. That's why you need to have your heart right and your house in order now, ready today for the return of Jesus Christ.

At the same time, the apostle Paul warned that "the day of Christ," including the Lord's climactic return, would not happen until the "man of sin" is revealed.[4] This is the Antichrist who "takes his seat in the temple of God, displaying himself as being God."[5]

If the Antichrist is going to be on the rise, wisdom says we should be prepared to go through some difficult days before the Lord's return. I know you are hoping that Jesus will come prior to the Tribulation period. So am I. But what if you are living right where you are today when the four horsemen of Revelation begin to ride, when unprecedented natural disasters strike the world, and when the Antichrist appears? What will you do? Will you even understand the significance of these developments? All of these things and more are definitely going to happen. The only question is when.

I encourage you to approach this book with an open mind. Be like the Bereans of Acts 17 who listened to what was being said by the apostle Paul and studied the Scriptures for themselves (Acts 17:11). I urge you to consider what I am presenting within these pages and study the Scriptures for yourself!

Why Is the Book of Revelation Relevant to Us?

While many people give the impression that Revelation is too complicated for most people to understand, others question its relevance to modern life. Certainly, some things in Revelation are difficult to grasp, and others might be quite disconcerting, but Revelation is actually an encouraging book. We shouldn't fear studying it or talking about it. In fact, there are many reasons why Revelation is vital to understand, and there are at least two reasons why this book is especially worth investigating. First, this is the only book you will ever read that carries a guaranteed blessing from God!

"Blessed is he who reads," the book begins, "and those who hear the words of the prophecy, and heed the things which are written in it; for the time is near" (1:3). God promises a special blessing to anyone who *reads* the book and who keeps, or *heeds,* its message. In other words, anyone who obeys the word in it. The verb here means literally to "read out loud." And that is probably the way the book was first read: aloud to the churches. I like to read the Scriptures aloud, not to insult anybody's intelligence, but because there is power in hearing the Word.

To begin, read through the entire book of Revelation in one sitting. Don't get bogged down trying to figure out what everything means. Just read. You will be amazed at how you see the complete picture of Revelation, and you will be surprised at how encouraged you are as a result.

Previews of Coming Attractions

Second, the book of Revelation is especially relevant today because it gives us insight into tomorrow's news. Besides giving inside information regarding the return of Christ, it gives us prior notice regarding the pressure-packed times about to come upon us, as well as essential information on how to survive them.

Current world conditions make us ripe for the rise of an antichrist. I believe that in all probability, "the man of sin" is alive right now and will be active on earth *before* Jesus Christ returns for His church. Jesus Himself said that, prior to His return, there will be a time of awful persecution and tribulation, like the world has never before seen (Matthew 24:15–22).

Moreover, the issues that troubled the people who originally received the book of Revelation are still with us. Similar to the internal problems that plagued the early church, personal compromise, complacency, immorality, and weak doctrine are all too common in Christian circles today. Externally, just as those early believers faced daily, fierce persecution, Christians today are increasingly the targets of abuse, physical harm, and in many places around the world, they are confronted with denying their faith in Christ or being put to death. In America, a nation founded on godly principles, our courts, media, and leaders seem obsessed with forcing Christians out of the public arena. Like the first-century Christians, we are facing a perilous future.

Nevertheless, we are people of hope! We know the truth and recognize the signs of the times. The world around us is searching for security and stability in the face of increasingly tumultuous events. It seems that every known bulwark of society is crumbling. Families are breaking up. Meticulously woven government coalitions are coming apart at the seams. We live with the potential onset of nuclear war and the threat of annihilation should that war come. The rise of Islamic radicals around the world has many people shaking in their shoes. Domestically and internationally, previously great economies seem to be teetering on the precipice of disaster. We seek to numb ourselves to the ominous fears of suitcase bombs, electromagnetic destruction, cyberwars, and chemical and biological attacks. We know these threats exist; we just don't want to think about them, because the possibilities are simply too scary. What can we do about these threats anyhow?

If you are a believer in Jesus Christ and have studied the book of Revelation, you *know* the answer to these questions. We are heading to a wedding! The wedding of Jesus Christ and His bride, the church, which is comprised of

Christians of every denomination, nationality, and generation. This is history's crowning event, a celebration that believers have been anticipating for centuries. If you have not sent back your RSVP, you still have time, but you'd better respond quickly. If you are a Christian, God will provide precise instructions about how you should get ready for the wedding. In fact, He's already done so in the book of Revelation.

3

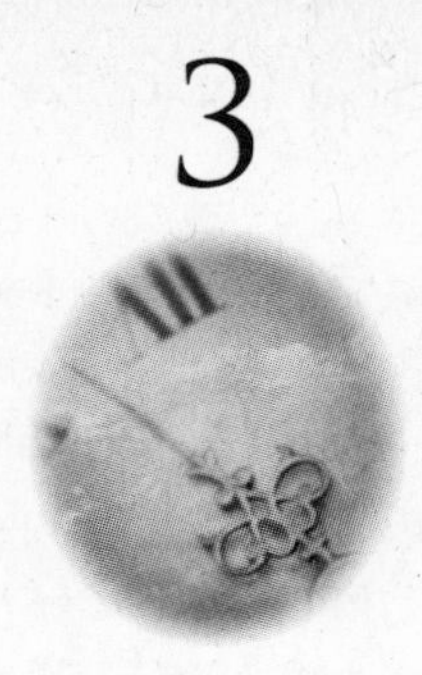

You Are Not in Darkness

W*hat can I do?* John pondered. *How can I warn my beloved children, my friends and family about what is soon to come upon the earth? They know we are experiencing tough times now, but they have no idea where we are in history. They've grown complacent and content in sinful society. They aren't ready to see Jesus.*

The banished apostle looked up from the quarry in which he was working. John took a rag and brushed at the perspiration on his forehead. *They have to wake up,* he thought, *and face the truth, even if it is not what they have been expecting.*

Many sincere people are asleep at the wheel. Some are cavorting with the devil, veering increasingly off course toward destruction. Others see the dangerous direction in which we are headed, but they naively hope that Jesus will come and save us before we hit the rocks. Escaping the coming Tribulation would be wonderful, but I'm convinced that we must go through many of these tribulation events. After decades of studying the Scriptures, I find little evidence that Jesus is going to return for Christians *before* the difficult times of Revelation begin to happen on earth. Although I'm certain Jesus is coming, we may indeed be here for what Jesus called the "beginning of sorrows" (Matthew

24:8, NKJV) and perhaps much more. We need to understand the signs of the times and recognize the events leading to the Lord's return.

In churches all across America, I've asked congregations, "How many of you believe that Jesus is going to come for us like a thief in the night?" It's a bit of a trick question, but I use it to make a point.

Most hands go up. Nearly everyone has a vague familiarity with the idea that Jesus will return when we least expect Him. Those who have made headlines in recent years for their foolish, unbiblical predictions of Christ's return tend to further convince us that we cannot know when Jesus is coming.

But if you look at this scripture carefully, you may be surprised. The Word does not say that He is coming like a thief in the night for *believers*.

> For you yourselves know full well that the day of the Lord will come just like a thief in the night. While they are saying, "Peace and safety!" then destruction will come upon them suddenly like labor pains upon a woman with child, and they will not escape. *But you, brethren, are not in darkness, that the day would overtake you like a thief*; for you are all sons of light and sons of day. We are not of night nor of darkness; so then let us not sleep as others do, but let us be alert and sober. (1 Thessalonians 5:2–6, emphasis added)

Do you see that? *You* are not to be in darkness. *You* are not of the night. *You* are to be watching and waiting, already prepared for the coming of the Lord. You will have advance information, namely, signs you can recognize that His coming is near. You will not be caught unaware. Or at least you should not be.

Jesus said, "My sheep know My voice."[6] They recognize not just the sound of His voice but the truth of His words. If you are a fan of John Grisham novels, you recognize the author's voice in each of his books. If you've read the great writers from the past, such as Shakespeare, you recognize their style. Similarly, if you study the Scriptures, you can know the voice of Jesus and recognize the truth of His Word. By becoming familiar with His voice, you will be able to recognize when something is consistent with what Jesus said or whether it is an idea concocted by someone else, well intentioned though they may be. There is no reason for you to be caught off guard by the cataclysmic events that are about to happen. Revelation will help you to be ready.

A Bit of Background

Around AD 90–95 the apostle John recorded the book of Revelation as divinely inspired from God. John was one of Jesus' closest companions, and five of his writings are in the Bible: the gospel of John; 1, 2, 3 John; and Revelation. John was one of the younger disciples. By the time he penned Revelation, he was an old man, but his mind was still sharp.

Most scholars believe that, under Roman emperor Domitian's rule, John was punished because of his uncompromising commitment to Jesus Christ and banished to the penal colony on Patmos, a tiny, mountainous island about forty-five miles off the southeastern coast of modern Turkey. Besides being a highly regarded leader of the Christian community, John's only crime was that he refused to worship the emperor. The pompous Domitian had demanded to be acknowledged as "Lord and God," so it was passed into law requiring the worship of the emperor at least once a year. Those who disobeyed received severe punishments. Christians believed that only Jesus is Lord, and they were not about to bow to any human authority.

For their part, the Romans could not understand what all the fuss was about. They were, after all, polytheists, which is to say they believed in many gods. To them, it was no big deal if the Christians wanted to add Jesus to the pantheon of gods so long as one day each year they acknowledged that their emperor is God.

Most early Christians refused to comply with Domitian's demands, and many were beaten or killed as a result. Perhaps because of his advanced age, or possibly because the Romans wanted to make an example of him, the apostle John was exiled rather than executed.

He was ripped away from his family and friends and dumped onto the island as slave labor, along with incorrigible criminals and dangerous misfits.

It was only through the goodness of God that he was not killed. Nevertheless, Patmos was no tropical retreat. Most likely, John was forced to work in the mines and allowed a subsistence lifestyle in a hillside cave. Sometime during his incarceration there, John was in the Spirit, in intimate communion with God on the Lord's Day when he experienced the visions that resulted in Revelation being written.

Although John was the writer, the message came directly from heaven. The astounding information in the book was communicated from God the Father, who gave it to the Son, Jesus, who shared it through His angel with the apostle John.[7]

The title "Revelation" comes from the transliteration of the Greek word *apocalupsis,* meaning "apocalypse." Today, this term is often used as a synonym for *chaos* and *catastrophe,* but it actually means "unveiling, to uncover, to make manifest." That's what the Revelation is: the unveiling of Jesus Christ. In the King James Version, the book was titled the "Revelation of Saint John the Divine," but that title is misleading. John was a human being like you and me, and while he was a saintly man, he was not divine. Moreover, Revelation is not the revelation of John. The accurate title reflected in many Bible translations is the "Revelation of Jesus Christ."

God is not trying to trick us. He wants us to know and understand this message. It is the unveiling of Jesus Christ, not the concealing of Jesus. So when we study the book, the Holy Spirit pulls back the curtain and lets us see the essential truths we need to know to survive the attacks of the Enemy in the days ahead. Certainly there is mystery here, and a great deal of symbolism, and you may not understand everything in the book. I certainly don't. But if we read and heed the words, we will be blessed now and forever.

The book raises questions for skeptics and believers alike. For instance, the collapse of the world economic systems and the present vacuum of effective leaders have set us up for the rise of the Antichrist, a strong leader who will soon come on the scene with solutions leading to prosperity, peace, and security. He will be welcomed by the world, and things will seem to go somewhat better for a short time, after which all hell—literally—will break loose on the earth. You will not be able to buy or sell anything without presenting some tangible evidence of your acceptance of the Antichrist's rule in your life.

But why would anyone acquiesce to take the mark of the Beast, the infamous 666? The answer is simple: to get food and the basic necessities for your family. If you must have a number—or some unique password-style indicator that will ostensibly protect you from identity theft and other modern crimes while allowing you to be part of the economic system—you will readily submit to such an invasion of your privacy for only one reason: your family's survival.

If you don't know the Word of God, you may be easily deceived. You won't know the eternal danger of buying into the Antichrist's economic system, and you may not understand the ramifications of your actions. God showed me that millions of people who have attended church services for years but were never taught the essential truths of Revelation will cry out to preachers, "Why didn't you tell us?" Many people who are merely religious, who felt that their religion was too personal and private for polite public conversation, will despair of their own lives.

How I Read the Book

Here is a simple, effective key to understanding the book of Revelation: watch for the words *see* and *hear*. I love to read the book and note every instance in which John calls attention to sight or sound. I try to put myself in his place and experience Revelation through his eyes and ears. If you interpret the book according to what John saw and heard, you will get a much clearer understanding of the message.

Nevertheless, I don't feel that I understand it all. God hates know-it-alls. He won't cater to our pride and arrogance, even if it is pride in our understanding of the Scriptures. I don't profess to have some private interpretation of this book. I'm continually willing to consider other ways of understanding it. But I have studied it, and I get excited about the message.

Although I encourage taking the words of Revelation as literally as possible, keep in mind that it is apocalyptic literature, so John includes a great deal of symbolism. Many times John provides us with a comparison, using something he has seen in his time to describe something from the distant future, of which he has no direct knowledge, yet he has seen it in a vision.

I do believe that some of Revelation was written in code. If people think the book of Revelation is strange, odd, and confusing, it may be an indication that they have not done our amount of homework throughout the Bible. There are approximately 400 verses in Revelation with over 800 allusions to the Old Testament within the book. I personally believe that without divine inspiration and illumination, it would be difficult, if not impossible, to truly understand the text. A little saying I learned in Bible college from one of my professors was, "The Word without the Spirit, you will dry up. The Spirit without the Word, you will blow up. The Spirit with the Word, you will grow up."

But why was code so necessary? Several reasons come to mind. John may have wanted to conceal some things in a spiritual code so only genuine Christians could understand that portion of the message. By the end of the first century, Christians were no longer popular. Quite the contrary, intense persecutions of Christians were common. So John had to be very careful with his words. After all, he was writing from a forced labor camp. His message to the struggling, persecuted Christian churches—to stand fast and to overcome—during the terrible reign of Domitian would be considered seditious if his meaning were obvious to all readers.

A second reason for symbolism involves a popular writing genre of the day. Similar to books and movies such as C. S. Lewis's *Chronicles of Narnia* and J. R. R. Tolkien's *Lord of the Rings* that make strong use of symbolism in our day, apocalyptic literature, which was a common literary form in John's day, was replete with symbolism. John had seen other materials written this way. Perhaps he knew that he could present his message in symbolic language and it would have an impact for centuries to come, which, of course, it has. Again, just because John used symbolic language to describe future events does not mean that the events and the scenes won't happen. The truths of the passages are real.

Symbols not only convey information, but they also impart values, arouse emotions, and paint pictures for us. For example, John could have said, "A dictator is coming who will rule the world." Instead he describes "a beast" (Revelation 13). He used Babylon as a synonym for Rome and possibly New York, as we will see. Babylon held deep significance and evoked strong emotions within readers who knew the Old Testament. In 586 BC, Jerusalem was destroyed by the army of the Babylonian king Nebuchadnezzar, and God's people were driven into exile in Babylon, which is modern-day Iraq. A mere twenty years prior to the time of John's writing, Rome had destroyed Jerusalem, once again dispersing the people of Israel, leveling the Jewish temple brick by brick to remove and rob the gold from Israel's most sacred house of worship. So when John used the term *Babylon*, his Christian readers instantly knew he meant Rome. The apostle Peter had done something similar at the close of his epistle: "She who is in Babylon, chosen together with you, sends you greetings."[8]

Is This Book Really for Me?

We know the apostle was writing to seven established churches in Asia Minor (modern Turkey) in Revelation 2 and 3. Because of John's stature as an original disciple of Jesus, many believe his message was repeated in churches throughout that region. Clearly, any believer in any age could read and profit from this letter. John was trying to encourage Christians, to give them hope while they faced vicious opposition and a perilous future. He wanted to help them keep their lives together as they saw their world collapsing all around them. He fervently wanted them to know that they could make it through the tough times ahead. Even if their faith in Christ cost them their lives, if they stayed true to Jesus, they would overcome the Enemy and reap an eternal reward. That is the dominant message of Revelation that we must constantly keep in mind. Jesus Christ is gloriously victorious over all of His enemies. The corollary to this point is that, in Him, we can overcome any obstacle or persecution as well!

How Will I Profit from All This Prophecy?

John did not send this book to the seven churches simply to satisfy their curiosity about the future. He sent it to help them survive the persecutions of their day and make it through the dark night of their despair. People he knew well were struggling. They needed hope and encouragement, and the elder apostle provided both. But even more, his Christian family was meant to hear the message and examine their own hearts in the light of it, to look deeply within themselves to determine if anything in their lives needed correcting. It is interesting to note that none of the churches saw themselves as Jesus saw them. To be blessed, they were not only to hear the word, but they were to keep it, act on it, guard it as a treasure, and practice what it prescribed. It is an invitation to examine yourself. That's the way the book should be approached today.

The Value of Peeking Ahead

Other than the first three chapters, the book of Revelation deals almost entirely with prophecy. Remember, John was writing to encourage people who were undergoing persecution. Why then would he spend so much time describing the future? Why didn't he talk more about the nasty present? Simply this: by seeing Jesus Christ presented in all His glory, these troubled, persecuted Christians were encouraged *today*, in the difficult days ahead, and for the tough task of witnessing for Christ in a very hostile world in the future. John's lasting message to them was, "We win!" When you know how a story ends, you can have great confidence despite any intervening difficult times.

I love the story of two young men who were reading an action-packed adventure story. One was fretting over the troubles and calamities striking the hero of the story, but the other was calm and cool as the story progressed.

"How can you be so confident?" the agitated fellow asked his friend.

"Easy," the friend responded. "I've read the end of the book, and I know the hero wins!"

That's one of the best reasons to study Revelation. We can read the end of the book and know that our Hero wins. And because He wins, we win too!

4

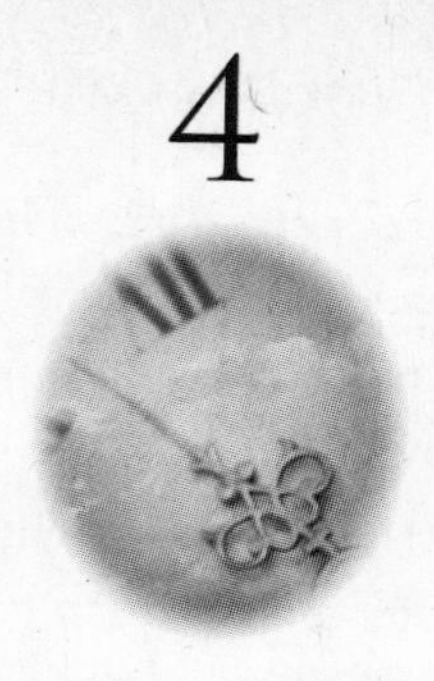

The Thirty-One Things

John carefully picked up the parchment on which he was writing and hurriedly stashed it under a sack. A guard passed by, and the apostle dared not let the soldier see his writing. John breathed a sigh of relief as the guard ambled past the makeshift tent John had assembled.

How long, O Lord? How long will evil triumph? Your people have been oppressed for so long now, they have almost given up hope. Will they even believe me when they read the words you have instructed me to write? They might mock me. Perhaps they will dismiss this message as the rantings of an old man whose mind is gone. Some of these things are so difficult to understand. Others are so hard to accept as viable possibilities.

Nevertheless, John returned to his writing. Indeed, some of the things he had seen were frightening even to him. He could only hope his readers would heed the message and prepare for what was to come.

In some measure, I can relate to the pressure and despair John felt as he wrote the book of Revelation at a penal colony. In 1989, I went to prison, but not as a visitor.[9] (If you are interested in the details, I wrote an entire account—how I got there, what I experienced, and what I learned—in my book *The Prison Years*[10]).

One of the most difficult aspects of prison life was the hopelessness I felt when first incarcerated. I was forty-nine years old when I was condemned to forty-five years in a federal prison. My punishment was essentially a death sentence. What was the use in living?

It was only after I rediscovered the Scriptures and rekindled my love for Jesus that my hope was renewed. I knew that, thanks to His redeeming love, whether I ever got out of prison alive or not, I would one day be free. If you know there will be an end to the suffering, you can endure almost anything.

While in prison, however, I studied the entire Bible, especially the book of Revelation. I began a daily concentrated study of the Scriptures, especially those relating to Jesus. Naturally, I wanted to learn about Christ's return, so I began searching out passages pertaining to this subject. I read every line over and over and looked up every word I couldn't understand. In fact, during my study of the book of Revelation, I looked up every word in the Greek to satisfy my thirst to understand what God has in store for our future. I prayed, *God, I have nothing but time. I want to know what this book means.*

Now, more than twenty years later, I am compelled to share with you what I discovered. I think I can understand something of the awe John felt as he received the visions of Revelation. Although I've never considered myself a prophet, I have experienced a few visions that have shattered my idealistic ideas about the future.

After serving five years in prison, the forty-five-year sentence imposed on me was commuted to eight years, and I was eligible for immediate parole and release. During the first few years out of prison, I kept a very low profile, rarely accepting any speaking engagements. I was as fragile as a frightened rabbit and needed time to heal, so I spent more time studying the Scriptures and trying to help others. Eventually I began writing a book and accepting a few speaking engagements.

In 1999 I received an invitation to speak at a prophetic conference to be held on New Year's Eve. This was not just another end-of-the-year celebration, with people praying and asking God's blessing on the coming year or partying as a giant ball slowly descended in Times Square. No, this was Y2K, an anagram for the year 2000, the eve of the new millennium. I was humbled and honored to be asked to speak publicly. I hadn't been out of prison that long, and I was still uncomfortable about standing behind a pulpit. But the people sponsoring the conference were friends, so I accepted their invitation.

Visions in the Night

I had spoken at a similar conference about eight months prior to my New Year's Eve invitation. The night before that conference, God spoke to my heart and mind. I had a vision and saw some extraordinary things, events that apparently were soon to happen around us. These were not happy visions. They were not scenes of life on Easy Street, especially for Christians. Quite the contrary. The visions horrified me and shook me to my core.

On New Year's Eve 1999, on the precipice of the new millennium, I publicly presented a message based on the vision I had experienced. At the time, I had little idea if or how this vision might be fulfilled, but looking back now, it staggers me to realize that God was showing me some things that were imminent. Similar to how the apostle John must have felt, I did not understand everything I experienced, but I understood enough to know that God was serious about this message.

Before I described the events I had seen in the vision, I told the audience, "The most important thing is to keep your family together in unity. The other things we spend our time, money, and energy doing may not matter much in the days ahead. Keep your family together and be part of the family of God. As the scripture says in Hebrews 10:25, we should not forsake assembling together, especially as the Day of the Lord approaches. Get ready. When you hear 'peace and safety,' sudden destruction is coming. Jesus said that, in the last days, perilous things will come. The key is 'fear not.' That's God's message throughout the Bible."

I began my recollection of the vision with the explanation that I believed the year 2000 would be the beginning of what Jesus calls "the beginning of birth pangs" (Matthew 24:8). The Bible describes this period as a time of great distress, but God assured me that during this period to come, it would also be a time of supernatural healing and supply for His people.

The Visions of the Thirty-One Things

One of the first things I remember God speaking to me was that two major earthquakes would be coming to the world. One of them was an earthquake coming to Japan that would signal the beginning of a total financial collapse of the world economy. Nearly twelve years later, on a live broadcast of my television show in 2011, I blurted out that a 9-point-plus earthquake was about to hit somewhere in the world. Little did I know at that time that a monstrous earthquake would trigger a powerful tsunami that would strike Japan on March 10, 2011, damaging a nuclear power plant and exposing millions to radiation. This occurred eleven days after that live broadcast. Early headlines claimed the magnitude to be 8.9, but I refused to accept that and told my production team that it was wrong. A few hours later, the authorities recalculated and adjusted the magnitude to 9.0, and some even calculated it to have been 9.1.

In the aftermath of the disaster, more than twenty thousand people were killed or declared missing. Estimates of the cost to restore the country were upwards of $300 billion, and over half a million people were left homeless.

I believe another earthquake is coming to Tokyo, and it may result in the total collapse of that country.

One of the prophetic things that God made clear to me was that a worldwide economic disaster was coming. I saw bank failures and stock markets collapse. The next item God showed me was that not only would the stock market collapse, but the most-trusted stocks would deteriorate. We have already seen this happen in our day with the collapse of Lehman Brothers, Kodak, Delta Airlines, Borders, American Airlines, Refco, Hostess, Circuit City, and many other banks, companies, and stocks.

In 2008, on the cusp of the market collapse, at least ten financial institutions—including Merrill Lynch, AIG, Freddie Mac, and Royal Bank of Scotland—all came within a breath of collapse and had to be rescued. Trillions of dollars had to be sunk into the system to prevent a total collapse. On

September 29, 2008, the Dow Jones Industrial Average plunged 777 points, the largest single-day drop in history. A leading economist said that commercial real estate (including church properties) would be the next shoe to drop in the collapse of the economy.

Another of the thirty-one things God showed me was a great void in the world's leadership—which is happening *now!* There would be great confusion in Europe, which we are seeing today with the fragility of the euro zone. Several member nations, including Greece and Spain, are on the verge of bankruptcy.

This leads us to the next item on the list: a call for a world leader. This is also happening *now!* Undoubtedly, this connects to the next item: I believe the Antichrist is alive today. I wrote down, "Keep eyes on Jesus, not miracles." In my study of Revelation, I came to realize that the Antichrist will have incredible power. His assistant also will be able to perform miracles. Don't follow miracles, though. Follow Jesus. The scripture is clear: "For they are the spirits of devils, working miracles" (Revelation 16:14).

One of the thirty-one things came to me just hours before going on stage on New Year's Eve 1999. I had seen in a night vision a terrible explosion in New York City and Washington, DC, at the same time. In the vision, I saw people covered in ash, running as they cried and screamed in terror. I remember God speaking that the one explosion and fire in Washington, DC, would be at a key military and defense location. Looking back on this, I suppose there could not have been a higher or more key location than the Pentagon, yet the date I was seeing these events was December 31, 1999. My wife, Lori, saw on my notes from the vision that I had written two things. The first was "great airplanes." The other word I had written was *tear-or-is-um,* but it came to me phonetically, so that's how I wrote it down. I saw terrorism from within the United States and from without.

On September 11, 2001, my daughter, Tammy Sue, woke us during one of the rare days I was able to sleep late. She was screaming on the phone, "Dad, Dad! They're bombing New York City!"

I scrambled for the television remote control. When I turned on the TV, I saw people, covered in ash, running in terror. I could not believe it! It felt as if I was watching the rerun of an old movie I had seen twenty months earlier. And then, before I could blink, I saw the second tower disintegrate into the earth—still the most unbelievable sight I have ever seen. How could two of the most important buildings in America just disappear? What I saw on TV was exactly what I had seen in my vision.

These nightmarish events gave me great insight into how the world systems, the Great Harlot, will be destroyed in an hour.

Since that time, our nation has experienced numerous attempted terrorist attacks, many of which have been foiled, but some, such as the attacks on military bases, have succeeded. Others came close to succeeding, such as the attempt in December 1999, when terrorists in Seattle were discovered trying to smuggle powerful explosives into the country.

Of course, domestic terrorism catapulted to an entirely new level on April 20, 1999, when we witnessed the deadliest school massacre in our nation's history at Columbine High School in Colorado. Again, I could not have imagined what sort of terrorism was soon to follow. But on July 20, 2012, a young man went on a shooting rampage at a movie theater in Aurora, Colorado, shooting seventy-one people and killing twelve in the worst mass shooting in U.S. history. The spirit of the Antichrist is running rampant.

This is only the beginning of the entire list. God showed me that cruise ships would be targeted soon. The water supplies for major cities will be contaminated and poisoned. I believe—in fact, I saw it in a vision—there is already at least one major nuclear weapon being assembled inside the United States. It was brought in piece by piece. Terrorists will use germ warfare against civilians and soldiers alike. Attacks will continue on airplanes and against airplanes as well.

I sensed God telling me that the United States has made too many enemies. It will become impossible to fight them all or even prevent them from harming us.

There will be great computer confusion, God spoke to me in 1999, not related to Y2K. At that time, many people were warning of potential computer breakdowns that would affect everything from the country's power grid to its water supplies. Even gasoline pumps would be unable to function due to the computer switchover to the year 2000. But God revealed to me a computer confusion that was not associated with Y2K.

I did not know what that meant. I had no idea what computer hacking was or the damage that viruses could do to computers. Yet I received messages that cyberwars would be much more subtle and would employ terror. Ironically, computer hackers attacked the FBI that same year.

I also saw that the Internet could be stopped suddenly—within a half hour. That is already happening. During the tumult in 2011 in Cairo's Tahrir Square that led to the downfall of Hosni Mubarak as Egypt's president, one of the tools the government employed against the protesters was a complete shutdown of the Internet. That was done because the protesters had organized demonstrations using social media networking sites. With a virtual flip of a switch, Egypt was suddenly plunged into Internet and cell phone darkness, with millions of people unable to communicate electronically. Think how often you send a text message, make a call on your cell phone, send an email, or search the Internet for information. Now imagine a world where such access is denied to anyone who refuses to acquiesce to the government. That is going to happen.

Today, in the United States, gangs are using social media and texts to organize flash mobs. On June 18, 2012, a flash mob took over a supermarket in Portland, Oregon, stealing merchandise and terrorizing patrons. Since then, other stores and gas stations have fallen victim to such mobs, all organized through texting and social media.

I also saw "weather more out of control than ever before." I saw floods and mudslides, with people suffocating, buried in mud. I was driving down the street, and in a flash I saw the picture of a horrible flood. Just a few days later, on December 15, 1999, torrential rains and flash floods created devastating mudslides in the state of Vargas in Venezuela. Tens of thousands of people perished, thousands of homes were destroyed, and the state's infrastructure completely collapsed.

One of the key phrases God gave me was *death by water.* This was six years before Hurricane Katrina. In front of a live audience on July 14, 2005,

I announced that God told me that New Orleans would be totally under water. There would be a sea of water over New Orleans. Seven weeks later, Hurricane Katrina hit, devastating the Crescent City and vast portions of the Deep South.

More ethnic cleansing will take place. This is happening currently in Russia, Sudan, and other places. Another thing I felt God clearly impress on me was that a third world war would begin when a nuclear bomb explodes in the Middle East.

I received a strong word that I did not understand: "Watch Turkey." The nation of Turkey had experienced violent storms and had also recently suffered the worst earthquake in its history. I thought the vision meant that we were simply to watch for earthquakes in that area. While that may be true, Turkey may also prove to be a major player in end-times events. The Turks may cooperate with Russia in a military move against Israel in the days ahead.

Other nations God included on the watch list were Egypt and China. Eleven years after my address on New Year's Eve, Egypt saw a change of administration, giving the presidency to the Muslim Brotherhood. Today, China is mobilizing and currently owns a majority of the U.S. debt. God emphasized that we should not trust old allies and new friends alike.

Another item was that there would be great betrayals in the world and in the church. The Bible teaches that people *will* betray one another (Matthew 24:10). There will be great disillusionment with superstar religion and impersonal churches. It saddened me as I saw that some megachurches would lose their buildings. Selfishness will be brought down by God's love. Spiritual pride must die. We must humble ourselves.

Now for Some Good News!

Besides these and some other frightening scenarios, I saw several encouraging signs in these visions. For example, I saw that great church leaders would emerge from minorities, especially from Hispanic and Native American groups and others as well. There will be people who come into your church who will shock you. They have been to hell and back. God is going to bring in people who will cause your hair to curl if you knew what they had done. But they have been redeemed, changed, and saved forevermore. My good friend Armando, a brother in the Lord, was once a gang member whose cohorts killed more than twenty people. Today, he boldly preaches the gospel in various parts of the world, often in inner-city settings.

I had a vision that angels will visit more frequently. True believers will come together, caring for each other and the needy among us. God will send seekers to us; they may be seeking food or water or shelter, but we will have opportunities to tell them about Jesus if we keep our hearts and minds open to the Spirit of God. It is going to be the greatest hour the church has ever known. We are going to see great healings, not necessarily through healing ministries, but through people praying for each other and seeing God do the work. Families will move in the Spirit, but don't forget the church. It will be important in the last days that we not neglect assembling together. Many souls will be saved during these days.

I saw blue explosions—many of them. I did not and still do not know what they mean. I don't know whether they were spiritual or physical manifestations.

At the time I experienced these visions, the events seemed so far into the future that I was reluctant to speak of them publicly. Nobody wants to sound like a fool. Although my reputation had long since been "laid on the altar," I did not relish having people mock me. But as we prepared to enter the new millennium, I felt strongly that I was supposed to share these visions. Keep in mind that none of these things had occurred when I spoke of them for the first time in public. There are dated recordings readily available of the message I presented. That's why I say I understand a bit of the conundrum in which the apostle John found himself, compelled by God's Spirit to share things that he did not fully understand.

As I delivered the message on New Year's Eve 1999, many people were uncomfortable with my words, thinking that I was obsessed with doom and gloom at a time when the entire world was celebrating. But all too soon I knew I had done the right thing.

Also, that night I related an earlier vision from 1997 when I had seen a horrendously powerful earthquake striking downtown Los Angeles. I was riding in the back of a car through the streets of LA at the time when I looked into the earth. I saw rocks bowing upward. God said this was the "pressure of the ages," and it was going to slip. I looked over Los Angeles and saw every building had collapsed.

A couple of years later, the front page of the *LA Daily Times* declared "Massive hidden fault threatens downtown." The article included a drawing depicting exactly what I had seen in my vision.

HELP ME, BROTHER JOHN!

What does a person do with that sort of knowledge? I confess I was afraid to do much. After all, who was I? I had been just recently released from prison. Who would believe that I was receiving visions from God? What right did I have to prophesy? Who would want to hear a warning message of impending death and disaster? So I said little about the visions until that New Year's Eve in 1999.

On the eve of the millennium, after I had spoken of the vision, including the horrific vision of a future Los Angeles earthquake, an elderly, highly accurate, well-known prophet approached me and said, "Jim, you have declared thirty-one prophetic events—and you are right on."

I did not know how many specific events which I had spoken about, but when I counted them out, they numbered thirty-one.

"But on one point," the prophet continued, "I have some insight for you. The Japanese earthquake will come first. When you see that, get ready. The next big event will be the California earthquake."

At this writing, that enormous Los Angeles earthquake has not yet happened. As much as it grieves me to say so, I am convinced that it will.

One of the prophets with an incredible track record is now saying, "I used to encourage people to pray about leaving the West Coast. Now I tell them to pray about whether they should stay."

In my visions I saw churches going bankrupt, their properties being foreclosed on and repossessed by banks. Keep in mind this was during the boom time of America's megachurches. Many churches were arrogantly competing for airtime on television networks, and some boasted that Christians would soon dominate the seats of government authority as well. Yet, I saw churches being repossessed by the hundreds.

Many scoffed at my words, purporting it was ludicrous to propose that forward-thinking congregations that supposedly enjoyed God's favor and prosperity could possibly be forced to close their doors. But in 2012 the beautiful campus of the Crystal Cathedral built by my dear friend Robert Schuller in Anaheim, California, fell to Chapter 11 bankruptcy and was later sold. Numerous lesser-known facilities have gone belly-up as well. While I was finishing this book, word came to me that a wonderful congregation was packing their church because a bank was foreclosing on their massive building that seated thousands of people in Branson, Missouri.

A Reuters news article portends a dire future for churches in debt, noting that a record number of churches are defaulting on their mortgages, and banks are foreclosing on churches in record numbers. In 2010, 270 churches defaulted; in 2011, 138 churches defaulted. The article notes, "That compares to just 24 sales in 2008 and only a handful in the decade before."[11]

Listening to some television evangelists, you would think they have won the entire world to Christ. The Bible, however, says, "The way is narrow that leads to life, and there are few who find it."[12] This is sobering, and I think we all need to examine our hearts. If we are truly in the last days, "the beginning of sorrows,"[13] things are not going to get better. For the Antichrist to arrive, mankind must be in a hopeless situation.

Certainly, just as in Hezekiah's time, when God granted the righteous king's prayer for fifteen additional years of life, our God may give us more time. If God's people repent and turn to Him, He can alter the timetable for future events. Yes, judgment will come, but it need not come in our generation or during the lives of our children. The key question, of course, is, will

God's people humble themselves and repent and turn from their wicked ways and seek His face? If we will do so, God has promised He will hear our prayer, forgive our sins, and heal our land.

OVERCOMERS

The theme of everything John saw and heard in the visions resonated in his heart and mind: Jesus Christ is victor, and we, as His people, are overcomers!

The word *overcomers* is used throughout the book of Revelation, from beginning to end. Clearly, God wants us to know that regardless of what trials, tribulations, or pressures we are enduring now, through our faith in Jesus Christ, we will overcome. Whatever circumstances we face in the future, He will help us to overcome through His power.

One of the first things John reminded us about is that Jesus is coming back with the clouds: "Behold, He is coming with the clouds, and every eye will see Him, even those who pierced Him; and all the tribes of the earth will mourn over Him. So it is to be. Amen" (Revelation 1:7).

To every believer this is a powerful and comforting verse. Jesus is coming again, and even those people responsible for His crucifixion will see Him again. You have God's word on it! The Bible is replete with references to the second coming of Christ. The big question for believers is not *if* but *when*. Regardless of when, we have a general idea of *what* is going to happen. More important, we know *who* is going to happen—Jesus!

5

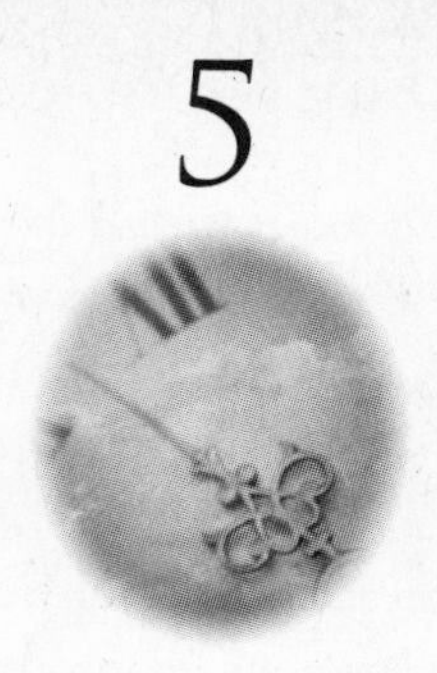

Seven Secret Messages to Seven Churches

John steadied the pen in his hand as he began to write the letters to the seven churches. He trembled at the weight of the words and the enormity of the consequences of ignoring them. If ever the church needed spiritual eyes to see and ears to hear the message, it was then. He wondered how his friends would receive the messages. Even though each letter contained words of encouragement, John also had been instructed to write some strong words of rebuke and warning.

The aging apostle missed seeing his friends at the various churches. He had lived in Ephesus for a while, and he knew the people there well. John grimaced as he thought of Polycarp, his faithful understudy who had served with him and then left to be a pastor in Smyrna. In that city, Polycarp was subsequently burned at the stake rather than deny his faith. John also thought of Artemis, who was martyred. And there were others too.

In contrast to these champions of the faith, the spiritual lethargy of the Laodicean church brought tears to the apostle's eyes. How could his little children (his term of endearment for the Christians he had taught) get so caught up in worldly things that they would allow their faithfulness to be compromised? It grieved him.

When his thoughts turned to his friends in the church at Philadelphia, a hint of a smile crossed his face. Philadelphia was home to a lovely group of people.

The other churches troubled him though. Sardis, for example, was the site of a supposedly impenetrable Roman garrison poised high atop a mountain. Yet the mountain had been breached at least twice, and the invaders destroyed not only the army but the people who depended on the Roman legions for protection. There was also Pergamum. What a beautiful setting for a city amid high pastoral hills, but the mountaintops were the sites of huge temples to false gods. In Laodicea John's many friends enjoyed relaxing in the hot springs. But just as the hot water descended the mountain and cooled as it reached the valley, likewise many of John's Laodicean friends had turned lukewarm in their relationship with the Lord.

Although the churches to whom John was writing were facing persecution and difficult times economically and spiritually, the challenge proffered by Jesus was clear: no matter how tough things get, it was paramount that Christians be rightly related to each other as well as to God.

EXTERNALS CAN BE DECEIVING

If you have ever moved to a new area, you know how hard it is to find a good church and how difficult churches are to evaluate. A church building might stand as a beautiful edifice, but the congregation inside may be spiritually dead or dying. Another congregation may have small, unattractive facilities, but inside you might find a dynamic group of believers. When we try to evaluate and examine a church, we can be easily fooled because looks can be deceiving.

But when Jesus Christ inspects His church, He sees what others might miss or ignore. He sees not only the external façades but the internal conditions. He judges accurately: "And all the churches will know that I am He who searches the minds and hearts" (Revelation 2:23). There is no hiding place from His keen vision. He sees both the good and the bad. He sees everything! Moreover, it is clear that Christ's messages transcended these seven groups. His words are intended for all of His churches. Perhaps that is why He uses the plural term *churches* at the close of each letter.

At the same time the Lord is also speaking to individuals through these letters. Notice the phrase, "He who has an ear, let him hear what the Spirit says" (2:29). Why? Because individuals make up churches, and the individuals who comprise the group determine the life, energy, integrity, spiritual depth, and effectiveness of any single church.

Why Are the Letters Even in Revelation?

If Revelation is a book about future things, why make such a fuss about seven ancient churches? I think the answer is that the Lord deals with His own people before sending judgment to others. The Bible says, "For the time has come for judgment to begin at the house of God; and if it begins with us first, what will be the end of those who do not obey the gospel of God? Now 'If the righteous one is scarcely saved, where will the ungodly and the sinner appear?'" (1 Peter 4:17–18, NKJV). God wants His church—believers from every race, nationality, and denomination—to be clean and ready for what is to come.

By implication the message Jesus is giving right up front in Revelation is this: "Before I judge the world, I will begin by judging My own church." This means He is going to examine our individual lives, because you and I are the temple of the Holy Spirit. Understand this: a purified church and a purified individual does not fear either the attacks of Satan or of other people. Historically, the church has been refined and purified by persecution. That is as true today as it has ever been.

Ephesus: Lost Love

The church at Ephesus (Revelation 2:1–7) could easily be called the church where love went wrong. Their initial love for Christ had grown cold.

Jesus noted several things about the Ephesians that pleased Him, so He started with a word of commendation, expressing what He approved about their church.

They were a serving church, doing the works of the Lord, and they were a sacrificial church, toiling to the point of exhaustion. Apparently the Ephesian church was also a suffering church. They bore their burdens patiently and without growing weary. Jesus acknowledged their enduring perseverance (2:2–3) and that they had not allowed physical, emotional, or spiritual fatigue to wear them down. In other words the Ephesians kept going, even when the going was tough. Even though they were persecuted, they refused to give up.

Additionally, the Ephesian Christians did not tolerate false prophets. The apostle Paul had warned them to guard against false teachers (Acts 20:28–31). Likewise, the apostle John told them to "test the spirits" (1 John 4:1–6) as to whether they were of God or not. The Ephesians obeyed. They separated themselves from false doctrine. They separated themselves from false deeds, and they apparently separated themselves from false teachers (Revelation 2:6).

HOW COULD THEY GO WRONG?

Since the Ephesians had all these good things going for them—service, sacrifice, steadfastness, saintliness, and suffering—we might wonder, how could they go wrong?

But Jesus did have an accusation against them. He said, "You have left your first love" (Revelation 2:4). The Ephesians had allowed their love for Christ to grow cold.

Many new believers begin their Christian lives with tremendous enthusiasm, fervor, and uninhibited, animated, open affection for Christ. And then, for some reason, their love for Jesus cools. The tragic lesson from the Ephesian church is that it is possible to start well, to serve, to sacrifice, to suffer, and then let love slip away.

Despite the serious warning in Christ's admonition to the Ephesian church, there is also good news (2:5–7). The Lord said that your first love can be *restored* if you do three things. First, He said to "*remember* from where you have fallen" (v. 5, emphasis added). Usually we say, "Forget the past." But Jesus says to remember where you were. Remember what you had! Remember what you have lost and cultivate a determination to get back to where you belong in your life with Christ.

The Lord's second command is to *repent.* To repent means more than being sorry that you were caught doing something wrong. The word *repent* means to turn around, to turn away from sin and turn to God. It involves a change of mind as you confess your sins, and then it demands a change of conduct, even a dramatic change of direction in your life.

The Lord's third command is to *repeat.* Repeat the works you did at first. Go back to square one. Where did you go wrong? Don't perpetuate wrong patterns. Restore your original fellowship that was broken by sin or neglect. Do those deeds, and you will find the Lord's favor.

Jesus clearly explained to the Ephesians what would happen if they did not do what He commanded. "I am coming to you," He warned. Coming in judgment, I might add. The implication is that Jesus would remove their lampstands (2:5). The light at Ephesus would go out.

Jesus told them, "To him who overcomes, I will grant to eat of the tree of life which is in the Paradise of God" (2:7). What a thought! The overcomers, the true believers who stick to the faith and continue to love the Lord through thick and thin, "will eat of the tree of life." It is interesting that Jesus mentions the tree of life in verse 7. In the garden of Eden, after they had sinned, Adam and Eve were prevented from partaking of the tree of life (Genesis 3:22, 24). But now the overcomers receive the promise that they can have eternal, abundant life in Christ.

Sadly the Ephesians were careless, compromising Christians who neglected their love for Christ and confused working for Christ and a relationship with Him. As a result they lost everything. Among the ancient ruins of Ephesus today you can visit several impressive sites, even the apostle John's home and the tomb in which he is thought to have been buried, but you cannot visit the church that served this city in the first century. It is gone, just as Jesus predicted. But His promise is still standing for individuals as well as the church today.

In light of Jesus' warning to the Ephesians, ask yourself:

1. Where do I spend most of my time, especially my discretionary time?
2. What do I think about most often?
3. What do I speak about most often?
4. On what do I spend my money?
5. Whom or what do I really love?

Do your answers indicate you are in danger of leaving your first love? Worse, have you already left your first love? If so, please remember . . . repent . . . return. You can restore a right relationship with Christ. If you will persevere, you can overcome. The Holy Spirit will help you. And one day soon you can celebrate with Jesus in paradise. I wouldn't miss Him for the world!

SMYRNA: DO NOT FEAR

The church of Smyrna was persecuted for its faith. Smyrna was an important center for propagating the worship of Caesar, what some have called the "Imperial Cult." That is probably why the Christians in Smyrna were heavily persecuted. When they refused to say, "Caesar is Lord," and rebuked the pagan religious system, they were ostracized and denied a livelihood. The guild system dominated the marketplace and controlled the economy. If you were not a guild member, you had no chance of finding a job. Consequently, many of the Christians in Smyrna were unemployed.

For these people persecution took various forms. They were forced to endure oppressive, economic pressures with no job, no money, and no hope. No doubt that is what Jesus referred to when He said, "I know your tribulation and your poverty" (Revelation 2:9). The word *poverty* here means abject poverty: possessing absolutely nothing. These Christians were not unemployed because they were too lazy to work but because a government-sponsored religion denied them any chance at a livelihood. We see this today in places such as Sudan. We may one day see something similar in America if we do not repent.

Despite the economic and spiritual persecution that left the Smyrnaean Christians impoverished, Jesus referred to them as *rich!* (2:9): "I know your tribulation and your poverty (but you are rich)." What was He talking about?

Jesus was saying that the Christians at Smyrna were living for eternal values that would never pass away. Thus, they were *spiritually* rich! Many people who are financially wealthy are spiritually poor. The Smyrnaean Christians were just the opposite. They were poor financially, but, oh, so very rich spiritually.

Interestingly, the Lord has no words of accusation against the church at Smyrna. Nowhere in this note does Jesus say, "I have this against you." They may not have had the approval of their neighbors, but these Christians certainly had the approval of God. This raises some interesting questions for us. Who are we trying to impress? The sinful world around us or Jesus?

Jesus was pleased with these financially strapped Christians; however, the Lord did give them a strong word of warning:

> Do not fear what you are about to suffer. Behold, the devil is about to cast some of you into prison, so that you will be tested, and you will have tribulation for ten days. Be faithful until death, and I will give you the crown of life. (Revelation 2:10)

Jesus knew Satan was planning to wreak more havoc on the Christians at Smyrna. Let that be a word of encouragement to you. Jesus already knows what the Enemy is planning to throw against you too. He gave the Christians in Smyrna three reasons why they should not fear:

1. The suffering won't be universal. Not every Christian would be imprisoned, but some would.
2. The sufferings would be limited to ten days. Ten days may seem like forever if you are in prison, but believe me, it is a relatively short time. And in the Bible, the phrase implies a brief period of time. The actual imprisonments may have been longer than ten days, but the imprisonment ahead of these Christians would not be unbearable.

3. The Lord implied that this suffering would test them, not destroy them. Yet He said, "Be faithful until death" no matter what sort of persecution comes.

Jesus was aware of how difficult it was to serve Him in Smyrna, but He did not sugarcoat His message to the Christians there. He honestly leveled with them, but He also encouraged them, saying, "Be faithful until death, and I will give you the crown of life" (v. 10). The "crown of life" is the winner's crown (*stephanos* in Greek) that was awarded at the annual athletic games, not a royal crown (*diadema* in Greek). Smyrnaeans were key players in the athletic games of the first century, so these Christians understood the promise of the victor's reward.

Because the Christians at Smyrna trusted Jesus, they were overcomers. As such, Jesus promised they would overcome "the second death" (v. 11), eternal hell—separation from God. So they had nothing to fear. Even if they were martyred, they would be ushered into glory and would receive the victor's crown from Jesus.

Always keep in mind that it costs something to be a disciple of Jesus, but it costs a lot more if you are not. The world may call us poor Christians, but in God's sight we are rich!

Pergamum: A Compromising Church

The greatest danger you face in your spiritual life is not from Satan, demons, or other religions; it is from compromise, namely, backing down from what you know God wants for your life.

Pergamum was once the greatest city in Asia. It was the first city in that part of the world to have a temple dedicated to the worship of Caesar, and the Pergamum people were fanatical devotees of the Imperial Cult. If Satan had an area headquarters, Pergamum would have been the place. The city was dedicated to false religion. In addition to its being a seat of emperor worship, Pergamum also was home to an enormous temple to the Greek god Zeus, which was high atop a prominent mountain. Also in the city was a temple to

Aesculapius (Asclepius), the Greco-Roman god of medicine, whose insignia was a snake wrapped around a staff.

This penchant to worship false gods may help us to understand a little better Jesus' words, "I know where you dwell, where Satan's throne is" (Revelation 2:13). Do you ever feel like that? That you are living in the middle of a satanic stronghold? Rest assured; God always has a witness, even in tough places. Maybe that witness is you.

What Did Jesus Approve About the Christians at Pergamum?

The Christians at Pergamum suffered severe persecutions for their faith, and at least one of their number, Antipas, had died because of his witness (2:13). We don't know much about Antipas. Whatever way he died, he did not die outside the notice of Jesus.

Despite intense pressure the believers at Pergamum refused to deny Christ and say "Caesar is Lord." Interestingly, the title that Jesus used for Himself in the letter to these people—"The One who has the sharp two-edged sword" (2:12)—was a direct swipe at the sword as a symbol of Roman power.

Jesus' Accusations Against the Church of Pergamum

Despite the steadfastness of the Pergamum, Satan the Dragon, the deceiving serpent, was making inroads here. A group of compromising people either infiltrated or had grown up in the church.

These compromises taught the doctrine of Balaam. You might recall that Balaam was a prophet of God who prostituted his gifts for money from Balak, the monarch of Moab, who hired him to curse the people of Israel. Balaam agreed, but when he attempted to pronounce a curse over Israel, the words that came out of his mouth were a blessing instead (Numbers 22–24). God turned those curses into blessings! He still does so many times today. He will turn your enemy's curses into blessings for you.

Unfortunately, if you read the whole story of Balaam and Balak, you will discover that Balaam advised Balak to befriend the Hebrews and seduce them into compromise by worshipping idols and engaging in sexual immorality. Eventually, God destroyed tens of thousands of His people because they disobeyed and compromised their faith at the instigation of Balaam and Balak.

You may ask, "What does this have to do with the church at Pergamum?" Apparently, some folks in this church took the easy road, the popular path, and compromised their faith. Who cares if you compromise? Jesus does. The Lord accused the Pergamum church of committing spiritual fornication by saying "Caesar is Lord." Of course, as soon as they did, the Romans said, "See, these aren't such bad guys. These Christians aren't so different, a little weird, maybe, but they are just like us." And of course, the ones who did compromise were allowed back in the guilds. They could get a job and get ahead in life. Compromise seemed sensible and comfortable, but it cost some of the Pergamum worshippers their souls. If you compromise your Christian values to get ahead in the world, you may gain a little, but eventually you will lose it all.

Ironically, the word *pergamum* means "married." Imagine if at your wedding your spouse said, "I pledge to you that I will be faithful *most* of the time." Would you agree to that? I certainly hope not! No, we want total commitment and fidelity from our spouse. In a similar manner and on a much deeper level, God wants a total, irrevocable commitment from us because, as His church, we are the bride of Christ. And what kind of bride should we be? A pure, holy bride. In contrast, in Revelation, the world system is pictured as a harlot.

ADMONITION TO PERGAMUM

Christ's admonition to the church at Pergamum was straightforward. "Repent," Jesus said, "or else I am coming to you quickly, and I will make war against them with the sword of My mouth" (Revelation 2:16). The Lord's implication was clear. Antipas felt the sword of Rome, but this church would feel the sword of Jesus if they would not repent. Do you get the idea that Jesus is serious about this compromise issue?

Jesus said, "To him who overcomes, to him I will give some of the hidden manna" (2:17). What a promise this is to those who will remain faithful.

Manna, of course, has a long history with God's people, introduced during the Exodus as a means of God's provision and stretching all the way to the ark of the covenant, where some manna was placed as a reminder of God's goodness. Jesus was reminding the Christians of Pergamum that He could and would nourish and take care of them.

In addition to the hidden manna, Jesus also promised the overcomers at Pergamum a "white stone." The white stone is intriguing and has at least two possible meanings:

1. In a court of law, a white stone was used by a judge when the verdict was for acquittal (a black stone meant the accused was guilty).
2. A white stone was often used as an admission ticket to a feast. The white stone was also a sign to the staff of a wealthy man's home that you were to be welcomed as an honored guest for lodging and dining as you travelled through his city.

Either or both of these metaphors would apply to believers who overcome. They have been declared not guilty because of faith in Jesus' blood. They have gained admission to the greatest feast of all—the marriage supper of the Lamb, the wedding feast of Jesus.

Thyatira: The Corrupted Church

Thyatira was a garrison city, a military town where soldiers were housed. It was a relatively small town between Pergamum and Sardis, but it was a bustling commercial center noted for its textiles and purple dye. Since only the extremely rich could afford to buy purple garments, purple came to be associated with wealth and royalty.

As an interesting sidebar, Thyatira was the hometown of Lydia, one of Paul's first converts in Philippi (Acts 16:14). Lydia was a seller of purple fabric and consequently was probably a wealthy businesswoman.

Because Thyatira was a commercial town, the trade guilds had a powerful influence on civic matters, and there were many guilds there. Wherever the guilds were strong, there were almost always two great enemies of Christ to be found within the city limits: idolatry and immorality.

Thyatira also had a special temple devoted to the worship of Apollo, the sun god, called Tyrimmaus in Greek, which may explain why the Lord introduced Himself as the Son of God (see Revelation 2:18), perhaps as a play on words that the Christians in Thyatira would catch.[14] This is the only time in Revelation this title is used for Jesus.

Interestingly, this fourth letter, the central letter of the seven, is to Thyatira, the tiniest town among the seven, and yet this is the longest letter. It is also the most sober letter, solemn in tone and context. Why? Because this was a good church that was being corrupted from within. So the Lord spoke a message through John of severe warning and judgment to this congregation.

Jesus reminds us of the description of His eyes and feet: "The Son of God, who has eyes like a flame of fire, and His feet are like burnished bronze" (2:18). This is a God who does not mess around; He is powerful and sees right through our spiritual façades.

Jesus said, "I know your deeds," and then He listed some traits about the Thyatira Christians with which He was pleased. Jesus said that He knew about their love, faith, service, perseverance, and motives. Their good works were increasing, and these were not just religious activities.

Although there was a lot of good about this church, Jesus was upset that they tolerated evil in their midst. God does not grade on a curve. No amount of good works can compensate for the tolerance of sin in our lives, homes, or churches. It's one thing to mess up, to do wrong. We've all done that. But to tolerate sin, coddle it, and make a place for it will lead to destruction.

What Was Going On?

The church permitted a false prophetess to influence and teach in the congregation, leading them into compromise similar to Jezebel's activities in the Old Testament (see Revelation 2:20). This Jezebel taught the believers to compromise with false religions, especially emperor worship, so they would not lose their jobs or their place in the guilds at Thyatira. Besides a lack of courage and commitment, the ready acceptance of these teachings by the believers indicates at least three negative character traits: selfishness, unwillingness to sacrifice for Christ, and unbelief that He can protect them.

The stakes for compromising the truth are high. Not only did this Jezebel bring destruction to herself, but she had an awful influence on many in the church who honestly wanted to please God. She led them astray with her great gifts and talents (2:20). She took their attention off the Lord and directed it to other things.

Jesus said, "I gave her time to repent, and she does not want to repent of her immorality" (2:21). The word He used here is *porneia,* the root from which we get the word *pornography.* Apparently this woman, and those she influenced in Thyatira, had grown stubborn, proud, and unwilling to repent. Even when confronted with her sin, she did not want to change.

When is the best time to repent? The short answer is, as soon as you know you have sinned. Keep a short account with God.

In the 1960s and 1970s, I served under Pat Robertson at the Christian Broadcasting Network for eight years where *The 700 Club* television show began. Pat gave me great opportunities to minister, which I gladly appreciated as his student and he as my mentor. Every time he entered the studio during a broadcast, I gladly turned the show over to Pat so he could talk to our audience, whether to teach or make an announcement. It always encouraged me whenever I saw him give an invitation to accept Christ. He continually taught people to keep short accounts with God, a lesson I have gratefully learned.

The most dangerous people in any church are those quasi-Christians who willingly compromise what they know to be true and refuse to repent, even when they are urged to do so. That's what the church at Thyatira was doing. And that is why Jesus said that He would use this church as a solemn warning and example to all the churches not to tolerate evil and compromise (2:23).

The result? Jesus said that people will die. "I will throw her on a bed of sickness, and those who commit adultery with her into great tribulation, unless they repent of her deeds. And I will kill her children with pestilence, and all the churches will know that I am He who searches the minds and hearts; and I will give to each one of you according to your deeds" (2:22–23). Notice that Jezebel is pictured as a harlot. The bed of sin often becomes the bed of judgment.

SOME GOOD NEWS

Thankfully, not everyone in the church had been unfaithful to the Lord. There were still some good folks there, and Jesus had a special word for them. "Hold fast until I come" (Revelation 2:25). In other words, hold on to the faith you have! Don't get mired down in the mud or sidetracked by false teachings. Keep on the right road.

Jesus condemned the "deep things of Satan" (2:24) at Thyatira. Perhaps these were blatantly demonic practices mixed with Christianity, but more likely these "deep things" included an early form of Gnosticism. The Gnostics loved to emphasize that they knew the deeper things and were teaching them.

Jesus said not to buy this nonsense. "I place no other burden upon you" (2:24). Keep the gospel message pure and simple. That doesn't mean we shouldn't seek to go deeper with God, but a continually deeper relationship with Christ is part of His original message and plan. Those who would add to it are condemned. Hold fast to your love, faith, service, and perseverance.

In encouraging believers to hold fast until He returns, Jesus promised them "authority over the nations" (2:26). Jesus then quoted from Psalm 2:8–9, promising that His rule or authority will be strong but also loving. To those who will obey, His rule will be that of a shepherd, but to those who resist, they will be like clay pots that are easily smashed. His rule will smash them to smithereens.

WHAT A REWARD!

In addition to the opportunity to rule, Jesus promised His followers another interesting reward, perhaps the ultimate reward, the morning star—the first bright light as the darkness of night dissipates. Later, in Revelation 22:16, we will discover that Jesus is the bright morning star. So He was basically saying here that He would give Himself to the one who overcomes!

One interesting side note can be found in Isaiah 14:12. There, we're told that Satan, who wanted the kingdom for himself, is named Lucifer, which in Hebrew means "bright star."[15] The compromisers at Thyatira were following the deeper things not of God but of Satan, which leads to death. On the other hand, God's overcomers will share with the true "Morning Star," Jesus Christ.

Sardis: It's Alive! Or Is It?

Back in my youth, a low-budget black-and-white film was produced in Pittsburgh and used university students as actors. That movie, *Night of the Living Dead*, became a cult legend.

In a similar way, the Christian church at Sardis could be called the "Church of the Living Dead." There wasn't much about the church of Sardis that reflected the living Lord.

Sardis was an important trade center about fifty miles east of Ephesus and situated at the junction of five major thoroughfares. The main religion in Sardis was the worship of Artemis, a fertility goddess and a sort of nature cult that worshipped the environment.

How the Mighty Fall

The people of Sardis were rich; their city was one of the greatest cities in the ancient world. They were a powerful population and lived in luxury. But they were overconfident, and consequently they became lazy. Five times the city fell to invaders because the Sardians believed their city was so high that nobody could touch them. In fact, when the enemy found a way to sneak up the rock formations by hiding in large fissures in the mountain range, they found the Sardis battlements completely unguarded.

After Alexander the Great conquered Sardis, the city thrived. But it fell again in exactly the same way to a later invader! Nobody was on guard.

Eventually, the Romans rebuilt the city after a devastating earthquake in AD 17, so when John wrote to Sardis, it was still a wealthy trade center, but the people were degenerate, morally sick, weak, lazy, compromising, and complacent. The Sardian church possessed no life, no spirit. The once-great city on a hill had been lost several times because it failed to keep watch. And in that lazy atmosphere, the church in Sardis reflected the attitudes and conduct of the Sardians.

Is There Any Hope?

There was still hope for the church of Sardis despite this sad scene. Even though they were the Church of the Living Dead, the good news is that God is in the resurrection business! There is hope because Jesus Christ is the head of the church, and He is able to bring new life by the fullness of His Spirit. Indeed, the great revivals in history have all been accompanied by a fresh outpouring of the Holy Spirit, the Spirit of Jesus.

In addressing the church at Sardis, Jesus referred to Himself as "He who has the seven Spirits of God" (Revelation 3:1). What does that mean? We know there is only one Holy Spirit, and it is the Spirit of Jesus, but He is described also as seven burning lamps (4:5) and seven all-seeing eyes (5:6). The phrase "the seven Spirits of God" may refer to Isaiah 11:2–5:

> The Spirit of the LORD will rest on Him,
> The spirit of wisdom and understanding,
> The spirit of counsel and strength,
> The spirit of knowledge and the fear of the LORD.
> And He will delight in the fear of the LORD,
> And He will not judge by what His eyes see,
> Nor make a decision by what His ears hear;
> But with righteousness He will judge the poor,
> And decide with fairness for the afflicted of the earth;
> And He will strike the earth with the rod of His mouth,
> And with the breath of His lips He will slay the wicked.
> Also righteousness will be the belt about His loins,
> And faithfulness the belt about His waist.

Here we see seven aspects or manifestations of the Spirit: wisdom, understanding, counsel, strength, knowledge, fear of the Lord, and righteous judgment. In other words, the phrase indicates the Spirit in His fullness and completeness.

It is the Holy Spirit who founded the church on the Day of Pentecost. It is the Holy Spirit who gives life and power to the church. And, of course, that is exactly what the dead church at Sardis was missing. But Jesus stands ready with the power of His Spirit to bring new life and revival.

We Need Some Good Leaders

Jesus also referred to the seven stars, possibly the pastors or church leaders (Revelation 3:1). Regardless, it is important to note that they are in Christ's hand too.

Unfortunately the church of Sardis had lost that concept and was now dead. Jesus knew it. Indeed, Jesus said, "I know your deeds, that you have a name that you are alive, but you are dead" (3:1). He was saying they may have fooled others by their external appearances and high and mighty reputation, but He knew what they were really like on the inside.

Shortly after I was released from prison, I was washing some windows in the house where Lori and I were living, and I fell off the ladder. I wasn't hurt, but the fall caused me to notice that vines had grown up all over the gardenia bushes. Everything looked green, prosperous, and healthy. But I noticed the vines had briars on them. I took some clippers to cut the vines off the bushes, and when I pulled out the vines I discovered that few of the gardenia bushes under the vine were thriving. In fact, when I cut out the vines and the weeds, there was very little left alive below the scruff. It had looked alive on the surface, but in actuality it was dead.

As I gazed at that strange scene, God spoke to me: "This is an example of a lot of religion today. It looks green and prosperous and healthy on the outside, but inside it is dead."

That was true of the church at Sardis.

This letter is different from the others we've examined so far in that there are few words of commendations to this body, except a commendation to "a few people" (3:4). Nor are there any major issues. There are no doctrinal problems mentioned that needed correction, no intense suffering. They might have been better off if they were suffering. No, this church was just *there,* comfortable, content, living on its reputation. It had a reputation without any present spiritual reality. They had a religious form without any spiritual force, a spiritual program without spiritual power. Frankly, although it grieves me to say, I fear a lot of Christians (including gospel singers, preachers, authors, and speakers) today could fit in easily at the Church of the Living Dead. This was the "Church of the Blahs."

The Christians at Sardis were decent people in a dying church with a dying witness. They allowed what they had to slip away. In fact, even what they had left was about to die.

Maybe that's why Jesus said, "Wake up, and strengthen the things that remain, which were about to die" (3:2). Be watchful! You're sleeping again, Sardis. Haven't you learned anything from your past? Wake up! The first step toward revival and renewal is to realize that something is wrong and to admit that you cannot go on this way any longer.

Jesus offered encouragement, but He also issued a warning to the church at Sardis. He said, "Therefore if you do not wake up, I will come like a thief, and you will not know at what hour I will come to you" (3:3). Jesus was not referring to the Second Coming; He was talking about coming when the Sardis church might least expect it, coming in judgment, here and now.

The Faithful Few

There is some good news. Like most churches, Sardis had a faithful few. We often make fun of the faithful few, but Jesus doesn't. The Bible speaks quite positively about the remnant of God's people. These few people in Sardis "have not soiled their garments" (Revelation 3:4), that is, they had not been unfaithful to Christ. As a reward, Jesus said, "They will walk with Me in white, for they are worthy" (3:4). Yet they were not worthy on their own merits, but rather because of their faith and their unwavering commitment to Christ.

Jesus went on to make a beautiful promise to this faithful few. First, they will be "clothed in white garments" (3:5), and white robes represent victory.

White is, of course, the color of purity. Traditionally, brides wear white at their weddings to signify purity. White robes may also stand for our resurrected bodies in heaven.

Part of the promise of Jesus is that those who overcome will be clothed in white, but there is also a second portion of the promise. Jesus said, "I will not erase his name from the book of life" (3:5). That is a powerful word of assurance from Jesus Himself. But what is the book of life? You may recall that Moses was willing to be wiped out of the book of life to save his people from the consequences of their sin (Exodus 32:31–33). The psalmist said, "May they [the wicked] be blotted out of the book of life" (Psalm 69:28). Daniel reported, "Everyone who is found written in the book [of life], will be rescued" (Daniel 12:1). And the apostle Paul appealed to the Lord, saying, "I ask you also to help these . . . whose names are in the book of life" (Philippians 4:3). Revelation 20:15 tells us, "If anyone's name was not found written in the book of life, he was thrown into the lake of fire." As for the faithful, Revelation 21:27 specifies that "nothing unclean, and no one who practices abomination and lying, shall ever come into it [heaven], but only those whose names are written in the Lamb's book of life."

A third part of the promise to those who overcome is equally fascinating. Jesus said, "I will confess his name before My Father and before His angels" (3:5). When He acknowledges us in heaven, all the privileges of His kingdom are ours. Can you imagine Jesus announcing your name in heaven? Jesus said, "Everyone who confesses Me before men, I will also confess him before My Father who is in heaven" (Matthew 10:32). One day soon He will do precisely that!

Philadelphia: Open Doors of Opportunity

The church at Philadelphia could easily be called the "Church of the Open Door," because it welcomed people in love and it sent people out to explore the opportunities God had opened before them. The city of Philadelphia was situated at a strategic site along a main road of the ancient Near East, where the regions of Mysia, Lydia, and Phrygia came together, and thus the town was known as a gateway to the East. Philadelphia was also known as Little Athens, because there were so many Greek temples there. In the context of the book of Revelation, you can view this city in two ways: either as an area of great opposition to the gospel or an area of great opportunity for the gospel.

Philadelphia was a border town founded with the idea that it would be a stepping stone for Greek culture and language to influence the regions of Lydia and Phrygia. So in a sense it was a missionary town even before the Lord's letter to the church was written, although its mission was not to spread the gospel but Greek culture. Philly was a relatively small town built on the edge of a volcanic plain. Not without reason, the area was known as "the burnt land." To get an idea of the land around Philadelphia, think of the pictures of the area around Mount St. Helens in the state of Washington after its eruption in May 1980.

Volcanic soil is extremely fertile, and the land around Philadelphia was especially good for grapes, which made winemaking one of the city's leading industries. Throw in the Greco-Roman pantheon, and the religion of the area revolved around the worship of Dionysus (or Bacchus), the wine god.

ROCK AND ROLL AND LOVE

One of the negative aspects about living near an extinct volcano is that the area is prone to earthquakes. Philadelphia was no exception. It was situated on top of a major geologic fault. The big one came in AD 17. Philadelphia was heavily damaged, and at least ten surrounding cities were destroyed. After the earthquake, a lot of residents were skeptical about returning to their homes, especially since this earthquake was not just one event; it was followed by numerous aftershocks.

Living in Philadelphia in the first century would be like living along the San Andreas Fault in California today. Everything would be fine and then suddenly a street would crack open or a wall would split down the middle. Many people decided to live on the burnt land in huts and tents and other temporary housing. Those who moved back into town spent much of their time repairing the destruction and trying to stay out of the way of falling buildings. Every time the earth shook, the city dwellers would run for their lives. That shaky setting is the background for this city and the Lord's letter to the church there.

Interestingly, of all the churches cited in Revelation, Philadelphia receives the greatest praise. It was a small, struggling church, yet very little if anything negative is said about this congregation. Of all the churches mentioned, the church at Philadelphia is the only one still thriving today. While there are Christian churches in Turkey, they are few in number and mostly underground because of Muslim laws against evangelizing—yet one of the strongest churches calls Philadelphia home. Some reports recently estimated there are as many as five thousand Christians in this town of about fifteen thousand people.

Jesus identified Himself to the church at Philadelphia with a powerful title: "He who is holy" (Revelation 3:7). Holy means "set apart, different, pure." Jesus also refers to Himself as "He . . . who is true" (3:7). This does not mean true as opposed to false or lying. He who is holy would not lie. Being true here means genuine as opposed to unreal, a substitute, or a cheap imitation. In other words, Jesus is real; He is not a manufactured god. He is the only one, true, authentic God.

Why is this important? It's important because there were hundreds of false gods in ancient times. As an example consider that there were dozens of Greek temples in Philadelphia. In the Greek pantheon, there were twelve primary gods and goddesses and thirty-nine lesser gods and goddesses. Amid this crowd, Jesus asserted that only He can rightfully claim to be God.

Jesus added that He "has the key of David, who opens and no one will shut, and who shuts and no one opens" (3:7). In the ancient Near East, keys are symbols of authority. In the New Testament, we read about the "keys of the kingdom of heaven" in Matthew 16:19 and the "key of knowledge" in Luke 11:52. Having all the keys is another way of saying that Jesus is the one who has final, absolute authority. Nobody gets to heaven except through Him!

We know that He also has the "keys of death and of Hades" (Revelation 1:18). The idea is that only Jesus can admit anyone into the New Jerusalem, heaven, the new city of David, the presence of God. Not Muhammad, not

Buddha, not the pope, not a cult leader, not a television preacher. Only Jesus. He holds the keys to your life and mine.

Jesus went on to tell the Philadelphians, "I have put before you an open door which no one can shut, because you have a little power, and have kept My word" (3:8). In the New Testament, an open door speaks of opportunity, especially opportunities for ministry. Jesus acknowledged that the Philadelphians had only a little power and strength, but because they did not deny His name, He told them He had much more for them to do.

But two big obstacles had to be overcome before the Philadelphians could take advantage of this open door. First, they were not strong. They had little power. That is, they were not a large church; but they were a faithful church: "You have kept the word of My perseverance" (3:10). You may not feel spiritually powerful, but in your weakness, God shows Himself to be strong. The Philadelphians had stayed strong in the face of persecution when others had not. It's not the size of your faith but the depth of your faithfulness and obedience to Christ that makes the difference.

Second, the Philadelphians had to overcome the opposition of some Jewish townspeople. These Jews were not Orthodox Jews, but they were nonetheless incensed at the ministry of the new Christians. Jesus referred to them as the "synagogue of Satan, who say that they are Jews and are not" (3:9).

It is not easy to witness for Christ when a lot of people are against you and spreading lies about you. But Jesus promised that one day He "will make them come and bow down at your feet, and make them know that I have loved you" (3:9).

For Pre-Tribulation Believers

In Jesus' promise to the Philadelphia church He said: "Because you have kept the word of My perseverance, I also will keep you from the hour of testing, that hour which is about to come upon the whole world, to test those who dwell upon the earth" (Revelation 3:10). The word translated here as "testing" can also be translated as "tribulation" or even "temptation" or "pressure." Usually the word does not have the article "the," but here it does, implying perhaps that this is no ordinary testing, tribulation, temptation, or trial. This is *the* temptation or *the* Tribulation. This particular usage of the word for testing occurs only one other time in the New Testament, John 17:15. Consequently, some scholars say this refers to *the* Tribulation, the time that John will describe later in Revelation.

Even if John was referring to the Tribulation, there is no reason to assume that Christians will have been raptured by that time. They may simply be kept safe by the power of God during that time, much as the Hebrews in Egypt were kept safe when the plagues struck prior to Pharaoh's letting God's people go. The region in which God's people lived, Goshen, was spared. Even though people all around them experienced the plagues, God's people went through it but were saved from it.

Regardless, Jesus gave the Philadelphia church a word of warning and a word of encouragement all in the same statement: "Hold fast" (3:11). Don't let anyone steal your crown! No false doctrine, no deceit, no dissention—don't allow anything to rob you as you run your race. Don't let anyone else take your crown because you are unworthy. The crown of victory will be given to those who have run the race and endured to the end.

Promises You Can Depend On

In almost rapid-fire succession, Jesus gave five promises to the overcomers at Philadelphia. First, He told them, "He who overcomes, I will make him a pillar in the temple of My God" (Revelation 3:12). In ancient times, cities honored outstanding citizens by erecting a pillar and inscribing their names on it. Jesus said that He was going to make the Philadelphians into pillars that could not be shaken by earthquakes, volcanoes, or anything else.

Second, Jesus promised, "He will not go out from it anymore" (3:12). While such a promise might sound constraining to us, imagine the impact of these words to a group of people who were constantly running for their lives at the slightest shaking of the ground beneath their feet. Jesus told them not to worry about that anymore. You won't have to run for your life ever again. There is incredible stability, safety, and security in Jesus.

Third, Jesus said, "I will write on him the name of My God" (3:12). In addition to the idea of inscribing our names on a pillar, this may refer to the Old Testament practice of branding a bond slave with the initials of the owner. This inscription of the name of God also reminded John's readers of the word that came through Moses, instructing him to have the priests bless the people: "They shall invoke My name on the sons of Israel, and I then will bless them" (Numbers 6:27). The idea is that this is the mark of God on those with whom He is well pleased.

Fourth, Jesus will write upon the overcomer the name of the city of God: "I will write on him . . . the name of the city of My God, the new Jerusalem, which comes down out of heaven from My God" (Revelation 3:12). This signature stands for citizenship in the city of God. Interestingly the phrase "new Jerusalem" is always said to be "coming down out of heaven from God" (21:2, 10). We tend to think of heaven as up there or out there, but apparently God is going to recreate this world into a new heaven and a new earth.

Fifth, Jesus will write on them a new name: "I will write on him . . . My new name" (3:12). This is a name that nobody knows yet, nobody but Jesus. Maybe it means that, at that time, He will show us His full glory. It may seem incomprehensible to us now, but then we will understand.

Laodicea: The Sin That Makes God Sick

Of the seven churches addressed in Revelation, the church at Laodicea was the one most soundly condemned. There is not one word of praise for this church, nothing good is said about it, and no redeeming qualities are listed. Yet as much as I hate to say so, I feel strongly that the majority of people sitting in our churches today would feel all too comfortable attending the Laodicean church. What was this church like?

Jesus described it as "neither cold nor hot" (3:15). He even said, "I wish that you were cold or hot. So because you are lukewarm, and neither hot nor cold, I will spit you out of My mouth" (3:15–16). Jesus was saying that lukewarm spiritual conditions make Him sick!

There are few things in life that we enjoy in lukewarm condition. If we don't accept lukewarm responses on a human level, how much more does He—the one who loved us so much that He gave Himself to a cross that we might be saved—demand a more vibrant, vigorous response? It is not enough to say "I believe in God" or even "I believe in Jesus." The devil believes in God and Jesus, too, and he will spend eternity in hell.

I am convinced that today God is saying: "Make up your mind, one way or the other. By vacillating, you make me sick." The truth is that wishy-washy, lukewarm Christianity has never pleased God, and it will not survive when the intense times described in Revelation occur.

How Do Good People Go Bad?

How did the Laodiceans allow themselves to get into such an anemic spiritual condition? Probably the same way we do: by neglecting the opportunities to grow spiritually, by allowing negative elements to creep into our lives and not dealing with them, permitting ourselves to tolerate pride, conceit, arrogance, self-delusion, self-righteousness, and indifference to the Spirit of God.

Pride Before a Fall

Laodicea prided itself on three things: their financial wealth, their outstanding clothing manufacturing, and a famous eye salve. Financially, the city was a major banking center. The residents had money and possessions. In fact, when an earthquake destroyed the city in AD 60, the Laodiceans did not seek help from anyone. They simply rebuilt their city using their own funds. The city boasted not one but two large amphitheaters, each seating more than twenty-five thousand people.

Laodicea was also known for an unusually soft black wool, which led local entrepreneurs to develop a thriving clothing manufacturing business. They had a reputation for providing the latest styles and the best quality of clothing.

The city was also a great center of learning. Local doctors were proud of the fact that they had developed a medicine used all over the world to relieve eye irritations. Even nonmedical Laodiceans took pride in this famous eye salve.

A proud and wealthy people with no need of anything, the Laodiceans saw no reason to change. No doubt, this arrogant attitude permeated the church to the point that the people were oblivious to their true spiritual condition.

Clearly, there was a drastic difference between how the Laodiceans saw themselves and how Jesus saw the Laodicean church. When Jesus described this church, He said, "You say, 'I am rich, and have become wealthy, and have need of nothing,' and you do not know that you are wretched and miserable and poor and blind and naked" (Revelation 3:17).

I can almost hear the rich Laodicean Christians protest: "Wretched? Miserable? Poor? Blind? Naked? Are you talking about us? Are you sure you have the right address on that letter?"

Oh, yes, they had money and possessions, but they were spiritually destitute. For all their fancy name-brand clothing, they were spiritually naked. No suit of clothes could cover the stain of sin on their hearts; no amount of makeup could hide the guilt and shame on their faces. Like the sovereign in Hans Christian Andersen's classic story "The Emperor's New Clothes," these people thought they were dressed in splendor but did not realize they were spiritually naked.

On top of all this, Jesus said they were blind. With all of their learning and great intelligence, despite their remedies for all sorts of eye ailments, the Laodiceans were blind to their own condition.

Sadly, this church typifies most of our modern-day congregations. It may well symbolize where we are in human history. Having begun on the Day of Pentecost in a flame of holy fire, we have now diluted the gospel to the point that our lukewarm message is useless to the world and unsatisfying even to the church.

WHAT CAN WE DO?

Jesus offered only one way out of this lukewarm, spiritually nauseating mess: "I advise you to buy from Me gold refined by fire so that you may become rich, and white garments so that you may clothe yourself, and that the shame of your nakedness will not be revealed; and eye salve to anoint your eyes so that you may see" (Revelation 3:18).

Isn't that interesting? Jesus tells us how to find true riches: gold refined by fire, things that will last forever. Like so many people today, the Laodiceans were obsessed with obtaining money and possessions. They were wrapped up in accumulating the riches of this world. But Jesus said, "Don't waste your time on temporary, transitory riches, things that will pass away with time. I want to give you true riches with eternal value, things that money, stocks, and securities cannot purchase."

Jesus also instructed the Laodiceans to purchase from Him white garments to cover their nakedness. As I mentioned earlier, white garments are a symbol of purity, forgiveness, righteousness, and holiness. That is the kind of bride for whom Jesus is returning. In Revelation, John saw a vision of the wedding of Jesus and His church, the bride, and he was instructed to write, "Blessed are those who are invited to the marriage supper of the Lamb" (19:9).

The third part of Jesus' advice to the Laodiceans was that they should buy eye salve to anoint their eyes so they could see better. I am convinced that one of our greatest needs is to see ourselves as we really are. What a difference it would make if we allowed the Spirit of God to remove the scales from our eyes so we could truly see ourselves!

Tough Love

Jesus explained to the Laodiceans why He was so hard on them: "Those whom I love, I reprove and discipline; therefore be zealous and repent" (Revelation 3:19). Moreover, this stern rebuke is accompanied by a promise: "Behold, I stand at the door and knock; if anyone hears My voice and opens the door, I will come in to him and will dine with him, and he with Me" (3:20). What an incredible invitation!

First, Jesus stands at the door and knocks. Think about it. How sad is that? The King of kings and Lord of lords stands outside the door of His own church, knocking, hoping that someone will open the door and invite Him to come inside. But we must take this invitation personally. He is standing at the door of our lives. That's what makes Christianity so radically different from other religions. It is not that you are seeking God, but Christ is seeking you.

Second, He won't crash through the door. You must open it. In Holman Hunt's famous painting *The Light of the World*, Jesus is depicted outside a large door as though He were knocking. But what is conspicuously absent from the door is a door handle or knob. That was not an oversight on the part of the artist. Quite the contrary, the artist was making a subtle, powerful, spiritual point that the door must be opened from the inside.

Third, Jesus promised that those who do open the door will enjoy His presence. He will enter and dine with you. Believe me, Jesus is no moocher. He will bring with Him everything you need for a banquet greater than anything you have ever imagined. On His menu will be love, joy, and peace, with heaven for dessert!

It is intriguing that Jesus instructed the Laodiceans to "buy from Me" the things they so desperately needed. That creates a problem. How can we who are poor, wretched, miserable, blind, and naked buy anything from Him who has no want or need, from our God who owns everything? What can we possibly give Him in return for the life He offers us? Gold? He walks on streets paved with the stuff. Houses? He is building us a home in heaven that far exceeds anything we have ever seen or imagined. Our service? With a snap of His fingers, He could have ten thousand angels do His bidding, and they would do a much better job than we might do, with far less complaining!

Seven Churches and Seven Words of Warning

From these seven churches we can learn at least seven things we need to know as we head into the times of testing, temptation, and tribulation ahead.

1. From **Ephesus**: We must be careful not to leave our first love.
2. From **Smyrna**: We must be ready to trust God in the midst of suffering.
3. From **Pergamum**: We must not water down what we believe.

4. From **Thyatira**: We must not compromise our morality or ethics.
5. From **Sardis**: We must guard against spiritual complacency and the accompanying dryness and deadness.
6. From **Philadelphia**: We should look for the open doors to share the gospel.
7. From **Laodicea**: We must guard against spiritual lethargy and lukewarmness.

It will serve us well to periodically review these admonitions as we see the events that John envisioned happening around us. Perhaps the greatest truth I learned from the seven churches is that no matter how deep in sin or problematic mankind becomes, there is always hope. Never give up! There is always a way back from the deepest pit.

6

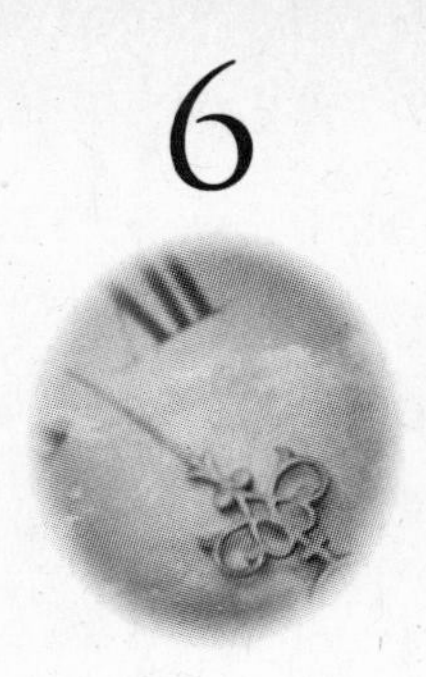

Where the Rapture Is Not

Most Christians believe that Jesus will one day return in power, glory, and judgment to reward His followers and to punish those who have rejected God. But the question that divides the hearts and minds of many believers—and sometimes even divides Christians into separate camps and denominations—is whether believers will experience some or all of the tough times described in the book of Revelation and other prophetic scriptures.

For many years I preached that Christians would not have to endure the horrors of the Tribulation, that Jesus would return and take His people out of this world. Admittedly, most of my thoughts on the matter were not original, nor were my views based on years of studying the Scriptures and reaching valid biblically-based conclusions. For the most part I simply believed what I had heard sincere men and women of God teach, namely, that Jesus was coming back before the seven-year Tribulation in an event called the Rapture.

Although the word *rapture* does not appear in the Bible, we based our ideas on a passage from Paul's first letter to the Thessalonians. The apostle encouraged believers with these words:

> For the Lord Himself will descend from heaven with a shout, with the voice of an archangel, and with the trumpet of God. And the dead in Christ will rise first. Then we who are alive and remain shall be caught up

together with them in the clouds to meet the Lord in the air. And thus we shall always be with the Lord (1 Thessalonians 4:16–17, NKJV).

Although this passage does indeed describe the Second Coming, we drew some unwarranted conclusions about when and how this event would occur. This "catching up" of the saints, which is what the word *rapture* means, was to take place secretly, as far as unbelievers were concerned. Only believers, it was thought, would be able to experience and witness the appearing of the Lord. Suddenly, Jesus was to appear in the air, and in the twinkling of an eye we would be gone, whisked off the ground to meet the Lord in the sky. The dead in Christ, believers who had died prior to His coming, would rise first, and together we would all meet Him in the air. From there He would take us to live with Him eternally. Later, Christ would return *again,* this time in power and glory to judge the world and set up His eternal kingdom. The Rapture was to happen, of course, *before* any events of the Tribulation began to pummel the earth.

One of my favorite prophetic scripture verses is, "Watch therefore, and pray always that you may be counted worthy to escape all these things that will come to pass, and to stand before the Son of Man" (Luke 21:36, NKJV). I placed a heavy emphasis on the word *escape*, because I was convinced it went against God's loving nature to allow His people to go through the horrors of the Tribulation.

My thinking on the subject changed when, in prison, I searched out the passages that described the Rapture that precedes the Tribulation. To my amazement, I could not find any. I found certain scriptures that other preachers and I twisted and conveniently interpreted to fit my "prosperity" messages, but when I allowed the Bible to speak for itself, I realized that my notions of a pre-Tribulation Rapture were not based in scripture.

Revelation 11 is where I now see the Lord's return and the catching away of Christ's church taking place, but many sincere and godly pastors, evangelists, and theologians preach and teach that Jesus comes back at the beginning of Revelation 4 (the pre-Tribulation Rapture). They base this on three points.

First, the church is not mentioned specifically again after Revelation 3. After each letter to the churches, Jesus concluded with a warning: "He who has an ear, let him hear what the Spirit says to the churches" (Revelation 2:7, 11, 17, 29; 3:6, 13, 22). But in Revelation 13:9, we find only, "If anyone has an ear, let him hear." Many theologians assume the church has been raptured, caught up, taken to heaven by this time.

Wait a minute! Throughout Revelation, John told us about believers and saints (for the latter, see 5:8; 8:3–4; 11:18; 13:7, 10; 14:12; 16:6; 17:6; 18:20, 24; 19:8; 20:9). Certainly, those Christians are part of the universal church that pre-Tribulation teachers assume is missing after Revelation 4.

Second, some conclude that because John used more Old Testament terminology in the different names for God—such as Lord, Almighty, and names other than Father, as in other parts of the New Testament—from chapters 4 through 19, this indicates that John was implying the Christians would be gone. Frankly, while these are interesting points, I don't find the evidence compelling that Christians will be in heaven while the rest of the earth's population suffers the Tribulation.

Third, most pre-Tribulation Rapture devotees assert that God would not allow His people to experience His wrath. I agree to some degree; I don't think God would allow His people to undergo the full measure of His wrath, but historically, God did not exempt His people from tough times. He brought them through them, however. And even if we assume a similarity to the plagues that struck Egypt, God allowed His people to live through them, protected in Goshen, while the rest of the nation was devastated by the plagues. Something like that may happen again when we see the wrath of God poured out around us, even though we may not be experiencing the worst of it ourselves.

Those who insist the church is gone sometimes point to the open door and the first voice like a trumpet that John encountered:

> After this I looked, and, behold a door was opened in heaven: and the first voice which I heard was as it were of a trumpet talking with me; which said, Come up hither, and I will shew thee things which must be hereafter. (Revelation 4:1, KJV)

Some teachers purport that this is the trumpet that calls believers to heaven, the same trumpet we read about in 1 Thessalonians 4:16–17:

> For the Lord Himself will descend from heaven with a shout, with the voice of the archangel and with the trumpet of God, and the dead in Christ will rise first. Then we who are alive and remain shall be caught up together with them in the clouds to meet the Lord in the air, and so we shall always be with the Lord.

But this voice in Revelation 4:1 in the Greek is not a trumpet but a "reverberation" or "quivering." John was describing the voice he heard, *not* the sounding of a trumpet. Moreover, the voice was talking to John, inviting *him* to see things that are about to happen in the future! This was the same voice (and the same Greek word) that John first heard in Revelation 1:10: "I heard behind me a loud voice like the sound of a trumpet." John is hearing a mighty, earthshaking voice reverberating in his ears. It is simply not a trumpet in either Revelation 1:10 or 4:1.

I teach with absolute confidence that this cannot be the Rapture. This is merely John's personal experience in which he receives an invitation to the throne room to see the future and receive the rest of the book of Revelation that he is about to write: it is not a call to a rapture in the sky. To think otherwise, I believe, is a twisting of the scripture and the basis for the pre-Tribulation Rapture.

Moreover, the fact that the seven churches that are so paramount in Revelation 2 and 3 are not mentioned again does not necessarily mean the body of Christ is not included in any further discussions throughout the book. Granted, the churches are addressed by their individual cities in Revelation 2 and 3. These congregations met in buildings and homes, but throughout the book, the church is made up of the saints, all true believers, the body of Christ. There is no reason to believe that the Christians are gone simply because there are no specific references to the church.

Why This Is *Not* the Rapture

How can I say with confidence that Revelation 4:1 is not the Rapture? Simply examine the scripture:

> Behold, I tell you a mystery; we shall not all sleep, but we shall all be changed, in a moment, in the twinkling of an eye, at the last trumpet; for the trumpet will sound, and the dead will be raised imperishable, and we will be changed. (1 Corinthians 15:51–52)

The same fellow who wrote those words also wrote the passage to the Thessalonians upon which so much of pre-Tribulation teaching is based. But notice in the above passage there is a key phrase: "at the last trumpet." We must look for the last trumpet! That is when the Christians will be raptured.

Jesus gave the definitive answer in Matthew 24. The disciples asked Jesus, "And what will be the sign of Your coming, and of the end of the age?" (v. 3). Jesus described a number of signs of the times, which we will examine in Revelation 11, and then He told the disciples:

> Immediately after the tribulation of those days the sun will be darkened, and the moon will not give its light; the stars will fall from heaven, and the powers of the heavens will be shaken. Then the sign of the Son of Man will appear in heaven, and then all the tribes of the earth will mourn, and they will see the Son of Man coming on the clouds of heaven with power and great glory. (Matthew 24:29–30, NKJV)

Notice, Jesus told us that His coming would be immediately *after* the "tribulation of those days" (v. 29). This event takes place *after* all the wars, famines, deceptions, earthquakes, and, yes, even the appearance of the Antichrist, as we will see ahead. Then the wait will be over. Jesus will return for us and take His bride, the church, to safety.

But in Revelation 4 there is not a resurrection of Christians who have already died; there is no mention of saints around the throne of God, but only the angels, the four living beings, and the twenty-four elders. Jesus does not return on the clouds. There is no final triumphant shout, no trumpet of God. There is merely a voice that reverberates loud enough to make the earth shake, the same voice that John heard previously. The King James Version has it wrong: the word is "reverberation" not "trumpet."

BEEN THERE, DONE THAT

I understand how easy it is to accept the teaching that Christians will be taken to heaven before the really tough times of the Tribulation begin. I received that same message from my church, my elders, my professors and fellow ministers, so I automatically accepted. But as I studied Revelation in prison, I asked, "What does this mean?" I marked indications of Jesus and God. Jesus said, "My sheep know My voice" (John 10:27). After thousands of hours of studying His Word, I can confidently say I know His voice coming through the Word.

And the Word of God tells us flatly that believers will go through some difficult times.

> For then there will be great tribulation, such as has not been since the beginning of the world until this time, no, nor ever shall be. And unless those days were shortened, no flesh would be saved; but for the elect's sake those days will be shortened (Matthew 24:21–22, NKJV).

People still turn to the Lord in the book of Revelation after chapter 4, and they will be a part of the universal church of Jesus. As the events of Revelation unfold, far more than 144,000 last-days Jews will be saved, as some pre-Tribulation teachers claim.

Moreover, God has given us a pattern in the Old Testament regarding His judgment and the deliverance of His people. He often brings His people *through* the tough times rather than remove them from difficult circumstances. For example, in the midst of the Assyrian invasion and the eventual collapse of Israel in 722 BC, many people in Israel died. Yet God brought a remnant through the Exile and reestablished His kingdom through them. Events took similar paths when, because of their sin and God's judgment, Judah went into exile in Babylon in 586 BC.

While some say the doctrine of a pre-Tribulation Rapture goes all the way back to the second century, I discovered that most pre-Tribulation preachers today base much of their interpretation on the notes of C. I. Scofield, whose popular reference Bible was first published in 1909. But although Dr. Scofield was a good man, a godly man, and a diligent student of the Scriptures, those notes are his *ideas*, not the Bible itself. In recent years a multitude of teachers have been influenced by these pre-Tribulation ideas.

In contrast, the number of outstanding Bible teachers and preachers throughout history who have *not* held to a pre-Tribulation view of the return of Christ is astounding. John Bunyan, Jonathan Edwards, Charles Finney, George Whitefield, Charles and John Wesley, John Knox, Charles Spurgeon, Matthew Henry, William Tyndale, George Mueller, and a host of other great spiritual leaders did not ascribe to the pre-Tribulation view, and some of them leaned heavily toward the idea that Jesus would return *after* the Tribulation.

From my own study, I am convinced that there is no reason to think believers will have been raptured by the time of the events described in Revelation 4.

God's Glorious Throne

When John was called up to heaven, immediately he was in the Spirit, and he saw "a throne was standing in heaven, and One sitting on the throne" (Revelation 4:2). Imagine that! One of the key words in Revelation is *throne*. The throne of God is mentioned in all but three of the twenty-two chapters of Revelation (it is not mentioned in chapters 2, 8, or 9). John referred to a throne forty-six times in his vision; fourteen of those references are in chapter 4 within eleven verses! So you might remember chapter 4 as the chapter of the throne.

Why is that important? Before he began to describe all the horrors that are about to happen (the rise of the Antichrist, the battle of Armageddon, the destruction of major portions of the human race), John placed the emphasis on the glory and sovereignty of God. He is totally in charge. *Our God reigns!*

Peeking into Eternity

The Jews thought of the world as a huge civic arena, almost as though the sky were like a dome of a planetarium that could be opened. Here John was again "in the Spirit," in a sort of spiritual ecstasy or euphoria, lifted up and beyond himself, almost like a trance, yet completely under the control of the Holy Spirit. In that state, he was given the privilege of looking into heaven. John saw the One who is on the throne, the Lord God. It is interesting that he described God in terms of awesome light and colors rather than size and shape. Usually when we try to describe somebody, we say things such as, "He's tall, slender, and handsome," or "She's cute, short, and pudgy." But John didn't do that. John said the one on the throne is "like a jasper stone and a sardius in appearance; and there was a rainbow around the throne, like an emerald in appearance" (v. 3).

I'm so glad that John included the rainbow in his description of God's throne. The rainbow is not a pagan symbol. The first recorded rainbow was a sign from God to His people: a promise!

Precious Stones

The stones John described implied preciousness and great worth. At least two of these stones were found in the breastplate of the high priest (Exodus 28:17). And if we flash forward in time to Revelation 21:19–20, we discover that these stones are among those that are the foundation of the Holy City, the New Jerusalem! Whatever they were, they were the best, most costly, precious materials conceivable.

1. Jasper today is usually considered dull and opaque. But in John's time, jasper was a clear, almost translucent rock, similar to a crystal or a diamond.

2. Sardius was a blood-red stone found near the city of Sardis, one of the churches mentioned in Revelation 3.

3. Emeralds are green, a peaceful, calming color.

Some Bible scholars see significance in these colors: jasper signifies purity, sardius indicates the wrath of God and perhaps the blood of Jesus, and emerald indicates the mercy of God.

God's Honor Guard

In Revelation 4 the rainbow goes completely around the throne of God, like a halo. And surrounding the throne are twenty-four elders also on thrones. They were "clothed in white raiment; and they had on their heads crowns of gold" (4:4, KJV).

Who are these guys? Most likely they symbolically represent the Old and New Testaments, the twelve tribes of Israel and the twelve apostles of Jesus. Why all twenty-four? Possibly because the kingdom of God is now comprised of both Jews and Gentiles.

More important, it is interesting to notice what these elders do. They are perpetually in God's presence and seated on thrones themselves (4:4), but they are not merely sitting there with a "Here's looking down on you" attitude. Oh, no. They are worshipping almighty God!

They are clothed with robes of purity (4:4) and have golden crowns (*stephanos,* victor's crowns) on their heads. They will cast their crowns before the throne—what He gave to them, they will give back to Him. They continually worship and praise the Lord as they bring to God the prayers of the saints (5:8). Later, at least one of them encouraged John when there was no one worthy to open the book with seven seals (5:1–5). One of them interpreted one of the visions (7:13).

What's it like around the throne of God? "And out of the throne proceeded lightnings and thunderings and voices: and there were seven lamps of fire burning before the throne, which are the seven Spirits of God" (4:5, KJV). These flashes of lightning and peals of thunder are reminiscent of similar signs in the sky at Mount Sinai as the people waited for the giving of the Law, right before God gave Moses the Ten Commandments.

The seven lamps or torches represent the seven Spirits of God. These are not seven separate spirits. Many scholars believe this is a reference to the Holy

Spirit in His fullness and completeness. For example, in Isaiah's prophecy about the first coming of Jesus, the prophet mentioned multiple aspects of the Spirit (see Isaiah 11:2, KJV).

In front of the throne there is a glassy sea (4:6), like a giant reflecting pool, and much grander than the reflecting pool between the Washington Monument and the Lincoln Memorial in Washington DC. The glassy sea implies three things. First, in the ancient world, glass was usually dull and hard to see through. But here the glass is crystal clear and as precious as gold (Job 28:17). Second, the glass represents dazzling purity, blinding light, too much for us to even look on, representing the purity of God. I don't think we will truly understand how pure God really is until we get to heaven. Third, the glassy sea suggests great distance. At this point, even in heaven, until we get to Revelation 21, God is somewhat distant from us. He is the awesome, majestic, glorious One.

THE FOUR BEASTS

John then saw four living creatures, or living beings (Revelation 4:6–8). In the King James Version, these beings are called beasts.

In this passage the King James Version—revered though it may be—does modern readers a disservice by referring to these living beings as beasts. That word confuses a lot of people, because they automatically think that beasts in Revelation are evil, and some are! Revelation 13 tells of two beasts who are intrinsically evil. But the beasts in 4:6–8 are not evil. The word used for the four beasts of chapter 4 is better translated as "living creatures," or the translation I prefer is "living beings." They are not dangerous creatures.

Who are they? Probably cherubim, which is the Hebrew plural for a cherub, perhaps a special sort of angelic being. These cherubs do not look like the ones we see nowadays on Christmas cards or decorations.

What do we know about them? They are always near the throne of God and near the Lamb of God (4:6; 5:6; 14:3). They have six wings and are full of eyes, front and back, similar to the seraphim in Isaiah 6:2. In other words, these living beings have all-seeing knowledge.

They, too, are constantly praising and worshipping God. In Revelation, we often see them worshipping in many of the same verses as the elders.

These beings perform certain duties in heaven. For example, the living beings give instructions concerning the wrath of God, releasing the infamous four horsemen (6:1–8). In Revelation 15:7 one of the living beings hands the bowls of the wrath of God over to the angels. This is certainly sobering when the seven angels pour out the seven bowls of God's wrath, which we will see in Revelation 16.

These four living beings seem scary, but they remind us of the visions of Ezekiel 1:4–28 in their appearance, and their praise reminds us of the seraphim in Isaiah 6:3.

Whatever else they do, they signify the wisdom of God. Maybe that is what is meant by the phrase "full of eyes."

Then comes an even more unusual description in 4:7 of a lion, a calf, a man, and an eagle. Some scholars see a parallel between the four faces of the living beings and the four ways Jesus is pictured in the Gospels. In Matthew, Jesus is pictured as the Lion of Judah. In Mark, the servant aspects of Jesus are emphasized. He was the servant who became the sacrifice for sin, which is what a calf was, a sacrificial animal (Hebrews 9:12, 19). In Luke's Gospel, Jesus is the compassionate Son of Man. In John, He is the reigning Christ, with emphasis on the deity of Jesus. Some think the eagle implies the heavenly Christ.

Whatever else, these beings know how to praise God. They praise Him for His holiness. They praise Him because He is the Almighty, the all-powerful One. And they praise Him for His eternal existence—"who was and who is and who is to come" (Revelation 4:8).

When the living beings start praising the Lord, the elders jump in, too, joining in the praise and worship. They praise God using an interesting phrase, "Worthy are You, our Lord and our God," which was the exact phrase used in the worship of the Roman emperor Domitian, who claimed to be Lord and God. But for the early believers there was only one Lord and God, and they refused to give Domitian the homage he demanded. That refusal, of course, reaped a lot of trouble for the early Christians.

In heaven, praise and worship of our God is perpetual and a natural part of everyday existence. If we are going to be comfortable in heaven, wouldn't it be a good idea to get started praising Him here on earth?

Jesus opened heaven to John, giving him a glorious image of the heavenly beings celebrating and worshipping God. The stage is almost set for the awesome events of the last days to unfold.

7

Game Changer

John's vision of heaven continues with his joining the four living beings and the twenty-four elders in worshipping God the Father. But here the focus changes. When John joins in, their worship moves from the Father to the Lord Jesus Christ. Yes, horrific events are about to unfold on earth, but before we begin to experience them, it is good to be reminded who is really in charge.

Worship means "to acknowledge worth." Our worship doesn't make Jesus worthy. He already is far more than worthy! When we worship, we are merely discovering and acknowledging the obvious.

Maybe with renewed emphasis on praise and worship—not merely in America, but worldwide—God is getting us ready. Just as worship precedes judgment in the book of Revelation, the next chapter in God's plan may well be the pouring out of His wrath in judgment.

A Book That Nobody Could Open

As Revelation 5 begins, John saw a scroll in God's hand (5:1). Some translations use the word *book*, and that is easiest for us to understand, but in this case the word *scroll* more accurately describes what John actually saw. But when John saw the scroll in the hand of Him who is on the throne in heaven, he noticed that it had writing on both sides. This could mean two things.

One, God has a lot contained in the scroll, which, of course, we know He does, and God has much more to say about what is to come.

Second, the writing on both sides may imply that nothing more could be added to it. What was written was complete and final. The scroll contains all that we will ever need to know about the future until we see Jesus face to face.

More important, John noticed that the scroll was sealed with seven seals. Again, this could mean two things.

One, the scroll was sealed similar to a last will and testament, a legal document. Under Roman law, when a man finished his will, it was sealed and then seven witnesses each put their seals on it, forming a sort of tape that fastened the scroll closed. The document could not be opened unless all seven witnesses or their representatives were present. So you could think of the scroll that John saw as God's final settlement of the affairs of our world. Indeed, the information within it, as we will see, stretches all the way to the end of time as we know it.

In the Old Testament, the prophet Daniel had a vision about the rise of the Antichrist and his ultimate destruction. The prophet was instructed to write, but then he was told to "close up and seal the words of the scroll until the time of the end" (Daniel 12:4, NIV). In a similar way, the scroll that John saw had been sealed, but for how long we don't know. It appears, however, that it is about to be opened (Revelation 5:2).

Second, the implication of the seven seals might be extreme secrecy. Nobody knows what is in this scroll except the One who wrote it. And none but God dares to open it.

About that time, we get the announcement in the form of a question: "Who is worthy to open the book and to break its seals?" (5:2).

Interestingly, this question comes not from John but from a "strong angel," a descriptive term we will see again later in John's vision (10:1; 18:21).

But no one is able to open the book. So John began to weep. He had been promised that he would see the future, but now that possibility dimmed because nobody was worthy to open the scroll or to look in it (5:4).

One of the elders tells John to stop weeping, that there is One who is worthy, and guess who that is? None other than "the Lion that is from the tribe of Judah, the Root of David" (5:5)—Jesus Christ.

Those two titles for Jesus are interesting. The Lion of the tribe of Judah refers back to Genesis 49:9 ("Judah is a lion's whelp; from the prey, my son, you have gone up. He crouches, he lies down as a lion, and as a lion, who dares rouse him up?"), when Jacob blessed his sons. What characteristics come to mind when you think of a lion? Power, majesty, strength, dignity, fearlessness? Yes, all that and more. That is a picture of the Messiah that the Jews held in their hearts, and that is the picture John saw.

The "Root of David" comes from Isaiah 11:1 and 10 ("Then a shoot will spring from the stem of Jesse, and a branch from his roots will bear fruit. . . . Then in that day the nations will resort to the root of Jesse, who will stand as a signal for the peoples; and his resting place will be glorious"), where the prophet predicted that a king would come from the family of Jesse. Jesse was David's father, and the prophet was saying that the Messiah would be born into his family. Ponder this: Jesus is the source, the root of David's family, yet Jesus was born into David's family. As confusing as that may sound, to early Jewish Christians this confirmed that Jesus was the Messiah. He is the only one who knows the secrets of God, so He can reveal the secrets of God.

The Game Changer

Next, John saw an awesome scene, one that would challenge the world's best artists to paint. He said, "And I saw between the throne (with the four living creatures) and the elders a Lamb standing, as if slain, having seven horns and seven eyes, which are the seven Spirits of God, sent out into all the earth" (Revelation 5:6). Picture this: John heard about the lion, but when he turned to look, he saw a lamb! And not just any lamb, but *the* Lamb, looking as though He had been slain. My mind is unable to grasp the full vision of this, but I recognize it as a turning point in the book of Revelation, because now the Lamb is on the scene.

The phrase *the Lamb* is used twenty-nine times in the book of Revelation, and yet curiously it is not the same word for lamb that John used earlier in the New Testament, nor is it the word used by any of the other writers in the New Testament. The usual word for lamb in the New Testament is *amnos*; here the word is *arnion*. It is the word that Jeremiah used when he talked about a lamb brought to slaughter (Jeremiah 11:19).

By this, John was saying, "This isn't the Jesus we knew around the Sea of Galilee. He is different in heaven. This is something new! He is the same and yet marvelously different."

First, John told us that this Lamb is "standing, as if slain" (Revelation 5:6). Isn't that interesting? Even in heaven, Jesus bears the marks of His crucifixion, the marks of His sacrifice for us. On the other hand, this same Lamb of God who gave His life for us—the one the Roman soldiers beat, mocked, and killed—is now the Lamb with seven horns and seven eyes! What does that mean?

Horns in the Bible stand for two things: power that cannot be withstood, and honor, as in the honor attributed to a hero. The Lamb has seven horns that signify completion, perfection, and fulfillment. So here you have the Lamb of God, the One who was slain, who is now the epitome of the might and power of God, the Lamb who can shatter and break His enemies.

The Lamb has seven eyes, and John explained that those are the seven Spirits of God—the Holy Spirit in fullness sent into all the earth. What does that mean? Jesus is the all-seeing God. There is no place on earth where a person can hide from Him. He is omniscient and all knowing as well as omnipresent. His Spirit can be everywhere at the same time.

What a picture this is of Jesus! He is the fulfillment of the messianic hopes and dreams. He is the Lion of Judah, the Root of David. He is the sacrifice that was slain for our salvation. But He is also the all-powerful One, the One with all knowledge. He is the all-conquering, all-seeing, ever-present God. No wonder the beings in heaven praise Him!

Living Praise and Worship

The praises roll across heaven in three waves: first the voices of the four living beings and the twenty-four elders, then the angels join them, and finally every created thing begins to praise Him (Revelation 5:6–14).

If we look closely, we can discover that the action heats up when Jesus takes the scroll from God's hand (5:7). As soon as that happens, the four living creatures and the twenty-four elders intensify their praises. The sound must have been beautiful and at the same time overwhelming to John.

As an interesting twist, here, each of the elders has a harp. Although sitting around and strumming harps is the way some people naively picture how we will spend eternity in heaven, this is actually one of the few places where you will find beings in heaven playing harps. Harps were used throughout the Old Testament as instruments of praise, so it shouldn't surprise us that these elders in heaven bring some instrumental background to the party.

The elders also have golden bowls full of incense, which are the prayers of the saints. They brought a similar collection of prayers to God previously, and they do so again. In addition to praising and worshipping God, praying seems to be an important part of what these elders do around the throne of God.

As all of this was going on, the elders sang a "new song." In Greek there are two words most often translated as "new." First, *neos,* which means "new in time" but not necessarily new in quality. For instance, you may buy a used car, and you tell people, "I just bought a new car." It's a new car to you, but to everyone else, it is still a used car.

Another word, *kainos,* means "new in quality," not simply recently produced. This word indicates a quality that has never before existed. This is the word we find in Revelation to describe the new quality of praise and worship, a new quality of joy, a new quality of strength, a new quality of peace, a new quality of *life* that comes only from Jesus!

And what a new song it is! The elders and the four living beings sing:

> Worthy are You to take the book and to break its seals; for You were slain, and purchased for God with Your blood men from every tribe and tongue

> and people and nation. You have made them to be a kingdom and priests to our God; and they will reign upon the earth. (Revelation 5:9–10, NASB)

Notice what this song says about the death of Jesus.

1. It was a sacrificial death, not an accident, not a disaster. Nobody took His life from Him. He willingly gave His life for us.
2. The song says His death was a liberating death. He purchased our salvation. He paid the price so we could be free.
3. It was a death for all, not just Jews, but for all, male and female, black, brown, red, and white. For God so loved the world.
4. It was a death with purpose, and it brought the proper results. He died for us. As a result, we are now part of His kingdom, and He has made us saints. One of these days, He is going to have us reign on earth.

Then comes the praise of the angels, generated by an enormous number of these beings! John reported, "Then I looked, and I heard the voice of many angels around the throne and the living creatures and the elders; and the number of them was myriads of myriads, and thousands of thousands" (5:11). Imagine the sound this multitude of angelic beings must have made as they said,

> Worthy is the Lamb that was slain to receive power and riches and wisdom and might and honor and glory and blessing. To Him who sits on the throne, and to the Lamb, be blessing and honor and glory and dominion forever and ever. (Revelation 5:12–13)

These angelic beings give Jesus the praise He rightfully deserves. The glory that belongs to God belongs to Him. We bless Him by giving Him our praise, worship, and gratitude. We need to praise and worship Jesus today for at least the four reasons we see in this chapter:

1. We should praise Him for who He is. He is the Lion of Judah, the Root of David, and the Lamb of God.

2. We should praise Him because of where He is. He is in heaven, right at the throne of God, right in the center of everything.
3. We should praise Him because of what He has done. He purchased our salvation with His blood, conquered death, beat the grave, rose again, and defeated the devil.
4. We should praise Him because He deserves the praise of every living creature and created thing.

No wonder the four living beings and the twenty-four elders fall down and worship Him, saying, "Amen," so be it, let it happen (v. 14)! They seem to sense that the praise and worship precedes and prepares the way for the remainder of the vision. And we are going to need the reminders of who is really in charge, because from here until we see Jesus return, life on earth is going to get ugly. Hold on tightly to Jesus. We're heading for a time of trouble!

8

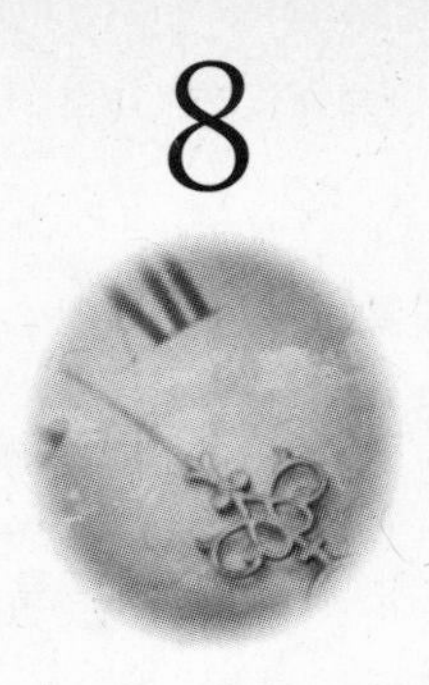

Now Generation

I am a builder. I have always enjoyed planning and working on new building projects and seeing them come together step by step. I learned early on that in reading blueprints, if I wanted to get the entire picture, I had to view each individual overlay of the master plan—an overlay for the foundation, one for the infrastructure, another for the plumbing and wiring, another for the interior walls, roofing, exterior surfaces, even an overlay for the landscaping and parking lots—and then lay them on top of each other. Only after studying the individual overlays together could I get an accurate picture of what was going to come into existence.

To truly understand the book of Revelation, you must review the prophecies of Daniel, ponder the words of Jesus from the Gospels, and then consider Paul's writings to the Thessalonians. As you add each of these layers to the book of Revelation, you can begin to see the entire picture as the Lord intended it to be seen.

One of the most important overlays to understanding Revelation is the Second Coming discourse given by Jesus to His disciples and recorded in Matthew 24 and Luke 21. Many of the "signs of the times" mentioned by Jesus are similar to those in the vision John received and recorded in Revelation 6.

John Kilpatrick is the former pastor of Brownsville Assembly of God Church in Pensacola, Florida, a place where a genuine revival broke out on

Father's Day 1995 and continued unabated with spontaneous services every night for five years, with more than four and a half million people going through the doors during that time. For years John studied the passages relating to the Second Coming. In regard to the words of the prophets and the predictions of Jesus, he said, "These days are not coming; they are here." John added, "Every major sign of the Second Coming is in motion right now."[16]

You don't need to be a Bible scholar to know that the planet is groaning. Populations are increasing while the resources needed to sustain them are decreasing. The oceans are dying, clean air and water are becoming scarce, natural disasters (earthquakes, tsunamis, wildfires, floods, crop failures, bacterial mutations, and shifting weather patterns), conflicts (terrorism and wars), false religions (cults and pseudoreligions), and a worldwide economic meltdown are reported daily in the news.

Something big is about to happen. We need to prepare to see Jesus! Knowledge that we are living in what the Bible refers to as the "last days" should motivate Christians to live closer to Jesus than ever before and to more actively seek out opportunities to share the gospel with people who don't yet know the Lord. The clock is ticking and time is running out. Yes, difficult days are upon us, but do not lose hope. Jesus Christ will return, and He will take you to live with Him eternally. Right now, however, we need to brace ourselves for some shocks.

How do I know this? Because Jesus Himself said so in Matthew 24.

The Most Frequently Asked Questions

What, when, and how is all this going to happen? Interestingly, these were the questions put to Jesus by His disciples just a few days prior to His crucifixion. They sat privately on the Mount of Olives, overlooking the city of Jerusalem. Gazing across the Kidron Valley, they could clearly see the magnificent beauty of the temple and its outlying buildings. The original temple was constructed during the reign of Solomon, around 960 BC, on that same site. It had been opulent and ornate beyond belief, but Solomon's temple had been razed when Jerusalem fell to Babylon in 586 BC. A second temple was erected, under the leadership of Zerubbabel, when a relatively small group of Jews returned to Jerusalem from exile in Babylon. Granted, this latest temple area, the panorama that Jesus and the disciples were looking at, paled in comparison to the grandeur of Solomon's temple. But recently Herod the Great had launched a massive building program to renovate the temple area. That restoration took forty-six years to complete. It was that work that impressed the disciples as they proudly viewed the temple.

Jesus, however, burst the bubble of their idealism with a strong dose of reality. "Do you not see all these things? Truly I say to you, not one stone here shall be left upon another, which will not be torn down" (Matthew 24:2). Jesus' prediction that the temple would be destroyed again shocked His disciples. Their consternation concerning Jesus' comment prompted them to ask three questions rolled into one: "Tell us, when will these things be? And what will be the sign of Your coming, and of the end of the age?" (24:3, NKJV).

Jesus' intriguing answer is recorded in Matthew 24:4–25:46 and became known as the Second Coming discourse. It is the second-longest discourse of Jesus recorded in the Bible; only the Sermon on the Mount (Matthew 5:3–7:27) comprises a longer, uninterrupted address by Jesus. In this talk, Jesus described a wide variety of the "signs of the times," things the disciples should look for before the coming of Christ and the end of the age. As with most apocalyptic statements in the Bible, Jesus' answer had a present-tense fulfillment, which could be applied to the ensuing destruction of Jerusalem during the disciples' lifetimes, and a future-tense fulfillment, which we are seeing come to pass today.

Jesus began with a warning: "See to it that no one misleads you" (Matthew 24:4). He explained that near the end of the age many false christs, false messiahs, and false saviors would appear. Jesus mentioned this sign three times within a few sentences (24:5, 11, 24).

While I am concerned about the rise of blatantly false christs operating with impunity in the world today, I don't see millions of Bible-believing Christians flocking after them. Nor do I see them going out to the desert, following after some guru who claims to be God. I am, however, shocked at the ever-increasing number of false christs we have *in the church* who are adored by millions of Christians who should know better. We have a proliferation of spiritual leaders with messiah complexes.

Worse still, we have many people preaching another gospel, a get-rich gospel, a feel-good gospel. By twisting and misinterpreting Scripture, they have unwittingly set the scene for another gospel that will eventually lead to the acceptance of not just another Christ, but the Antichrist. As we will see in the pages ahead, one of the main methods the Antichrist will use to control people will be manipulation of money and material goods.

A second sign Jesus said would indicate His imminent return is the increase of "wars and rumors of wars" (Matthew 24:6). Skeptics are quick to interject, "But we have always had wars." Unfortunately, that is true. Nevertheless, the obvious tenor of Jesus' statement is that wars, nation rising against nation, kingdom against kingdom, will drastically intensify.

Jesus said there would be an increase of wars before He returns, but you need not be afraid: "See that you are not frightened, for those things must take place, but that is not yet the end" (Matthew 24:6).

Other disturbing signs of the times mentioned by Jesus, "birth pangs," as He referred to them, include famines and earthquakes in various places. Devout Christians will be hated; many others will fall away from Christ and even deliver up their brothers and sisters to the opposition. Lawlessness will increase, and most people's love will grow cold (Matthew 24:7–12). In Luke's account of the Second Coming discourse, Jesus mentioned pestilences along with an increase in natural disasters. This may mean an increase of new killer bugs and vermin, but it might also indicate the rise of killer diseases spawned and spread by animals and birds.

I believe the earth itself is groaning in anticipation of the Lord's return (Romans 8:19–22). This groaning may include floods, volcano eruptions, tidal waves, hurricanes, earthquakes, droughts, wildfires, mudslides, tsunamis, and other signs. Certainly, these things have always occurred on earth, but the thrust of Jesus' message is when you see all these things increasing in frequency and intensity and converging on one point in human history. Get ready because we are nearing the end of the age.

Some Good News

On the positive side, Jesus gave us some good news to anticipate. He said, essentially, yes, things are going to get bad, "but the one who endures to the end, he will be saved. This gospel of the kingdom shall be preached in the whole world as a testimony to all the nations, and then the end will come" (Matthew 24:13–14). Jesus didn't say that everyone in the world would be saved; nor did He say that everyone in the world would believe. He did not even say that everyone on earth would hear the gospel. He merely said that His gospel would be preached "to all the nations." With our modern means of communications—television, radio, the Internet, and new communication technologies to come—we are the first generation in history with the potential to see Jesus' words fulfilled.

More important than our human wherewithal to communicate the message, God is pouring out His Holy Spirit in a fresh way all over the world. Despite the evil in our world, I believe we are on the cusp of the greatest period of Spirit-anointed evangelism the world has ever known.

The Key Sign

Another sign unique to our generation—and perhaps one of the most significant signs of the times that Jesus told us to watch for—is found in Luke's Gospel, where Jesus predicted that the Jewish people will "fall by the edge of the sword, and will be led captive into all the nations; and Jerusalem will be trampled under foot by the Gentiles until the times of the Gentiles are fulfilled" (Luke 21:24). Bible scholars may debate the various meanings of "the times of the Gentiles," but basically Jesus was telling His disciples that He would not return until Jerusalem is back in Jewish hands and under Jewish control.

Following the destruction of Jerusalem in AD 70, the nation of Israel was wiped out and non-Jews controlled the Holy Land. For nearly two thousand years the Jewish people were scattered all over the earth. But on May 14, 1948, the nation of Israel was reborn, and since then, Jewish people living around the world have been streaming back to Israel in fulfillment of the prophet Ezekiel's words uttered nearly twenty-six hundred years ago: "Behold, I will take the sons of Israel from among the nations where they have gone, and I will gather them from every side and bring them into their own land; and I will make them one nation in the land, on the mountains of Israel" (Ezekiel 37:21–22).

In June 1967, against overwhelming odds, Israel defeated a coalition of Arab nations in six days and reclaimed the Old City of Jerusalem, including the site where the Jewish temple formerly stood. We are the first people to see that happen since AD 70.

I believe the Jewish temple will soon be rebuilt and some sort of renewed sacrificial system will be restored. Then, at the halfway point of the seven-year period known as the Tribulation, the Antichrist will desecrate the rebuilt Jewish temple in some abominable way, and he will declare to the world that he is God (2 Thessalonians 2:4).

Jesus recognized this "abomination of desolation" as a pivotal point in the end-time scenario: "Therefore when you see the abomination of desolation which was spoken of through Daniel the prophet, standing in the holy place (let the reader understand), then those who are in Judea must flee to the mountains" (Matthew 24:15–16).

He warned people "there will be a great tribulation, such as has not occurred since the beginning of the world until now, nor ever shall. Unless those days had been cut short, no life would have been saved; but for the sake of the elect those days will be cut short" (Matthew 24:21–22).

Yet as difficult as these days may be, Jesus told His disciples that as we see the signs of the times coming to pass, we should not despair or go around with a doom-and-gloom attitude. Quite the contrary, Jesus encouraged us to have the opposite outlook: "Now when these things begin to happen, look up and lift up your heads, because your redemption draws near" (Luke 21:28, NKJV).

This Generation Will Not Pass Away

Jesus then gave His disciples an easily understood object lesson concerning the last days: "When you see all these things, recognize that He is near, right at the door. Truly I say to you, this generation will not pass away until all these things take place. Heaven and earth will pass away, but My words shall not pass away" (Matthew 24:32–35).

Jesus made it very clear that the generation that sees these things come to pass will be the same generation to see His triumphant return. That word *generation* can also be translated as "race of people," but the word is more often used in the Bible for a specific period of time. Some Bible scholars believe that period to be forty years. They base this number on the forty years it took for a generation of unbelievers to die off in the wilderness, before God led Joshua and the Israelites into the Promised Land. But this forty years of wandering in the desert was part of God's punishment for their sin, not a normal generation. God said, "I was angry with those people for forty years. I said, 'They are not loyal to me and have not understood my ways.' I was angry and made a promise, 'They will never enter my rest'" (Psalm 95:10–11, NCV).

My friend and fellow Revelation student John Shorey points out that a biblical generation might more likely be considered *seventy* years, based on Psalm 90:10 (NCV): "Our lifetime is seventy years or, if we are strong, eighty years." Obviously, some people live longer than seventy or eighty years, many others live less. But on average, the seventy-year figure for the length of a generation is interesting, especially in light of Jesus' statement indicating that the generation that saw the rebirth of Israel would be the one to see the ushering in of climactic events of history.

Shorey's studies are detailed in his book *The Window of the Lord's Return 2012–2020.*[17] He arrived at the dates listed in his title by taking into consideration May 1948 as the beginning of "this generation." Is it possible that the time comprising this generation may be fulfilled between these dates, that the tumultuous times described in Matthew 24 and Revelation 6 could happen within our lifetime and Jesus could return?

Certainly, Jesus warned us against trying to set a date for His return, and those Christians who have ignored His admonition have been sorely embarrassed. On the other hand, Jesus encouraged us to read the signs of the times and to be ready: "Therefore be on the alert, for you do not know which day your Lord is coming. . . . For this reason you also must be ready; for the Son of Man is coming at an hour when you do not think He will" (Matthew 24:42, 44).

In addition to the reestablishment of Israel as a nation, John Shorey listed six major events that must take place before Jesus returns:

1. The Antichrist must be revealed.
2. There must be a falling away of many Christians from the faith.

John based the necessity for these two events on the insight given by the apostle Paul to the Thessalonians, who were concerned by rumors that the Lord had already come. To correct this mistake, Paul wrote:

> Concerning the coming of our Lord Jesus Christ and our being gathered to Him, we ask you, brothers, not to become easily unsettled or alarmed by some prophecy, report or letter supposed to have come from us, saying that the day of the Lord has already come. Don't let anyone deceive you in any way, for that day will not come until the rebellion occurs and the man of lawlessness is revealed, the man doomed to destruction (2 Thessalonians 2:1–3, NIV).

The rebellion that the apostle Paul wrote about was also referred to as the *apostasy*, "a great falling away," a walking away from the Christian faith by many who once were believers. We are seeing this today. In Christian churches many young people and adults who have grown up in the church and have known the Lord are gone. Paul also mentioned the "man of lawlessness," known as "the man of sin," or the Antichrist. Don't miss what Paul was saying: Jesus will not return until the Antichrist has been revealed!

Moreover, the parallel passage in the Gospel of Mark makes it clear that the coming of the Lord will not happen until *after* this time of tribulation.

> But in those days, after that tribulation, the sun shall be darkened, and the moon shall not give her light, and the stars of heaven shall fall, and the powers that are in heaven shall be shaken. And then shall they see the Son of man coming in the clouds with great power and glory. And then shall he send his angels, and shall gather together his elect from the four winds, from the uttermost part of the earth to the uttermost part of heaven. . . . Verily I say unto you, that this generation shall not pass, till all these things be done." (Mark 13:24–27, 30, KJV)

I like the way the New Century Version describes this conclusion: "I tell you the truth, all these things will happen while the people of this time are still living" (Mark 13:30, NCV).

John Shorey's remaining points that must happen before Christ's return are:

3. A one-world government must be in place.
4. Heavenly events must also take place—the sky darkens, stars fall from the sky, the moon turns blood red (Matthew 24:29–31; Revelation 6:12–13).
5. The temple must be rebuilt in Jerusalem.
6. The Antichrist must desecrate the temple.[18]

We will look more closely at all of these points in the pages ahead, but I mention them here before we plunge into Revelation 6 because these events are going to happen so quickly. Why? Because I believe, as I have been saying for more than a decade, that the horses are out of the barn!

9

The Horsemen Are Riding Now

The old apostle pondered the meaning of the vision as he wrote, pausing often, after nearly every other word, to pray. *These are difficult things to describe, Lord. I feel I am telling of a time that many people are hoping will never happen. But God, You have revealed Your plans to us in advance. We know these things will come to pass. Please Jesus, show me the good here.*

The marvelous, heavenly, worshipful atmosphere of Revelation 4 and 5 are in marked contrast to the judgment and wrath we encounter in Revelation 6 through 19. Judgment itself seems strange to us because we don't really understand God's holiness and His utter hatred of sin. But in the chapters ahead, along with His judgment on sin, we'll see God vindicate and reward His servants. As the old saying reminds us, it is always darkest before the dawn.

Beginning of Sorrows

Before we begin, let's not forget the road map to Revelation that we found in Matthew 24. The parallels between Matthew 24 and Revelation 6 are astonishing! Let me recap for you here:

1. False christs and false prophets appear (Matthew 24:5).

2. Wars and rumors of wars (Matthew 24:6–7). I think Jesus may be referring to the final world war here.
3. Famines and no food to eat (Matthew 24:7).
4. Earthquakes (Matthew 24:7).
5. The Tribulation (Matthew 24:21–22).
6. Cosmic disturbances the earth has never seen before (Matthew 24:29).
7. The sign of His coming and appearance (Matthew 24:30).

In Revelation 6 the seals of the scroll that we saw in Revelation 5 are opened—and only one person is able to open the seven seals. The Lamb! *Jesus.* One by one, He opens these seals and history begins to unfold before John's eyes!

Keep in mind the overall outline of what is going to happen in the future. According to Daniel 9:27, the Antichrist will rise to worldwide power and will rule for seven years, beginning with a peace agreement he will sign with Israel. In the middle of those seven years, the Antichrist will violate that agreement, invade Israel, and desecrate all that is holy to Israel. At the end of that period, Christ will return to judge the earth and to establish His kingdom.

Generally, that is what the future holds. As to the *when* of those events, very devout Christians disagree. While I do believe these events are precursors to the Tribulation, I believe these are the sorrows and beginning of birth pangs that Jesus described in Matthew 24:8. I do not believe the Rapture will have already occurred when these things begin to happen.

In Revelation 6, we find one of the most intriguing visions recorded by John: as the Lamb of God—Jesus—opens the first four seals on the scroll, the four horsemen of the apocalypse are released. These horses and their riders are not Kentucky Derby winners, but you would not be gambling if you put your money on the fulfillment of the prophecies regarding them.

Horses in the Bible often represent God's activity on earth, the force He uses to get His work done. In Zechariah 6:1–8, for example, horses are agents of God's wrath and vengeance upon sinful men. In Revelation, they serve the same purpose.

What do these four horses and their riders represent?

The White Horse: A Ghostly Imposter

John watched in awe as the Lamb opened the first seal on the scroll. And as Jesus peeled back the seal, John heard one of the four living beings speak with a voice that sounded like thunder, "Come!" But he wasn't calling John. The living being was summoning the first of the four horsemen.

The first horse was white. John wrote, "And I looked, and behold, a white horse. He who sat on it had a bow; and a crown was given to him, and he went out conquering and to conquer" (Revelation 6:2, NKJV).

Some people think the rider of this white horse is Jesus because of a similar description of the conquering Christ in Revelation 19:11, but there are two reasons why I am convinced the horseman of Revelation 6 is not a description of Christ. In fact, I think this horseman is the Antichrist or, at the very least, the spirit of the Antichrist.

First, the rider of the white horse in Revelation 6 has a bow but does not have any arrows. In the Old Testament, a bow is a symbol of military power. So it seems that the white horse with the rider carrying the bow symbolizes military conquest. But because he comes with a bow without arrows, it is thought that he will rise on a platform of peace, no doubt assisted by temporary economic prosperity and real or manipulated miracles. The Antichrist will offer amazing, practical, peaceful solutions to the world's most perplexing problems, and as a result, he will be hailed as a great leader and liberator.

No doubt he will be a smooth talker who employs an intricate type of spiritual warfare, engaging in a war of words and information, saying that good is evil and evil is good. He will not have to use any weapons to conquer the world and evoke the worship of much of the earth's population. Instead, he will use words—his charming and cunning words and moving and motivating speeches. His talk will be slick and enticing; he will promise peace and prosperity to a world that by this time will be ready to hand the keys of authority to anyone who holds out hope of escaping the chaotic events that will be happening on earth at that time.

The gradual erosion of America's Christian heritage that we're seeing now is not accidental, and it subtly sets the stage for the man of sin who will use words to wreak havoc upon the world. Even more confusing, the Antichrist will most likely invest religious language with new meaning, using words such as *salvation, redemption, spiritual*, and even *Christ* to mean something other than the usual, traditionally accepted Christian concepts. His new insights will find a ready acceptance. Then, after three and a half years, as his name implies, the Antichrist will speak against Christ, indeed, speaking the opposite of Jesus or instead of Jesus. Sadly, this smooth-talking devil will influence many people to follow him to death and destruction. But mark this: his initial victories will not be with the sword so much as with the tongue.

The second reason why I believe the rider on the white horse is the Antichrist has to do with the type of crown he is wearing. This crown is not the *diadema* (royal crown), the one Jesus is wearing in Revelation 19. Instead, it is the *stephanos* (victor's crown), which is awarded to the winner of an athletic contest.

John has told us in advance that the Antichrist will ride out to victory (6:2). Indeed, the Antichrist will win some big races. He will win public opinion polls and perhaps even elections, as our world willingly hands him the reins of power. And for three and a half years, the Antichrist will be the most popular person in the world. He will provide a form of peace and some measure of calm. But this happiness will be short-lived.

A Serious Warning from History!

The Antichrist to come will have the power to conquer and deceive. His spirit is already hard at work in the world. For Exhibit A look at how the Bible applies to today's society and consider 2 Timothy 3:1–7:

> But realize this, that in the last days difficult times will come. For men will be lovers of self, lovers of money, boastful, arrogant, revilers, disobe-

> dient to parents, ungrateful, unholy, unloving, irreconcilable, malicious gossips, without self-control, brutal, haters of good, treacherous, reckless, conceited, lovers of pleasure rather than lovers of God, holding to a form of godliness, although they have denied its power; avoid such men as these. For among them are those who enter into households and captivate weak women weighed down with sins, led on by various impulses, always learning and never able to come to the knowledge of the truth.

Is that not a description of much of the content of today's websites, television shows, and motion pictures? Can you agree with me that the filth presented by these mediums has degraded the quality of our lives and well-being? What's more, society's moral degradation has led to prayer being removed from our schools, public readings of the Bible banned in schools, and even the removal of the Ten Commandments from city halls and judicial courts throughout the nation. I personally wonder how much longer it will be before the Ten Commandments are removed from the Supreme Court building in Washington, DC. I fear what may happen to America on the day that we do such a thing!

Modern media and secularism have caused many to become lukewarm in the eyes of God, and in such we have been deceived! Our deception has given rise to another gospel—the love of money being preached from many of our pulpits. In the end of days, when money has no value and many choose to end their lives because they trusted those leaders who falsely led them to believe that they would only prosper, the platform will be ready for the Antichrist to take power.

We were warned at least twice about this. First, Jesus said, "See to it that no one misleads you. For many will come in My name, saying, 'I am the Christ,' and will mislead many" (Matthew 24:4–5). A common misunderstanding here is that Jesus was referring to the Antichrist. Look closely. Jesus said that *many* will come in His name and lead people astray! These will be preachers who believe completely in the false gospel they are preaching to their congregations.

Jesus even warned in Matthew 7:21–23 what would happen to those who preached and believed this aberrant gospel, and He concluded, "I will declare to them, 'I never knew you; DEPART FROM ME, YOU WHO PRACTICE LAWLESSNESS!'" These deceivers preached that Jesus is Lord, preached from the Word of God, performed mighty miracles in the name of Jesus, and prayed for the sick, but because they did not preach the true gospel of Jesus Christ, they will not be allowed entry into heaven. In their practice, they paved the way for the Antichrist, but they themselves were not him.

The second warning comes from the apostle Paul in 2 Thessalonians 2:3–4:

> Let no one in any way deceive you, for it will not come unless the apostasy comes first, and the man of lawlessness is revealed, the son of destruction, who opposes and exalts himself above every so-called god or object of worship, so that he takes his seat in the temple of God, displaying himself as being God.

According to scripture, the falling away comes *first,* which means that there must be something to fall away *from.* Whether it is an economic collapse, devastation from war, a lack of food, or even a mass realization of a great deception, this falling away will open the door for the Antichrist.

The Red Horse: Terror!

As the Lamb opened the second seal, another living being called out, and John saw a second horseman come forth, ready to ride:

> When He opened the second seal, I heard the second living creature saying, "Come and see." Another horse, fiery red, went out. And it was granted to the one who sat on it to take peace from the earth, and that people should kill one another; and there was given to him a great sword. (Revelation 6:3–4, NKJV)

This is no ordinary horseman and this is no ordinary sword. This is an assassin's sword, wielded by terrorists. The word could be translated "a loud sword," and its effects will certainly get the world's attention. The red war-horse's purpose is to take peace from the earth and, along with it, the prosperity on which so many people are depending. Throughout Revelation the color red denotes terror and death. The Dragon of Revelation 12:3 is red, as is the Beast in Revelation 17:3. This red horse in Revelation indicates a time of unbridled bloodshed, when there will be crime in the streets, people butchering one another, when the world has become a seething caldron of bitterness and hatred.

Just think about how concerns over terrorism affect our everyday lives. In a post 9/11 world, the unthinkable has become not merely possible but our new reality. We fret about the nuclear threat, concerned about nuclear bombs getting into the hands of terrorists, but meanwhile, Iran (ancient Persia) moves forward with a nuclear program that the entire world fears could go rogue at any moment. The new nuclear-armed terrorists do not have a commitment to play by any rules that the United States and the old Soviet Union had during the Cold War. The deterrent of mutually assured destruction that helped hold nuclear-wielding nations in check in the past century no longer exists. Today's terrorists do not concern themselves with their own survival. In fact, many Muslim terrorists have been deceived into believing that they will receive a special reward if they lose their lives by attacking Israel or the United States. In addition to these threats, who knows how responsible the leaders will be in China, Russia, India, Pakistan, and even Israel, all of whom have nuclear weapons in their arsenals?

I believe the prophet Joel saw this "great sword" to which John refers:

> A fire devoureth before them; and behind them a flame burneth: the land is as the garden of Eden before them, and behind them a desolate wilderness; yea, and nothing shall escape them. The appearance of them is as the appearance of horses; and as horsemen, so shall they run. Like the noise of chariots on the tops of mountains shall they leap, like the noise of a flame of fire that devoureth the stubble, as a strong people set in battle array. Before their face the people shall be much pained: all faces shall gather blackness. (Joel 2:3–6, KJV)

This reminds me of a nuclear warhead being detonated. Pictures of people burned by radiation reveal faces scarred beyond recognition and bodies burned horribly, but not by fire. The color of these burns? Black.

But nuclear terrorism is only the tip of the iceberg. Imagine what havoc terrorists could wreak if they were able to set off bombs simultaneously in the nation's malls or schools, or if they could poison the nation's water supply or destroy a major portion of the nation's power grid. Or, think if you dare, of the death and destruction that would occur with the release of sarin gas over New York, Chicago, or Los Angeles. Imagine the terror that would spread like wildfire if a bacterial agent were released in a commercial flight, with hundreds of passengers transmitting a fatal disease wherever their travels might take them.

I am convinced that as the red horse rides, we will see terrorism on an unprecedented scale. In addition to terrorism, we are likely to see an increase of wars at this time. Isaiah 19:2 says, "They will each fight against his brother and each against his neighbor, city against city and kingdom against kingdom." Zechariah 14:13 says, "They will seize one another's hand, and the hand of one will be lifted against the hand of another." Jesus said something similar:

> And you will hear of wars and rumors of wars. See that you are not troubled; for all these things must come to pass, but the end is not yet. For nation will rise against nation, and kingdom against kingdom. . . . And then many will be offended, will betray one another, and will hate one another. (Matthew 24:6–7, 10, NKJV)

Loyalty will be a thing of the past. Clearly, the red horse is ready to ride.

THE BLACK HORSE: FAMINE!

Similar to the events leading to the emergence of the first two horses, when the Lamb opened the third seal on the scroll, John heard the third living being call out, "Come!" The third horse and rider responded as John watched in awe.

> When He opened the third seal, I heard the third living creature say, "Come and see." So I looked, and behold, a black horse, and he who sat

> on it had a pair of scales in his hand. And I heard a voice in the midst of the four living creatures saying, "A quart of wheat for a denarius, and three quarts of barley for a denarius; and do not harm the oil and the wine." (Revelation 6:5–6, NKJV)

The rider of the black horse carries with him famine and economic collapse, signified by the scales in his hand and the exorbitant food prices. During this time, food may still be available in certain areas of the world, but at a steep price. In John's time, the denarius was considered a fair day's wage. A measure of wheat would be about one quart, which was considered enough for a person's daily needs, certainly not an entire family's. Ordinarily, a person would buy between eight to twelve quarts of wheat for a penny or about twenty-four quarts of barley, which was an even cheaper grain.

To John's astonishment, when the black horseman rides, people will work all day and not have enough income to feed themselves, much less their families. The implication is that we could easily spend a day's wages for a loaf of bread.

The phrase "do not harm the oil and the wine" could indicate that this will be a perverse time when luxuries are readily available but basic necessities are scarce.

Regardless, John saw that there is going to be a time of horrible famine, a severe worldwide shortage of food. This may work right into the Antichrist's hands when he devises a way to control the food distribution (13:17).

During the summer of 2012, I dreamed that I was going through the factories of America and finding the buildings and warehouses empty. No people were working, nothing was being manufactured, and no food was being grown, harvested, or prepared for market. Two Christians were talking with me when a foreign woman came into the room. One of the Christians gave me a nine-inch square loaf of hard bread and then a half loaf.

The woman grabbed the bread out of my hand. "Don't let him have that!" she commanded. "That is a month and a half of food. He is not allowed to have that!"

Jesus, too, warned His disciples in advance that this time of war and famine and upheaval is coming (Matthew 24:7–8, NKJV). He said that we should expect it but not fear (v. 6).

It is hard to imagine the impact a major famine might have in economically developed nations. Most of us have never experienced famine. We get upset when we miss a meal, much less when there is no food in the pantry or refrigerator. The closest most of us have gotten to real famine is seeing images of starving children on television. We cannot comprehend that such a thing could happen in our country. Yet the Bible states that it will. Indeed, even in the United States, known as the breadbasket of the world, we now have so few food products in storage that the nation could be plunged into famine by the effects of a major drought over a single growing season. In 2012, the United States experienced one of the driest summers in history. More than 55 percent of the country suffered what climatologists described as a "flash drought," because drought conditions developed so quickly, with topsoil turning to dust while crops died in the fields.[19] Should such devastating conditions continue long term, the food supply for the entire world could be seriously affected.

Worse yet, most of the food industry, like many other commodities, has implemented a "just in time" shipping policy, which means that rather than stockpile food in warehouses, suppliers plan their growth and delivery cycles so the food gets to the stores just in time for purchase. But how does food get to the stores? Mostly by truck. What if there is no fuel for the trucks because of terrorist activity, wars, or some natural calamity? Food will not get through to people but will rot in place. In a best-case scenario, it will be fodder for scavengers trying to find something to feed their families.

Imagine the economic effects brought on by the galloping black horse as the prices for whatever food is available—which may be sparse—skyrocket. What good are paper dollars or stocks or bonds when people do not have access to food? Beyond that, economic turmoil is certain to bring out the worst in people. Hunger and hopelessness will turn ordinarily law-abiding citizens into thieves or worse as they attempt to provide for their families. People devoid of hope often turn to violence, and that is certain to ensue during difficult economic times. Witness, for example, the blatant anarchy, burning, looting, rioting, and even killings that occurred in New Orleans in 2005 in the aftermath of Hurricane Katrina. Now, multiply that city by city across the nation and around the world. Civilized society, not to mention economic markets, will tumble into a global tailspin as the black horse romps.

What Should We Do?

The Bible says we're going to work a whole day for enough pay to buy a loaf of bread. There will be no food to speak of, but the church should not be a victim, whether the setting is the Tribulation or a hurricane or a tornado. I am convinced we should be preparing for tough times by stocking up on food, water, medical supplies, solar-powered generators, water purifiers, and sanitation equipment.

I can honestly say that God has impressed this message on my heart: *we need to prepare for some difficult times!* I've seen visions of children crying. I've heard Larry Norman's song "I Wish We'd All Been Ready" playing over and over in my head, and I believe that is an important message not just for me but for this entire generation. I'm glad to say that many people are responding positively to this call to prepare.

If you own land, hang on to it. Christians are going to need places of refuge in the days ahead, and I believe God is telling a number of people these days to secure land where food can be grown, where water can be stored, and where there is enough room for people to congregate safely. More than ten years ago, God impressed on me that in the last days the church will need to be a refuge, a place where people can find shelter, food, and most of all, a message of hope in Jesus.

We've all heard the adage that an ounce of prevention is worth a pound of cure. Many of our grandparents had gardens in their backyard, where they grew some of their own food. If your grandma was like mine, she may have canned food for the winter to feed the family. We've all heard similar admonitions, encouraging us to think ahead.

Have some nonperishable food on hand, just in case. If I'm wrong, you can always use it should you be hunkered down during a blizzard, hurricane, or tornado. But if I'm right, that nonperishable food may save your life someday. There are reputable resources for prepackaged food. Take advantage of the opportunities that are available today. Prepare now. In the days ahead, food will be more valuable than gold.

It will also be wise to stockpile other basic necessities. Use them and replenish your supply every so often so you can keep things fresh, but always keep enough for a long-term problem. Remember how Joseph prepared when God instructed him to be ready for difficult times ahead. Thanks to Joseph's forward thinking and preparation in Egypt, his family was protected and all of Egypt survived because Pharaoh took Joseph's interpretation of his dreams as a word from the Lord.[20]

While I appreciate President Ronald Reagan's use of the metaphor of the United States as a city on a hill,[21] the church should be a storehouse, the light in the darkness—not America. Every church should have a food pantry, not simply to help meet the needs of members of the congregation who are hurting today, but also to serve as a food resource for the future. Sadly, most churches I know of are so in debt or caught up in raising enough money to build a new facility or scraping enough money together to function, meeting today's needs, that they have little resources to help anyone in the days ahead.

I believe God expects us to be wise and to do our part in getting ready to serve the masses of people who are going to be looking for help. When the events of Revelation begin to unfold, you will not have a lot of time. You cannot be scrambling to grow food, indeed, you may not even be able to grow food quickly enough. Be prepared.

A True Harvest Time

We need to see our advance preparations not so much as a means of survival but as a means of winning souls to Christ. The hard times ahead will be the greatest hour the church has ever known. Truly, the difficult time ahead will be the best of times and the worst of times. It will be a great hour for soul winning, but it will also be a difficult time. The King James Version refers to these days as "perilous times," a time of sorrow. When the events of Revelation begin to happen, people are going to be shaken. Some will harden their hearts toward God, but many will seek His face, possibly for the first time in their lives.

Furthermore, during that time when all the earth is in upheaval, because they will come to us for food and other basic necessities, we may have a marvelous opportunity to introduce people to Jesus.

God showed me that if people are hungry, we will not be able to lead them to Christ. But if all you are doing is trying to feed them, even the best stockpiles will eventually run out. I believe God wants us to prepare to feed people physically so we can feed them spiritually, pointing them to the only One who can truly satisfy: Jesus Christ.

When the Antichrist comes to power, he will eventually control the food supply. What is necessary for an Antichrist to arise? Why would intelligent people accept such a system? A lack of food, possibly accompanied by a worldwide economic collapse, will create such distress among nations that there will be an international cry for leadership. Satan's man will be ready.

We are almost there. But another horse must yet ride.

The Pale Horse: Disease

This fourth horse, pale and ashen—more accurately, a sickly, pale green horse—emerges on the scene, following quickly after the first three horsemen. Clearly, this fourth horseman will bring death, plagues, and pestilences, with Hades—the abode of the dead—following closely behind. The color of the horse is even associated with death:

> When He opened the fourth seal, I heard the voice of the fourth living creature saying, "Come and see." So I looked, and behold, a pale horse. And the name of him who sat on it was Death, and Hades followed with him. And power was given to them over a fourth of the earth, to kill with sword, with hunger, with death, and by the beasts of the earth. (Revelation 6:7–8, NKJV)

This evil equestrian will be given power to kill a fourth of the world's population. People will die by weapons—the sword in fact may be a reference to a type of bomb—hunger, pestilence, and wild animals. All these elements would accompany war, but also people will die because of diseases associated with animals.

When I first studied this passage during my years in prison, I was horrified by its straightforward message of death. More than that, I was baffled. How could one-fourth of the world's population—presently more than seven billion people and rising at the rate of another person every fraction of a second[22]—be wiped out in such a short time? As I frequently do when I find something in the Bible that doesn't make sense to me, I turned to the Greek and discovered that the word in the second sentence of verse 8 translated as "death" could also be translated as "plagues or pestilence." The New Century Version simply states it as "disease." I pondered the connection between diseases and animals.

Today, we know all too well that HIV—the virus that leads to AIDS—has been linked to monkeys. Other frightening diseases, such as Ebola fever, mad cow disease (bovine spongiform encephalopathy), bird flu and other variants of avian influenza, severe acute respiratory syndrome (SARS), and H1N1 (originally known as the swine flu) originate from animals. Think also about *Salmonella* and *E. coli,* which can wreak havoc on the human body, and you can begin to understand that even without a nuclear war, should these diseases be purposely spread, the possibility of one-fourth of earth's population being wiped out is very real.

Other Possibilities

Strange phenomena within plant life may contaminate much of the water supply, which we are starting to see happen today, killing a large portion of the world's fish population and leading to human deaths due to freakish diseases such as necrotizing *fasciitis*, namely an infection caused by a flesh-eating bacteria. That is to say nothing of the evil among us. We know now that some sources of germ warfare—many of which incorporate toxins, such as from the anthrax bacteria present in soil, and ricin, a toxin that can be obtained from a common house plant—are easily within the grasp of those intent on doing evil.

While I am deeply saddened by our inhumanity to one another, and I am horrified by the machinations of new technologies that continually create new ways for us to kill each other, I have given up trying to figure out how this fourth horseman will accomplish his purposes. I read John's words and I know they will come to pass. Moreover, I am convinced these things will happen *before* Jesus returns for believers. The fact that we see evidence that these atrocities could happen in our lifetime should motivate us to help our generation prepare to meet the Lord.

Who's Really in Charge?

Despite the unsettling nature of these events, always keep in mind who is in control. Who is the one breaking the seals? The Lamb!

When the Lamb opened the fifth seal, John saw two responses (Revelation 6:9–17), almost like a split screen: what was happening in heaven and what was happening on earth at the same time. First he saw the events from the viewpoint of some souls under the altar, "who had been slain for the word of God and for the testimony which they held" (6:9, NKJV).

Remember what Jesus said in Matthew 24: "Then they will deliver you to tribulation, and will kill you, and you will be hated by all nations because of My name" (6:9). Those killed for Jesus' sake are in heaven with a front-row seat to see the wrath of God poured out on those who persecuted them for their faith. We on earth call these saints by their Greek name: martyrs.

The word *martyr* simply means "witness," but it is obvious that these saints had suffered death for Christ's sake. They were slain by the Enemy because of their witness for Christ, which they would not compromise! This is not merely figurative language. These people had not simply been insulted or passed over for a promotion or mocked because of their faith. They had been *killed!* These people died rather than deny Jesus as Lord.

Why would there be an altar in heaven? We don't really know, but perhaps the patterns for the Jewish tabernacle and temple on earth are replicas of something in heaven. Regardless, this is a picture out of the Old Testament about sacrifices in which a priest poured the blood of the sacrifice at the foot of the altar area (Leviticus 4:7). In other words, the lifeblood of these martyrs has been poured out for the Lord as a sacrificial offering.

These martyrs shouted a poignant question to God: "How long, O Lord, holy and true, until You judge and avenge our blood on those who dwell on the earth?" (6:10, NKJV). How long, indeed? How long are the heathen going to get away with murder? Have you ever felt that way? Have you ever wondered why God's people so often seem to be suffering while the devil's crowd seems to be prospering? Psalm 73 tells us that the pagans will eventually receive their just punishment, but the cries of these dear saints in heaven who have given their lives for Christ certainly resonate with many of us.

Moreover, these saints seem to want to see their persecutors punished (6:10). What kind of Christian attitude is that? In Luke 23:34, didn't Jesus pray for those who killed Him? Stephen did too (Acts 7:60). In Matthew 5:44, didn't Jesus tell us to pray for those who persecute us? What's going on here? How can these martyrs be so bold in demanding vengeance?

For one thing, the question is not whether the martyrs' persecutors will be punished. The only question is when. I believe the saints in heaven now know that God is going to judge sin, that He will soon establish His eternal kingdom. It is only a matter of time.

Second, although it is hard to judge the motives of people in heaven, you have to assume that their motives are pure, and it is not revenge these saints are seeking. It is the vindication of God's holiness and wanting to see His kingdom truly come.

Nevertheless, the martyred saints are given white robes, robes of victory and honor, and told to wait a while longer, that more believers in Christ will die, that their number is not yet complete: "until both the number of their fellow servants and their brethren, who would be killed as they were, was completed" (Revelation 6:11 NKJV). More simply stated, "others will be joining you." Understand, nothing happens by accident to God's faithful. He knows what is going on, why, and for how long.

When you are going through tough times, don't think God is not aware. He is and He has allowed your circumstance for some reason. The real question is, who are you going to trust? modern society? television newscasters? the systems of this world? your friends? yourself? Or will you trust the God who knows?

10

The Day the Sun Goes Dark

The scene shifts as John watched the Lamb open the sixth seal. What he saw was enough to make a courageous person's pulse quicken.

The opening of the sixth seal results in cataclysmic convulsions across the face of the earth. Here we experience the first of three gargantuan earthquakes (Revelation 6:12; 11:13; 16:18–19). Beyond that, all nature comes unglued! The sun, moon, stars, sky, mountains, islands, everything is in a state of upheaval.

The whole earth seems to be disintegrating. John saw five devastating effects. First, a major earthquake. This is not merely a shake up; no, this is a megaquake that affects the entire planet (Amos 8:8; Ezekiel 38:19; Joel 2:10). The idea is that when it all starts to come down, the earth is going to start breaking apart!

Second, John wrote that the sky turned black. Scripture is replete with references to the darkening of the sun and moon (Amos 8:8; Isaiah 13:13, 50:3; Ezekiel 32:7; Joel 2:31; Matthew 24:29; Mark 13:24; Luke 23:45), yet if you are like most Christians, you have never heard these mentioned in a sermon.

It is hard to miss the explicit statement of Jesus, quoting the prophet Isaiah: "Soon after the trouble of those days, 'the sun will grow dark, and the moon will not give its light. The stars will fall from the sky. And the powers of the heavens will be shaken'" (Matthew 24:29, NCV). The apostle Peter picked up on this message on the Day of Pentecost when the Holy Spirit was poured out on the believers in the Upper Room (see Acts 2). In explaining how the outpouring fit into God's time line, Peter quoted the prophet Joel and said, "God says, 'In the last days I will pour out my Spirit on all kinds of people. Your sons and daughters will prophesy. Your young men will see visions, and your old men will dream dreams. At that time I will pour out my Spirit also on my male slaves and female slaves, and they will prophesy. I will show miracles in the sky and on the earth: blood, fire, and thick smoke'" (Acts 2:17–19, NCV).

We love all that talk about dreams and visions and miracles. But that's where most preachers stop. I've heard hundreds of messages about the Spirit being poured out on all kinds of people in the last days, and that is a marvelous and much-needed message—probably now more than ever. But the next couple of verses say, "The sun will become dark, the moon red as blood, before an overwhelming and glorious day of the Lord will come. Then anyone who calls on the Lord will be saved" (Acts 2:20–21, NCV).

That is every bit as much a part of the last days' message as the previous verses, but nobody talks about the sun going dark. It is as though we want to avoid the subject of the terrifying darkness that the Bible clearly states is going to cover the earth. Granted, part of the reason for that may be that we don't fully understand these references, but there are many other difficult subjects in the Bible with far less scripture that entire denominations have staked their existence on.

How Will the Sun and Moon Go Dark?

This darkness could be the result of a nuclear war or an asteroid hitting earth. Or maybe God will simply do it supernaturally (Joel 3:13–15). In describing the judgment that God will bring on Egypt, the prophet Ezekiel looked at the future and reported,

> When I make you disappear, I will cover the sky and make the stars dark. I will cover the sun with a cloud, and the moon will not shine. I will make

> all the shining lights in the sky become dark over you; I will bring darkness over your land, says the Lord GOD. (Ezekiel 32:7–8, NCV)

Ezekiel's report sounds a lot like a nuclear winter, with ash and debris filling the sky for long periods of time and blocking the rays of the sun or the light of the moon. Scientists have informed us that climatic events similar to nuclear winters happened previously on earth, as far back as the Ice Age. Perhaps God will simply do it again.

I believe this darkening of the sky most likely will be the result of a volcanic eruption that will spew so much ash into the air that it will be impossible to see the light of the sun or the moon from earth. We have experienced such phenomena when Mount St. Helens erupted in 1980. More recently, air traffic all across Europe was shut down because of volcanic eruptions in Iceland, which spewed so much ash into the air that the airlines dared not fly. But possibly the eruption to surpass all others is presently seething below the western United States, in one of our favorite recreation areas: Yellowstone National Park.

In "Supervolcano,"[23] a BBC docudrama on Yellowstone's seismic potential, scientists have estimated that an eruption of the megavolcano now percolating below Old Faithful is a "restless caldera," twenty-five by thirty-seven square miles of bubbling volcanic activity, a size slightly smaller than the state of Rhode Island. When it blows, as it undoubtedly will, there may be enough ash to darken the skies for at least a year or more, which could cause an event similar to a nuclear winter, which means no food will grow due to lack of sunlight. When that happens, the light of sun and the moon would be darkened, just as Jesus and John and the prophets said they would.

DON'T TRY TO CATCH THESE FALLING STARS!

John reported that the stars fell (Revelation 6:13). The word for "stars" that John used is the word *aster,* from which we get the word *asteroid.* I believe what John saw was most likely a massive asteroid shower. The phrase implies that the stars not only fall but are strewn all over the sky. To the Jews, this was especially bad news, because the order in the heavens was a clear sign of

God's unchanging attitude. Take away the heavens and there's nothing left! To the Jews, the ultimate chaos would be for the stars to fall from their place in the heavens—but John said that's exactly what is going to happen. Before he described the fall of the stars, it was prophesied centuries before by Isaiah ("All the host of heaven will wear away, and the sky will be rolled up like a scroll," Isaiah 34:4). Jesus concurred, quoting Isaiah: "The sun will be darkened, and the moon will not give its light, and the stars will fall from the sky, and the powers of the heavens will be shaken" (Matthew 24:29).

I sincerely believe that the stars in the heavens will not fall from the sky, because one star alone would literally decimate the entire planet. I always go to the Greek for complete clarity of New Testament scripture. In my studies, I have come to believe these stars John saw were in fact an asteroid shower.

Something like John described has happened many times before. One of the greatest of these occurred on October 8, 1871, when legend tells us that Mrs. O'Leary's cow kicked over a lantern. Within minutes, the O'Leary farm was fully engulfed in a raging fire, with the entire city of Chicago, Illinois, soon to follow.

What many don't know is that, on the same night as the Chicago fire, there was another deadly fire about 250 miles north of the city in a Wisconsin town named Peshtigo. In Peshtigo, fire literally fell from the sky and quickly consumed the entire city, burning it to the ground. Over 1,000 people perished in the fire. To this day, Peshtigo holds the title of the deadliest fire in American history.

Several cities in Michigan burned that same night, including Holland, Muskegan, Manistee, and Port Huron. Scientists believe that great fire was started by an asteroid shower, as indicated by the fragments found near Port Huron, Michigan, not long after the fires had gone out.

John saw the sky split and fold up like a scroll that has been stretched open and then suddenly sliced down the middle. After the opening of the sixth seal, John saw the repositioning of mountains and islands (Revelation 6:14). The most unshakable things on earth will be shattered when Jesus opens the sixth seal.

I believe that every tectonic plate is going to move. The resultant earthquakes, volcanoes, and tsunamis will be unlike anything we could ever imagine. In a fascinating article in *U.S. News & World Report,* Charles W. Petit wrote about volcanic action in the Canary Islands that could wreak havoc on the eastern coast of the United States. If this seismic activity involved one hundred cubic miles of rock, it could send numerous tsunamis across the Atlantic Ocean. A computer simulation suggests that a rockslide of this magnitude could generate a half-mile-high splash, which could spawn a dozen or more eighty-foot waves rushing toward the U.S. East Coast. Those waves could travel inland a few miles, covering densely populated cities, such as Boston, New York, Washington, DC, and others, especially along low-lying shores.[24]

Earthquake activity on the Canary Islands is almost constant. On April 4, 2012, seventeen earthquakes rattled the islands in one day! Admittedly, they were all rated less than a three on the Richter scale, but the perpetual seismic activity may soon take its toll. On several occasions the islands have experienced tremors, tiny seismic shudders, numbering as many as four hundred to six hundred per day! How much shimmying will it take before the fault line will crack and a portion of the islands plummets into the sea, sending a wall of water roaring toward the U.S. East Coast?

Who's Laughing Now?

As the camera angle shifted, John saw the response of the people on earth after the breaking of the sixth seal and the calamities that follow. John noticed first that it will be a time of universal fear. As had been prophesied in Zephaniah 1:14 and Luke 23:30, even strong men, the great and the rich, will weep. Nobody will be exempt from the judgment of God—everyone will be shaking with fear.

Second, John saw that people will be looking for somewhere to hide (Revelation 6:15–16), just like Adam and Eve did when they realized they had sinned and offended almighty God. Comedians, movie stars, politicians, and others who have mocked God will be looking for a place to hide. In fact, John said they will be looking to hide in caves among the rocks. Many will cry out to the mountains and the rocks, "Fall on us and hide us from the presence of Him who sits on the throne" (v. 16).

John noticed a third curious response: people will flee from . . . a lamb. Fleeing a lion makes sense, but a lamb doesn't seem all that scary. The Lamb of Revelation, however, is no meek, docile lamb. He is the Lamb of God!

God is holy. There is no sin in heaven. If there is sin in us, now is the time to deal with it. This is merely the first series of judgments. We will reign victoriously—but not yet.

11

The Great Tribulation Begins

John looked into the future and saw what is going to happen in the last days, the terrible days of the Tribulation. Revelation 7 is like a flashback in which John took time out from describing the opening of the seven seals to fill us in on the Great Tribulation. This vision raises all sorts of questions about the Tribulation, some of which we won't be able to answer with certainty but must accept by faith. We do know this: the time of tribulation that Jesus predicted will be an awful time (Matthew 24:21–22)!

The Tribulation to which Jesus referred will be a time of demonic power, devastation, desolation, and destruction. But before this time is unleashed in all its fury, a group of God's faithful will be sealed so they can survive it. They are not sealed so they will be exempt or won't have to go through this period of time, but John saw that they will be brought safely through it. That is the thrust of Revelation 7.

John saw three things of note in this regard. First, he saw a warning: tribulation is coming soon! Second, he received an assurance: the faithful ones will suffer, but they will come through because they are set apart by God. Third, he received a promise: when they have made it through these days of tribulation, they will enjoy the blessing of being in God's presence for eternity. So even though John saw some difficult things in this portion of the vision, it is nonetheless an encouraging message.

As the chapter opens, we see four angels holding back the winds until the sealing of the faithful ones is completed (7:1, 3). In Jewish thought, there was an idea that the winds originating from the north, south, east, and west were good, but winds that moved diagonally were harmful. These angels are at the corners of the earth, as though each is holding a corner of a sheet and getting ready to shake it, which will unleash the diagonal winds. When they do, watch out!

About that time, John saw another angel ascending "from the rising of the sun" (7:2) from the east. Why the east? The sun, which is a source of light and life rises in the east. Remember, too, when Jesus was born in Bethlehem, the magi saw the star in the east.

More important, this angel has the seal of the living God (7:2) and apparently the authority that goes along with it. That term, *the living God,* was a favorite phrase of biblical writers, often juxtaposing the living God against the dead gods of the heathen (for example, Isaiah 44:9–17, which comes close to being a comedy sketch about man-made gods). For the people living through these difficult days, only a living God can help them in their struggles. Men and women need and want to know the living God. He is the only One who can satisfy, but there is also a hint of a threat and a promise in that phrase: the living God is a threat to those who live in disobedience to Him and a promise to those who are faithful to Him.

What about the seal of God that the angel carries and the instructions: "Do not harm the earth . . . until we have sealed the bond-servants of our God" (7:3)? The idea goes back to Ezekiel 9:1–7. In the Hebrew alphabet, the letter Taw looks like an X or a plus sign. Every king possessed a signet ring, worn not merely as a decorative piece of jewelry, but to authenticate a document as coming from the king with the king's authority and power. Documents were sealed and then impressed with this special mark of the monarch. So when these people in Revelation are sealed with the seal of the living God, it is a clear sign that they belong to God and that the angels operate under the power and authority of God.

The seal of God was placed on the foreheads of God's servants. Keep that in mind, because later Satan will attempt to counterfeit this mark of God by implementing the mark of the Beast in Revelation 13:16–18.

Here, the primary purpose of sealing God's people will be to protect them from the coming horrors of the Tribulation period. The apostle Paul also wrote about believers being sealed by the Holy Spirit as proof that we belong to God (Ephesians 1:13–14).

Similar to the Old Testament Passover, in which the blood of the lamb on the doorway sealed the people in as the angel of death passed over them on a deadly mission to kill every firstborn child of the Egyptians, this seal will protect God's people through even more terrifying events.

Who Are the 144,000?

The big question involves the 144,000 who receive the seal of God (7:4–8). Some say these are Jews who accept Jesus as Messiah during the Tribulation period; others suggest the 144,000 are Jewish evangelists who are saved during the Tribulation and then stand up to the pressures from the Antichrist as witnesses for Jesus. I believe, however, there are going to be many more believers who make it through the Tribulation than the 144,000.

Most likely, 144,000 is a number that represents perfection and completion: 12 times 12 times 1000. Whatever the number symbolizes, John heard the number of those who were sealed: 12,000 from each of the 12 tribes of Israel. The message here is that a lot of believers will be caught up in the Tribulation, and they are going to experience some tough times, but they *will* survive it! We don't know much about the 144,000, but we know they are special to God, and we will see them again in Revelation 14:1–5, where they seem to be a special group of saints that will be saved during the Tribulation.

Their Suffering Will Be Worth It

Next, in Revelation 7:9–10, John saw the glory of the great multitude dressed in white robes. Obviously, this group of people numbered far more than 144,000. This is meant to be an encouragement to us. Notice four things about the enormous group of believers. First, the number is so huge no one could count it. They are from every nation, tribe, people, and language. There will be no segregation in heaven; we will be one people.

These saints in heaven are victorious; they are not beaten down, battered, or worn. They have come through some tough times, but they are still rejoicing, just as some of us have come through some difficulties. They have not turned their backs on Jesus.

These victorious believers are dressed in white robes and waving palm branches. In John's time, conquering Roman generals wore white robes, and palm branches were often waved to celebrate a victory or some other special occasion. John was reminding his persecuted readers, "You will be the real conquerors if you stay true to Jesus." Clearly, he saw and heard these people celebrating the biggest win of all.

John especially noticed the shout of victory, not congratulating themselves for making it through, but giving glory to the one who empowered them to make it: "Salvation belongs to our God!" (6:10, NKJV). Glory to God! He has brought them through—not that He extracted them from persecution, but He brought them through. Let this be an encouragement to you: in Christ, a person can endure any kind of trouble and come out to glory!

WHAT A TESTIMONY!

The angels and the four living beings and the twenty-four elders around the throne of God can barely contain themselves at this beautiful acknowledgment of God's goodness and grace. They fall on their faces and begin to praise God along with the saints! Every word that pours out of their mouths is a marvelous acclamation of perfect praise to our God:

1. Blessing!
2. Glory!
3. Wisdom!
4. Thanksgiving!

5. Honor!
6. Power!
7. Might!

We need to praise Him like that. Before approaching God with your needs and requests, address these words of praise to the One who is on the throne and to the Lamb. You will find yourself so immersed in a flood of joyful appreciation for God and His love for you. Thoughts of your own needs may not even occur to you. But God hasn't forgotten them. He knows what you need before you ask.

A Beautiful Picture

John had an interesting exchange with one of the elders, who asked him, "Who are these people dressed in white robes? Where did they come from?" (Revelation 7:13, NCV).

John instantly replied with one of the greatest answers in history: "You know." This is his version of *Are You Smarter Than a Fifth Grader?* He bounced the question right back to the elder, who then informed the apostle, "These are the ones who come out of the great tribulation, and they have washed their robes and made them white in the blood of the Lamb" (7:14).

Some people believe the Rapture takes place at this point. I do not think so, because most of the signs of Christ's return are not recounted here. There's no cloud, no final trumpet, no resurrection of the dead.

The King James Version reports that these people have come "out of great tribulation." Consequently, many people think of these tribulations as troubles, tough times, or suffering, all of which may be true, but this is not true to the original language. The Greek here says that these people come "out of *the* tribulation," not merely a tough time. They came through *the* Tribulation period, the time that Jesus referred to in Matthew 24, through the toughest of times ever known!

The elder then provided a description of an amazing reward for these believers. He told John that these saints have washed their robes in the blood of the Lamb (7:14). He saw white robes washed in blood. These robes of purity have been purchased by the blood of Jesus.

It is fascinating to note, however, that the saints have washed their robes; Jesus did not wash them for the believers. It is His blood, His purity that makes our lives clean. He makes salvation available, but every individual must do something too. We must do our part by accepting His sacrifice for our sins and allowing that cleansing process to work in us. All that Jesus did for us is useless unless we also participate. There will be no one in heaven whose robes have not been cleansed, purified, and made absolutely clean by the blood of the Lamb.

That phrase, *the blood of the lamb*, is also interesting. We think of blood as death, but the Jews thought of blood as life, because life is *in* the blood. The elder reminded John that victory comes from the blood of Jesus in our lives! It is the blood that cleanses us from all sin (1 John 1:7). His blood is the propitiation for our sins; He paid the penalty for us (Romans 3:25). We are justified through the blood of Jesus (Romans 5:9), redeemed by the blood (Ephesians 1:7); our salvation was purchased with precious blood, as of a lamb unblemished and spotless (1 Peter 1:18, 19). His blood cleanses our consciences and gives us the power to serve Him (Hebrews 9:14).

John saw these redeemed saints in heaven in the presence of God, "in His temple." Remember, no Jew ever dared to go into the Holy of Holies, the inner sanctum of the temple, except for the high priest. But John saw these true believers in the heavenly temple of God, serving before the throne of God night and day (Revelation 7:15).

Isn't it interesting that people who are honored so highly are servants in the presence of God? Most of us want to be served, but the best jobs in heaven will be those of servants. Apparently, during their lifetimes, these people experienced great hardships, because part of their reward is that they will never have to experience those things again. The Lamb will lead them to fountains of living water, and God will wipe away every tear. We must endure everything for Jesus' sake, persevere, and He will nourish our bodies and souls, He will bring peace to our hearts.

12

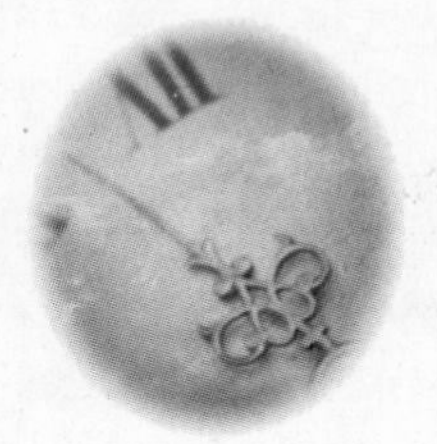

The Calm Before the Storm

John knew his message would not be easy for his readers. As a candle flickered in the darkness, casting shadows on the parchment on which he was writing, he felt a flickering ambivalence about the vision. He wanted to write the vision—he knew he must be obedient to the voice of Jesus—but he wished he did not have to reveal some of the things he had seen. He delighted in the glories of heaven, but he shuddered at the thought of showing the horrors of the events about to come upon the earth.

First, John showed us the glory of chapters 4 and 5, giving us a glimpse of what is going on there, then he showed us the horror of the birth pangs before the Tribulation in chapter 6, and then the beauty of the redeemed lives in chapter 7. It's as though we couldn't take it all in if we didn't know that this is the Revelation of Jesus Christ and that in these chapters we come face to face with God's wrath as it is poured out on sinful society.

Perhaps the most astounding and horrific part of the Tribulation period is that the majority of people who are alive during these unimaginable days of suffering and chaos will not repent. It amazes me that the same events cause some people to cry out to God for forgiveness while others curse God and die.

As we move into Revelation 8, we hope for a break in the drama being described to us. After the opening of the six seals, we see the seventh seal ahead, bringing a new series of judgments. But there is a brief pause in this action; we have reached the calm before the storm.

SILENCE ISN'T GOLDEN

When Jesus broke open the seventh seal, "there was silence in heaven for about half an hour" (Revelation 8:1). Every other scene of heaven that we have witnessed so far has been replete with loud voices, as redeemed people as well as angels praise and worship God. This silence is a strange, staggering development. During this awful, awesome silence, everything stops. Time seems to stand still. It's as though the beings in heaven collectively gasp at the sight of what is about to happen on earth. Their praises suddenly stop. They are awestruck, somber and stunned at what is coming.

When the seventh seal is broken, we see the seven angels who stand before God, not merely in a place of honor, but ready to serve Him, to do whatever He commands. The seven angels are each given a trumpet, but before they blow the trumpets, there is a fascinating scene in heaven in which the prayers of the saints are recognized. These are the prayers of people like us! True believers, holy ones—saints.

Two very interesting events occur. First, an angel in addition to the seven trumpeters stands at the altar with a golden censer (8:3). In the Bible, the sweet smell of incense symbolizes the prayers of God's people rising to heaven. The angel in Revelation 8:3 is given "much incense," so we are talking about a lot of prayers by God's people. Interestingly, as the prayers go up, the judgment comes down! Then the angel fills the censer with fire and hurls it at the earth (v. 5), which results in thunder, lightning, and another major earthquake.

Something big is about to happen. But before we look at that, we have to ask if there is a connection between the prayers of the saints and the judgment falling on the earth. I think there is; namely, God always answers our prayers for justice. The prayers of the saints are answered, and in some way they are involved in unleashing the vengeance of God's wrath upon those who hate Him and ignore Him on earth. We saw something similar in Revelation 6, when the saints in heaven asked God "how long" before their deaths and the great name of God would be vindicated?

Revelation 8:6 returns us to the seven angels with the seven trumpets, but as we will soon see, seven is not a lucky number for those folks alive during the Tribulation. John described the total terror that will reign on earth at that time, including a series of plagues that are amazingly similar to the plagues with which God struck the earth prior to delivering His people from Egyptian slavery (Exodus 7–10). But the coming calamities encompass far more territory, include far more natural resources, and affect far more people. These horrors will take place, most likely, just prior to the Lord's return.

According to Revelation 8:7 (NKJV), when the trumpets begin to sound, "hail and fire followed, mingled with blood" and "a third of the trees were burned up, and all green grass was burned up." The sounding of these trumpets is going to usher in one of the most frightening times in human history. Believe it or not, another series of judgments is to come after the trumpet judgments. Those judgments will be the seven bowls of God's wrath being poured out on the earth. For now, let's consider the trumpet judgments.

In the Old Testament, trumpet blasts served three purposes: they called the people together for meetings, such as when the Law was given at Mount Sinai (Exodus 19:16–19); they announced war or summoned the people to battle (for example, the conquest of Jericho; Joshua 6:13–16); and they announced special or unusual events that the Lord was doing in and through His people. Of course, one such special event involved trumpet fanfares to announce the presence of royalty or the anointing or enthronement of a king (1 Kings 1:34, 39).

In Revelation, the sounding of the seven trumpets is like a declaration of war as well as an announcement that God is ready to judge His enemies. The first four trumpets have to do with events that are going to affect the natural world. From America to Australia, from the Arctic to the Antarctic, the earth will experience an ecological upheaval that will make toxic waste dumps seem like playgrounds. The first trumpet affects the land (8:7). Hail and fire are mixed with blood and hurled out of the sky, resulting in one-third of the earth being burned. One-third of everything green will be gone. Next, one-third of the sea, the saltwater bodies and one-third of all sea life will be destroyed (v. 8). This could be caused by a volcano or an asteroid or meteor strike, as the second angel sounds his trumpet and "something like a great mountain burning with fire was thrown into the sea; and a third of the sea became blood, and a third of the creatures which were in the sea and had life, died; and a third of the ships were destroyed" (vv. 8, 9). Once again, this sounds like what scientists say will probably happen if the seismic activity at the Canary Islands causes parts of the islands to fall into the sea, triggering massive tsunamis to devastate the coasts outlining the Atlantic Ocean.

Imagine yourself on a cruise ship, a naval vessel, or a cargo ship, and suddenly the sea turns blood red and one-third of all the ships in the world are destroyed. I was at Sanibel Island in Florida a few years ago when the "red tide" came in on the beach. It was one of the scariest, foulest things I have ever seen or smelled. Thankfully, it lasted only a short time. But imagine Waikiki Beach, South Beach, the French Riviera, and every other famous beach suddenly plagued by waters turning into blood. The putrid smell alone will be stifling.

Then came the third angel's trumpet blast. In addition to one-third of earth's saltwater bodies being contaminated, the freshwater supply will be severely affected as well. Rivers and springs will be poisoned by the great star or asteroid named Wormwood. It "fell from heaven, burning like a torch, and it fell on a third of the rivers and on the springs of waters," causing them to become bitter (8:10). John said "many men died from the waters, because they were made bitter" (v. 11). Again, this sounds suspiciously like the results of an asteroid or meteor strike. Regardless, drinkable water is going to be rare.

When the fourth angel sounds his trumpet, things get even worse. John reported, "A third of the sun and a third of the moon and a third of the stars were struck, so that a third of them would be darkened and the day would not shine for a third of it, and the night in the same way" (8:12).

It is hard to visualize one-third of the heavenly bodies snuffed out and darkened, but as we've seen previously in Revelation 6, this is going to happen.

In the Second Coming discourse in Matthew 24, Jesus, too, confirmed that the sun would be blotted out before He returns. After listing some of the signs of the times of which His followers should be aware, Jesus said,

> Immediately after the tribulation of those days the sun will be darkened, and the moon will not give its light; the stars will fall from heaven, and the powers of the heavens will be shaken. Then the sign of the Son of Man will appear in heaven, and then all the tribes of the earth will mourn, and they will see the Son of Man coming on the clouds of heaven with power and great glory. (Matthew 24:29–30, NKJV)

The parallel passage in Luke's Gospel is equally calamitous:

> And there will be signs in the sun, in the moon, and in the stars; and on the earth distress of nations, with perplexity, the sea and the waves roaring; men's hearts failing them from fear and the expectation of those things which are coming on the earth, for the powers of the heavens will be shaken. (Luke 21:25–26, NKJV)

Notice that Jesus said the "signs in the sun" will occur *before* His return in power and glory—not after.

I believe the events John described in Revelation 8 will lead us to the point of Christ's return. The devastation will literally wipe out a third of our vegetation, water supply, and sea life as well as a third of the sun's light. Could a nuclear attack create such conditions? Possibly. Could a meteor or an asteroid striking the earth cause the calamities John described? Absolutely. He may never have seen a meteor or an asteroid or a comet, but he described a realistic picture of a meteor strike. Possibly the burning mountain John saw could be a combined event: a volcanic eruption caused by a meteor strike.

Amid this eerie scene, John saw "an eagle flying in midheaven, saying with a loud voice, 'Woe, woe, woe to those who dwell on the earth, because of the remaining blasts of the trumpet of the three angels who are about to sound!'" (8:13). The eagle's message is, "The *worst* is yet to come!"

13

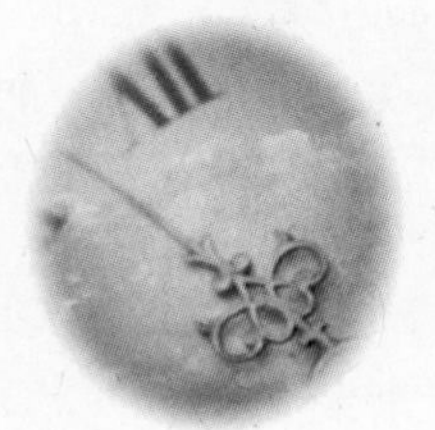

Demonic Warfare

The apostle cringed as he prepared to write out the vision of the final three trumpets of Revelation. The first four angels trumpeted natural disasters that were about to come upon the earth. Now, the final three trumpets were going to herald something even more earth-shattering. In fact, at the sound of the fifth and sixth trumpets, the earth would become downright demonic. In Revelation 9, John saw two frightening armies unleashed upon human beings.

When the fifth trumpet sounded, he saw "a star from heaven that had fallen to the earth; and the key of the bottomless pit was given to him" (9:1). This star is not a comet or a meteor; it is a person. He is the king over the pit, the abyss. He is given the key to the abyss. He has no authority of his own, except what is given to him by God. Even when all hell breaks loose on the earth, our Lord God is still in control.

Who is this star? I believe it is Satan. One of the names for Satan is Lucifer, which means "brightness." He is referred to as the "morning star" in Isaiah 14:12–14, NIV. In Luke 10:18, Jesus said, "I was watching Satan fall from heaven like lightning."

What Is the Abyss?

The abyss is "the bottomless pit" or simply "the pit." Interestingly, it is basically the same word as found in Genesis 1:2. Originally the abyss was a dark, formless, endless, subterranean "watery place," the primeval deep (Genesis 7:11). In the New Testament, the word is used only nine times, with seven of those references in Revelation. What do we know about it?

It is the abode of demons (Luke 8:31), the place where demons live—if you call that living. The abyss is also the temporary place of punishment for fallen angels, which would include demons, the Beast, the False Prophet, and, of course, Satan himself. We also know that the Antichrist, the Beast, will rise out of this pit in some way (Revelation 11:7; 17:8). The abyss is not exactly a nice neighborhood.

The abyss is apparently the place where Satan will be imprisoned for one thousand years, during the millennial reign of Jesus. Then he will be released for a short time. Why? I don't know. If I were writing this story, I certainly would not want these guys on the loose again after they had been penned up in their place. But God has His reasons.

One thing the abyss is not: it is not the lake of fire that will be the final place of punishment for Satan and those who follow him. We will see more about that in Revelation 20:10, 14, 15. But it is part of that netherworld.

In Revelation 9, the star—the devil, Satan—opens the abyss like a furnace door, and the sun and sky are darkened from the smoke. That would be bad enough, but what comes out of that smoke is really terrifying! An army of locust emerges from the smoke (vv. 3–11). Locusts in the Bible are always a symbol of destruction. Whenever God judged His people, He often sent a swarm of locusts to devastate the land and irritate the people. Again, it sounds like a bad horror movie, but if you have never had to battle these insects, you may not realize how destructive they can be.

In the first two chapters of the book of Joel, the prophet described a locust invasion. The results are devastating. The vines are laid waste. The locusts strip the bark from the trees. The fields are devastated, and the corn crop is destroyed. Every tree in the field withers and dies. No vegetation escapes the locusts, so consequently, the flocks and herds of sheep and goats starve because there is no pasture for them and no corn.

When locusts swarm, they travel in huge columns more than a hundred feet deep and four miles long. It's no wonder that John says these bugs will darken the sky. Furthermore, the sound made by their wings in flight will be maddening, further magnified by the sound of their munching on everything in sight. The noise will be like the crackling of a huge forest fire, and their aftermath will be no less devastating than that of a wildfire. Famine usually follows in the wake of locusts.

But in Revelation 9 it gets worse, because these are not ordinary locusts. These locusts come from the demonic pits. These creatures don't eat vegetation. In fact, they are instructed not to touch any vegetation (v. 4). Their attack is focused on human beings. They are allowed to torment all men, women, and children who do not have the seal of God on their foreheads. While normal locusts are destructive to vegetation, these vermin have the sting of scorpions.

Do you remember the saints who were sealed in Revelation 7:3? This is why it was so important that they be protected.

Palestinian scorpions look like small lobsters, with claws and a long wire-like tail with a poisonous barb. The sting is far worse than that of a hornet and can be fatal. These demonic locusts have a sting to torment people, and the effects of their attack will last for five months (9:5). The torturous attacks will evoke strong responses from their victims. The tormented people will want to die, but for some reason, they will not be able to do so (v. 6).

Interestingly, John reminds us that these locusts have an overlord: "They have as king over them, the angel of the abyss; his name in Hebrew is Abaddon, and in the Greek he has the name Apollyon" (9:11). The names Abaddon and Apollyon mean the same in either language: "the destroyer," or "destruction."

The Sixth Trumpet Sounds

When the sixth angel sounds his trumpet, a second demonic attack is unleashed (Revelation 9:13–21). Whereas the locusts are allowed to torment but not kill, this second demonically inspired army of mounted troops is going to wipe out one-third of humankind. An army two hundred million strong will storm through the Euphrates area of the Middle East. For years the Parthians lived beyond the Euphrates, and they had a reputation of being the most dreaded warriors in the world. For John to even hint of an attack coming from beyond the Euphrates would strike fear into most of his readers. Today, scholars suggest this massive army coming through the Euphrates region might be Chinese, due in part to a later reference (16:12) to the "kings from the east." And the Chinese have long been able to field an army of two hundred million soldiers.

Regardless of who actually fields this army, we know that this is not an arbitrary uprising. It has been planned for a long time ("So the four angels, who had been prepared for the hour and day and month and year, were released to kill a third of mankind" [9:15 NKJV]). We also know that the attack after the sounding of the sixth trumpet is going to result in the death of one-third of the human beings who have survived the calamities that have already befallen the planet. That means that a quarter of the world's population will already have been killed because of the natural disasters, wars, and diseases announced in Revelation 6:8. Thus, another third of the population is going to die.

By the time the first six trumpet judgments are completed, more than half of the world's population that was alive at the beginning of the Tribulation period will have died. Wouldn't you think that such horrendous events would cause you to consider calling out to God for mercy? Wouldn't you contemplate the benefits of repentance? Would you not deduce that the God who controls these events is nobody to mess with? Would you not wonder if you are ready to meet Him in judgment? Would you not ponder where you will spend eternity?

Apparently, those thoughts never crossed the minds of the people being pummeled by the tribulation woes. In fact, they refused to repent, and they continued in their sins ("The rest of mankind, who were not killed by these plagues, did not repent of the works of their hands, so as not to worship demons, and the idols of gold and of silver and of brass and of stone and of wood, which can neither see nor walk; and they did not repent of their murders nor of their sorceries not of their immorality nor of their thefts" [vv. 20–21]). It is frightening to think that some people will persist in their sin while mired in the midst of God's judgment. Not only do these people figuratively thumb their noses at God, but also they will continue their demon worship, their idolatry, and their false religions. These are "dead" sinners worshipping dead gods.

Meanwhile, God is still working out His plan through all these awful events. At this point in the book of Revelation, we are about three and a half years into the Tribulation period. The Antichrist will be making his bid as a peacemaker soon, if he hasn't done so already, offering peace and stability and prosperity to a world that has been bludgeoned by tribulation. Things do not look good right now, but remember, this is God's plan that John was describing to us. It is not the Antichrist's plan, nor is it the devil's grand scheme. It is the Revelation of Jesus and those who believe in Him and who will endure to the end will overcome. In the end, we win, because Jesus Christ has already won!

14

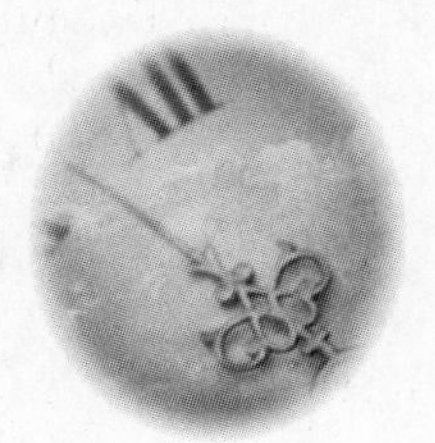

A Great Mystery Solved

In the previous section of the vision, John saw that demon-inspired warfare is coming, but God is going to seal His people so we will not be tormented. Not long ago, I saw a photo of an Apache helicopter. Its bulging windshields, giant propellers, and weaponry struck me as being very similar to John's description of the locusts in Revelation 8. Keep in mind, John was trying to convey to us things that his eyes had never seen or even imagined. Could it be that these helicopters are part of the force that will destroy millions of people during this horrific period?

I loved Charlie Chan mysteries when I was a boy. Charlie was the quintessential detective, piecing together clues to get to the truth. That's similar to our task of gathering clues throughout Revelation, discovering how the pieces fit together in astounding ways, showing us what to expect and when we can anticipate the return of Jesus Christ.

Revelation 10 is another breather after all the horrors of chapters 8 and 9. It is as though the Lord said, "John needs a break." If you've ever watched a television show with one intense scene after another, you almost long for a commercial, a break where you can catch your breath and allow your mind to process some of the information you've gathered during the show. That's where we are in Revelation.

Time Has Come

So far we've seen the horrors that followed the opening of the seven seals and horrible judgments announced by the first six trumpets. Now, there's a short break between Revelation 10:1 and 11:14. Here, John saw some fascinating images.

A Different Sort of Angel

First, John saw a mighty angel coming down from heaven (Revelation 10:1). Who is this mighty angel? There are more than sixty references to angels in the book of Revelation. We don't understand everything about them, but they are intriguing. We think of angels as benign creatures, but check out what the Bible says about angels.

The word *angel* is used in the King James Version in various ways. Sometimes the word refers to angelic beings, sometimes to pastors or leaders, and occasionally simply to messengers. For example, in Matthew 11:10, John the Baptist is referred to as a messenger ("Behold, I send My messenger ahead of You, who will prepare Your way before You"), which is the same Greek word that the apostle John used for angel here in Revelation 10:1. Most of us know that John the Baptist was not an angel.

This angel in Revelation 10 is different from others you will study. This angel was "dressed in a cloud with a rainbow over his head. His face was like the sun, and his legs were like pillars of fire." He held a "small scroll" and placed "his right foot on the sea and his left foot on the land." He shouted "like the roaring of a lion," and in response to his shout, "the voices of seven thunders spoke." John prepared to write down all of this, and then "a voice from heaven" stopped him, saying, "Keep hidden what the seven thunders said, and do not write them down" (10:1–4, NCV).

Many of the characteristics of this messenger are similar to the Lord Jesus. First, John described the angel as "mighty." Second, this angel was robed in a cloud. At least 156 passages of scripture identify God's presence with clouds. In Exodus 16:10 God led Israel by a cloud. I believe this cloud was the presence of Jesus. Dark clouds covered Mount Sinai when the Ten Commandments and the Law were given (Exodus 19:9). When God appeared to Moses, He did so in a cloud of glory (Exodus 24:15, 34:5). Leviticus 16:2 says, "I will appear in the cloud over the mercy seat." Numbers 11:25, Deuteronomy 31:15, and 1 Kings 8:11 all talk about the glory of the Lord filling the temple. The psalmist said, "[God] makes the clouds His chariot" (Psalm 104:3). When Jesus ascended into heaven, forty days after His resurrection, He was received by a cloud (Acts 1:9). We also know that when Jesus returns, He will come in the clouds and with power and great glory (Matthew 24; Luke 21:27; 1 Thessalonians 4:16; Revelation 1:7). Thus, when John saw this angel (messenger) in Revelation 10:1 coming down from heaven, robed in a cloud, you can be sure of what John was thinking, especially when you observe the other aspects of his description of this angel.

Third, a rainbow spanned his head (10:1). After the Genesis flood, the rainbow was God's promise that He would not destroy the earth again by water (Genesis 9:9–16). Every time I see a rainbow, I rejoice in that promise of God. The rainbow in Revelation 10 reminds us of the rainbow that is around the throne of God (Revelation 4:3). Even in the midst of God's wrath, He is still merciful. With all the death, destruction, and horror the world has seen in Revelation 8 and 9, there is still hope in Jesus.

Fourth, the angel's face was like the sun (10:1). Recall the description of Jesus in Revelation 1:16. That is also the description of Jesus' face at the Transfiguration (Matthew 17:2).

Fifth, the angel's legs were like fiery pillars (Revelation 1:15). His voice was like the roar of a lion (10:3), which reminds us that Jesus is also known as the Lion of Judah (5:5). Matthew 2:6 says, "And you, Bethlehem, land of Judah, are by no means least among the leaders of Judah; for out of you shall come forth a ruler." Interesting, isn't it? Jesus came from the tribe of Judah.

A Different Kind of Prison Ministry

As I studied this passage of scripture in prison, I thought, *This cannot be just any angel. This must be Jesus. Nobody else fits this description.* Each morning in prison, for exercise, I walked around the exercise field and listened to a small transistor radio. One morning, I heard David Jeremiah teaching on Revelation

10. "This must be Jesus," he said. "It cannot be anyone else." I was ecstatic. It was as though God were confirming His Word to my heart and mind through my little transistor radio.

Two other points also might suggest this messenger is Jesus in some manifestation. First, that angel had a book, actually a small scroll, in his hand (10:2). This tiny scroll contained the rest of the prophetic message John was to deliver. We can assume that since Jesus is the only one worthy to open the scrolls by breaking the seals in Revelation 5:5, He would be the only one worthy to give the remainder of the message.

Second, notice the stand that this messenger took in 10:2, namely, that of a conquering king (10:5–6), astride land and sea. What does this mean? To me, it indicates *dominion,* that the strong angel is claiming the whole world, everything, every universe, every galaxy as His own. Only a victorious Savior could rightfully do that, not an angel, only Jesus.

These and the prior points are my reasons for believing this mighty messenger is a manifestation of Jesus. At the very least, we know this angel comes from the heart and presence of God.

John saw this messenger and heard the voices of the seven thunders, which is probably the voice of God, which is described elsewhere as thunder (Psalm 29:3–9).

HOLD IT RIGHT THERE, JOHN!

John was about to transcribe the message, but a voice from heaven stopped him, instructing him to "seal up the things which the seven peals of thunder have spoken and do not write them." This is the only message in Revelation that remains sealed; everything else is revealed, opened, unsealed. In fact, in Revelation 22:10, we see that a message sealed up in Daniel 8:26; 12:4, 9 is finally revealed. These prophecies were to be sealed until the last times, when they will be opened.

We are not told why these words were sealed or what the message contained. There is little use in speculating. God has not told us what these seven thunders said, so that tells me there is more information yet to come. In 2 Corinthians 2:12, the apostle Paul described the experience of "a man in Christ" who "was caught up to the third heaven," where he heard "inexpressible words, which a man is not permitted to speak." Thus, God does not disclose everything to us on this side of heaven. Still, I cannot help wondering if the date and time for the Second Coming were contained in those seven peals of thunder in Revelation 10:3.

Notice the declaration of the angel in 10:5–7. It has been variously translated as "there will be no more time" or "time will be no more." But perhaps a better translation is "there should be delay no longer." Any way we translate it, there's only one person who could authoritatively make that declaration: Jesus! Yes! Only Jesus or His Father can declare that time is up.

What does this mean? I think there are two possibilities. First, it could mean there is literally no time left before the climactic events of history transpire. The Antichrist is about to burst on to the scene, and the terrors are about to come upon the earth. Jesus' return is imminent. Second, it could mean that it's all over. Eternity has begun.

Either way, notice the seriousness of this scene. The angel raised his right hand, like a person would take an oath. There are a number of places in the Bible where God places Himself under oath, for example, when He made covenants with Noah (Genesis 9:8–17), Abraham (Genesis 17:1–27), and David (2 Samuel 7:12–17; Psalm 89:3–4, 27–28). God did not have to make an everlasting commitment to any man, but He did, and He continues to honor those covenants to this day.

So why would God delay His judgments today? I believe God is allowing people time to repent. He is not willing that anyone be lost (2 Peter 3:9), therefore He withholds His judgment so that people can have time to repent. Yet at this point in Revelation, the angel says, "Time's up! Prepare for judgment!"

Mystery Solved

In Revelation 10:7, the strong angel refers to the "mystery of God." What is he talking about? What mystery? I thought this was supposed to be an unfolding, a revelation. But now we are told the mystery of God will be accomplished, finished, completed. In other words, God's whole purpose for human history has been fulfilled: God has won the victory over evil.

In the Bible, that word *mystery* is often used to imply a truth hidden to those outside of the kingdom of God but revealed to His people. Both Jesus and the apostle Paul spoke about this mystery. Jesus did so in parables, although His disciples often did not understand them. This almost always prompted Jesus to share the meaning, to uncover the mystery for them (Mark 4:11).

Paul, too, spoke about this same mystery. See Romans 11:25, 16:25; 1 Corinthians 2:7, 15:51–52; Ephesians 1:9, 3:3–9, 5:32, 6:19; and Colossians 1:26–27, 2:2. In commanding the Ephesians to wear the full armor of God to defend themselves and present the gospel, the apostle asked for prayer to "make known with boldness the mystery of the gospel" (6:19). In Colossians 4:3, Paul said that he was writing the letter from prison because he was sharing the "mystery of Christ." All of Ephesians 3 is dedicated to this mystery, with Paul's goal declared as bringing "to light what is the administration of the mystery which for ages has been hidden in God" (v. 9, also alluded to in Romans 16:25). The mystery hidden throughout the ages is the same mystery found in Revelation 10:7, before the seventh angel sounds the seventh and final trumpet to call the bride to meet the bridegroom in the air.

We know this mystery is the gospel of Jesus Christ. Notice in Revelation 11:14–19 that the signal for the completion of this mystery is the seventh trumpet. After that trumpet volley, the angels will start to pour out the bowls of God's wrath, and we cannot fathom how awful that scene will be.

Sweet and Bitter Tastes

In Revelation 10:8 a voice from heaven told John, "'Go, take the book which is open in the hand of the angel who stands on the sea and on the land.'" John reported, "I went to the angel, telling him to give me the little book. And he said to me, 'Take it and eat it; and it will make your stomach bitter, but in your mouth it will be sweet as honey'" (10:9). John did as he was told, and the results were just as the angel said. It's interesting that John was instructed to "take" the scroll from the strong angel. The book was not given to him; he must grasp it, eat it, and digest it. Similarly, God offers His Word to us, but we still must take it, read it, digest it, and make it part of our lives. It is not enough to possess God's revelation; we must internalize it.

The image of John eating the little book comes right out of Ezekiel 3:1–3, where the prophet was told to "fill your body with this scroll which I am giving you." The idea is that the message must become a part of the believer.

The sweetness of God's Word is another idea repeated often in scripture. Psalm 19:10 says that the judgments of God are "sweeter…than honey and the drippings of the honeycomb." Psalm 119:103 says, "How sweet are Your words to my taste! Yes, sweeter than honey to my mouth!"

Notice that the little book initially was sweet to John's taste, but then it turned bitter after he swallowed it (Revelation 10:9–10). What does this mean? I believe this describes the full scope of the great message we carry of the gospel. Yes, it is a message of hope (sweet), but it is also a warning (bitter). It's a good news–bad news message. The good news is that Jesus is coming! The bad news is that He comes in judgment! The rapture is bad news for the unsaved.

More to Come

After John ate the little book and his stomach turned sour, he was told, "You must prophesy again concerning many people and nations and tongues and kings" (Revelation 10:11). He must declare God's prophetic truth, not "before" many peoples, but "concerning" many peoples. In other words, John was instructed to preach to the "nations," which in the New Testament usually means the Gentile nations. John was told that he would have a lot to tell people about what's coming.

15

THE RAPTURE CHAPTER

To me, Revelation 11 is one of the most exciting chapters in the Bible, because I am convinced that we see the Second Coming in these verses! The chapter begins with some strange instructions for John to measure the temple (11:1–2). The prophet Ezekiel was directed to do something similar after God's people had been taken captive and exiled in Babylon (Ezekiel 40–43). What's the purpose of these measurements? In Ezekiel, I believe God was reminding His people that the temple belonged to Him and it would be preserved. I think that same message underlies these initial verses in Revelation 11.

PREPARATIONS FOR THE TEMPLE TO BE REBUILT

I believe the temple will be rebuilt in Jerusalem. The temple was destroyed in AD 70, about twenty-five years before John wrote the book of Revelation. There's evidence today that many Jews are preparing for the temple's reconstruction and preparing to worship there (see www.templeinstitute.org). Because the Antichrist will secure peace in Israel, it is not beyond the realm of possibility that the Antichrist may help or encourage the Jews to rebuild the temple.

Interestingly, John was told to "leave out the court which is outside the temple" from his measurements (Revelation 11:2). The outer court of the original temple was known as the court of the Gentiles. There were three other courts in the temple area: the court of women, the court of the Israelites, and the court of the priests. Within the latter was a special area known as the Holy of Holies, where the presence of God resided in a special way. Only the high priest could enter the Holy of Holies, once a year, on the Day of Atonement.

The idea of the various courts emphasized the separation and exclusivity of certain groups as well as a separation of the holy from the profane, with the people outside the courts excluded. That's why, when Jesus was crucified and paid the price for our sins, the veil of the temple was torn, indicating that there was no longer any separation between God and people, that the way into God's presence was open to all. John was instructed to measure the courts in preparation, I believe, for the building of another temple, but the instructions also included a dire warning: the court of the Gentiles, the area outside the temple, would be given to the Gentiles—that is, people who are not Jews—to use for three and a half years: "They will tread under foot the holy city for forty-two months" (11:2).

According to God's previous commands, the temple was to be built on Mount Moriah, the place where Abraham prepared to offer his son Isaac to God. That site creates a problem, because the Temple Mount is the site today of the Dome of the Rock, the second most revered shrine in the Muslim religion. Could it be that the new temple will be built on land adjacent to an Islamic shrine? If so, there would be no need to measure the outer court, so that may be why the outer court was excluded in the instructions to John.

Asher Kaufman, a professor of physics at Hebrew University, says the temple site is twenty-six meters from the Dome of the Rock, which means the new temple could be built on its ancient location without disturbing the Muslim shrine.[25] Why is that important? Well, if the Muslim world suspected that Christians or Jews had any intention to destroy their sacred site, a holy war unlike anything we have ever seen would follow. But if the Jewish temple could be built without disturbing the Dome of the Rock, Muslims would be perceived as gracious and benevolent neighbors, despite Islam's antipathy to Christianity and Judaism.

The Two Unusual Witnesses

In Revelation 11:3, John is told about the two special witnesses who will preach in Jerusalem for 1,260 days (three and a half years). The Bible doesn't tell us specifically who these two are, but some scholars say the two are representative characters, not real individuals, but symbols of the law and the prophets, the law and the gospel, the Old Testament and the New Testament. Most scholars, however, believe the two witnesses are two individuals, and they speculate about their identities.

Some say the two witnesses are Enoch and Elijah. Enoch walked with God and the Lord "took him" (Genesis 5:24). Similarly, the prophet Elijah was taken up "by a whirlwind to heaven" (2 Kings 2:11). Neither of these men experienced death. As such, some see them as the two witnesses of Revelation 11.

The two may be Zerubbabel and Joshua the priest, because John seemed to refer to Zechariah 4 (Zechariah's fifth vision in which a golden lampstand and two olive trees highlight the important positions of these two men in the restored community). Joshua and Zerubbabel helped to reestablish Israel and rebuild the temple after the Exile.

Most likely the two witnesses are Moses and Elijah, either literally or figuratively. Moses was the great lawgiver of the Old Testament, the man to whom God gave the Ten Commandments, and Elijah was the greatest prophet of the Old Testament. These two also appeared with Jesus at the Transfiguration (Matthew 17:1–3). Just as ten plagues preceded the deliverance of the Hebrews from Egypt, the two witnesses in Revelation 11 perform similar miracles in verse 6: "These have the power to shut up the sky, so that rain will not fall during the days of their prophesying; and they have power over the waters to turn them into blood, and to strike the earth with every plague, as often as they desire."

If anyone attempts to harm the two witnesses, "fire flows out of their mouth and devours their enemies" (11:5). The fire reference is similar to what Elijah did when some soldiers tried to shut down his ministry (2 Kings 1:1–17). Elijah was also famous for prophesying to Ahab that there would be no rain until he said so, and his words came true. We also know, according to Malachi 4:5–6, that someone like Elijah, or possibly Elijah himself, is to return before the great and final day of the Lord: "Behold, I am going to send you Elijah the prophet before the coming of the great and terrible day of the LORD."[26] If these two witnesses are not Moses and Elijah, they will be similar to them.

In Revelation 11:3 notice when the ministry of the two witnesses takes place and for how long: 1,260 days. According to the Jewish calendar, a month equaled 30 days. Thus 1,260 days equals 42 months—three and a half years.

We see similar terminology in Revelation 12:14, "a time and times and half a time." This is the same time frame referred to in Daniel 7:25 and 12:7 ("a time, times, and half a time").

These three and a half years comprise the first half of the Tribulation. During this time, Israel will rebuild the temple in Jerusalem, possibly with the protection, cooperation, encouragement, and assistance of the Antichrist. This arrangement will require some elaborate negotiations, but it is going to happen. The Antichrist may even encourage the restoration of the sacrificial system. For three and a half years, Israel will prosper under this pact, but then the Antichrist will break this agreement (Daniel 9:27), turn against the Jewish people, and desecrate the temple of God.

The message of the two witnesses apparently has to do with Israel and the temple. They are clothed in sackcloth (a dark, coarse cloth made from goat or camel hair, with a rough texture similar to a burlap sack). The sackcloth indicates mourning, grieving, humility, and contrite repentance. It's interesting that during this time the Word of God and the power of God will be outside the temple rather than within it.

Notice, too, that these two men are designated as prophets (Revelation 11:3, 6). Prophesying in the Bible is often more forth telling than foretelling, and that seems to be the tact of these two witnesses. They call the nations to repent and to return to the Lord. They also perform miracles (11:5–6). They will certainly have divine protection until their work is completed, because their message will not be popular with the powers of the earth.

When they have finished their work, the Beast—the Antichrist, possessed by Satan—will ascend from the bottomless pit (the abyss) and will cause the two witnesses to be killed (v. 7). He will not allow their bodies to be buried (v. 9), which to Jews was an unthinkable offense. An unburied body was an outrage and an insult to the dead. All of this will be done under the auspices of the Antichrist in order to humiliate God's messengers and ultimately God Himself.

It is also significant where this will happen. Using coded language, John told his readers that these things are going to take place in Egypt (a biblical euphemism for bondage) and Sodom (a euphemism for gross sin). To make sure his readers understood, John added, "where also their Lord was crucified" (11:8). He was referring to Jerusalem.

It's interesting to see that Jerusalem is called the "great city" eight times in this chapter, but it was great only from a human perspective, not God's. To Him, Jerusalem had become as corrupt as Sodom and Egypt.

A News Event That Rocks the World

Apparently this event is going to receive worldwide attention, because everyone around the world will be transfixed by the images they will see on their televisions, computers, smartphones, and tablet computers, not to mention the amount of traffic on social media outlets. The news media will be overwhelmed trying to describe and analyze the significance of these developments in the Middle East. The Antichrist will want the whole world to see that he has won and that God's prophets are dead (Revelation 11:9).

Worse still, the world will respond happily, even gleefully. The scene will be like a satanic Christmas celebration, a counterfeit yuletide, as people rejoice over the deaths of God's messengers (v. 10). Ironically, this is the only rejoicing we'll see in Revelation until Christians get to heaven. Obviously the preaching of these two prophets will anger most people.

The merriment of sin, however, doesn't last long. Three and a half days after the two messengers have been killed, they will be raised up (v. 11) and summoned to heaven by a *voice*. This voice will startle everyone on earth. Fear will grip observers when they see the two prophets ascend to heaven (11:12). Imagine seeing that on YouTube!

The enemies of God will shake with fear because simultaneously the earth will begin to quake. One-tenth of Jerusalem will be destroyed (11:13), and seven thousand people will be killed in the earthquake. The rest of the population of the planet will be terrified.

Ironically, the survivors of these catastrophes will react to the destruction of the earthquake and give "glory to the God of heaven" (11:13). Do these survivors repent and turn to God after these events? Perhaps some will. Maybe some will be saved. Maybe they will acknowledge that in some way this is an act of God. Regardless, as we will see in the chapters ahead, their response does not have a long-term effect in their lives.

In 2012, Rabbi Jonathan Cahn and I had a number of discussions regarding his book *The Harbinger*, in which he compares the description in Isaiah 9:10 of the aftermath of the Assyrian invasion of the Northern Kingdom and the prophetic signs relating to what America experienced on September 11, 2001. The parallels are stunning and frightening, especially if we do not repent and seek God's forgiveness. Cahn added that those who attacked the United States are direct descendents of the Assyrians who attacked Israel.

America was committed to God on the day our first president, George Washington, was sworn into office at St. Paul's Chapel, a small stone church still standing today near Ground Zero of the September 11 attack, but God's hand of protection was lifted because of our sin, allowing the attack on our soil. More important perhaps is that America's attitude in 2001 was strikingly similar to Israel's in 733 BC. Rather than acknowledge our sinfulness, repent and seek God's favor once again, the predominant theme among our leaders was identical to the eighth-centry Israelites who said,

> The bricks have fallen down,
> But we will rebuild with smooth stones;
> The sycamores have been cut down,
> But we will replace them with cedars. (Isaiah 9:10)

The arrogance of the Israelites, rather than humble repentance before God, led to their total destruction a few years later. Rabbi Cahn lists nine harbingers, or warnings, of things to come, showing how the details of Isaiah's prophecy were fulfilled and, astonishingly, how they were replicated by the events immediately after the 9/11 attacks. Ironically, almost to the word, America has repeated Israel's defiance. The question Rabbi Cahn poses for the United States is, are we to experience a judgment similar to that of Israel in 722 BC when the Assyrians conquered the Northern Kingdom and deported the ten tribes, relocating the Israelites across their empire?

Israel failed to follow God's admonition in 2 Chronicles 7:14: "If my people who are called by My name will humble themselves, and pray and seek My face, and turn from their wicked ways, then I will hear from heaven, and will forgive their sin and heal their land." So far the United States has failed to obey this command, and we are not alone. Most other countries with a large population of God's people have not followed through on God's command. We have not repented of our disobedience, rebellion, or the murdering of more than fifty million babies, along with all that God had planned for them and their future children. If Rabbi Cahn is correct, and I believe he is, America is on a collision course with God's judgment.

The Turning Point

The third woe found in Revelation 11:19 is the turning point in the visions given to the apostle John. Clearly, the best and the worst will happen now.

The seventh angel blows the seventh trumpet (11:15), the last trumpet blast mentioned in the Bible. This is it! Time has come! Jesus is coming back with this last trumpet! We know from the other overlays of scripture that the following events will occur simultaneously.

> For the Lord himself shall descend from heaven with a shout, with the voice of the archangel, and with the trump of God: and the dead in Christ shall rise first: then we which are alive and remain shall be caught up

> together with them in the clouds, to meet the Lord in the air; and so shall we ever be with the Lord. (1 Thessalonians 4:16–17, KJV)

Notice, when the trumpet sounds, instantly the Christians who are alive as well as those who are dead will be caught up together to meet Jesus.

> But look! I tell you this secret: We will not all sleep, but we will all be changed. It will take only a second—as quickly as an eye blinks—when the last trumpet sounds. The trumpet will sound, and those who have died will be raised to live forever, and we will all be changed. (1 Corinthians 15:51–52, NCV)

Whether we are alive at Christ's coming or whether we have already died, we will all be instantaneously changed at the sound of the last trumpet. In a moment, in the blink of an eye, our earthly bodies will be transformed into bodies suitable for heaven.

> At the same time, as Jesus said: "Then shall appear the sign of the Son of man in heaven: and then shall all the tribes of the earth mourn, and they shall see the Son of man coming in the clouds of heaven with power and great glory. And he shall send his angels with a great sound of a trumpet, and they shall gather together his elect from the four winds, from one end of heaven to the other." (Matthew 16:27; 24:30–31)

The events we commonly associate with the Rapture will take place at this point in Revelation. This, I believe, is the true Rapture—to use a familiar term—the Second Coming! All that Paul described in 1 Thessalonians 4:16–17 will happen here. The victory has been won!

Those who believe in a pre-Tribulation Rapture do not consider the trumpets mentioned in 1 Corinthians 15:52 and 1 Thessalonians 4:16 as being the same as the one John mentioned in Revelation 11:15. Scripture does not delineate between the trumpets described as the last. Had God wanted to distinguish between the trumpets—as He did with the seven trumpets noted in Revelation 10–11—He could have done so, but He did not. That's why I believe these trumpets are the same. Furthermore, I believe this is the same trumpet to which Jesus referred in Matthew 24:31.

The unusual aspect about this event in Revelation, though, is that John wrote about it as though it had already happened. He told the story as if the victory had already been won (even though there are still eleven chapters to go in the book). I believe John wrote it this way because God wants us to know that the final victory is assured.

When the seventh trumpet sounds, three dramatic events occur: (1) an announcement of victory; (2) an acclamation of praise; and (3) the ark of the covenant revealed as the temple of God in heaven is opened. Let's look at each of these more closely.

First, there is the announcement of victory by "loud voices in heaven" (Revelation 11:15). The voices could come from angelic choirs or the saints who are already in heaven. The Bible doesn't say specifically. What is important is the content of their announcement: "The kingdom of the world has become the kingdom of our Lord and of His Christ; and He will reign forever and ever" (v. 15). This is the moment we believers have been waiting for—the Rapture!

What leads me to view this moment as the true Rapture? I noticed that prior passages referred to Jesus as "Him who is and who was and who is to come" (1:4; 4:8). In Revelation 11:17, however, He is referred to as the One "who is and who was" (NIV). The King James Version includes the phrase "and art to come," but these words are not in the Greek. In fact, John no longer needs to include the words "and is to come" because, at this point, Jesus has returned!

We then hear the praise of the twenty-four elders as they give thanks for three specific, special blessings (11:16–18): (1) that Jesus reigns supremely (v. 17), (2) that He judges righteously (11:18), and (3) that He rewards His faithful followers (11:18). In short, He reigns. Previously, in Revelation 4:10–11, the elders worshipped and praised the Creator and the Redeemer. Now they worship Him as conqueror and King!

In 11:18, He *judges*: "The time came for the dead to be judged." The Lamb is now the Lion. This is not the babe of Bethlehem. He is the ultimate Judge before whom everyone who ever lived will have to give an account of their lives.

In 11:18, He also *rewards*: "The time to reward Your servants, the prophets, the saints, and those who fear Your name, the small and the great, and to destroy those who destroy the earth."

In verse 18 we also find a table of contents for the rest of the book. Notice, "The nations were enraged." This foreshadows the coming hostile attack that will be finally and completely defeated. Why were the nations angry? The short answer is that they want their own way. So many people are obsessed with taking God out of the equation, attempting to exclude His Word from all public discourse, to marginalize His messengers, and to worship the creature rather than the Creator. After the final trumpet call, God is not going to allow any of this to happen any longer.

In verse 18, His wrath is loosed on the world: "Your wrath came." New Testament Greek has two words for anger. One is *thumos*, which means "rage or passionate anger." Most of our anger is of this sort. We're angry because we've been hurt, insulted, or exploited. The second Greek word is *orge*, which means "indignation, a settled sense of wrath, not like an outburst of anger or a temper tantrum, but a well-controlled, deliberate expression of anger." John uses *orge* in verse 18, which shows us that God's wrath is not temperamental but rather an expression of His deep hatred of sin. God is angry at what sin has done to us and at what we have allowed sin to do to us. Finally, God's astounding patience toward sinful people has reached its limits. While He rewards His faithful, He finally looses His wrath on those who have rejected Him for the final time.

In this moment, the time has come for the dead to be judged. This could be the final judgment of unrepentant sinners (20:11–15). Or this could be the final judgment of the saints, true believers (Romans 14:10–13; 1 Corinthians 3:9–15; 2 Corinthians 5:9–11). While I have plenty of questions about these judgments, I have no question about the fact that every person who ever lived will be judged.

The good news is that God will reward His servants, the small and the great (Matthew 16:27; Revelation 22:12). The bad news is that He will "destroy those who destroy the earth," not just ecologically, but through the effects of their sin. Ironic, isn't it? The people who live for the earth and its pleasures are often the ones who are destroying the very world they worship. In truth, the world does not belong to them.

The third dramatic event centers on the opening of the temple of God in heaven, "and the ark of His covenant appeared in His temple" (11:19). The ark disappeared in 586 BC after the Babylonians stormed the walls of Jerusalem and razed the temple. The ark contained a jar of manna, Aaron's rod, and the tablets with the Ten Commandments. The ark was a reminder to the people of God of His special covenant with them and a promise that His presence was with them. Originally, the promise was to Israel, but now it is to all who know Jesus. The full display of God's glory is going to be revealed. This is a sign of God's faithfulness, although seeing it at this juncture makes it sound rather scary. In the Old Testament, the glory of God rested upon the ark and God's Law was within the ark, which incidentally reminds us that those two go together and are never separated.

In this scene, the temple is opened, and the long-lost ark is revealed. What is implied by the reappearance of the ark? I believe the return of the ark is a subtle statement that the undeniable glory of God is on display for all to see. In the face of God's obvious glory, the enemies of God are destroyed and God fulfills all His promises! His Word is validated by the return of the ark and confirmed as true.

Not surprisingly, amid this grand revelation of the ark in God's temple, a raft of tumultuous calamities assails the earth: hail, lightning, thunder, and earthquakes. Notice the contrast: the coming of the glory of God is encouraging and exciting to those who know and worship Him, but it will terrify those who don't. Note also that the situation is either-or, yes or no, with nothing in between. God reigns. He rules. Jesus is Lord today. Stay close to Him, and your faith will be vindicated. This is not the time to be complacent or compromising. Nor is it a time to drift idly along in your faith. Stay as close to Jesus as you can, and you will be safe from the wrath of God.

The Rapture chapter begins with the temple on earth being restored and then desecrated. It closes with the opening of the temple in heaven.

I believe that Jesus will not return until the Antichrist is on the scene, and in Revelation 11 we see the Antichrist appear as an advocate of peace and a prophet of prosperity. The world will view him as a leader who can do no wrong. I believe he will make arrangements for the temple to be built alongside the Dome of the Rock, and he will encourage the Jews to reinstitute the sacrificial system. For the first three and half years, the Jews will prosper under this system, but then God's wrath will be unleashed on earth. When this happens, John warns us, don't despair, because it is almost time for the King of kings to return!

16

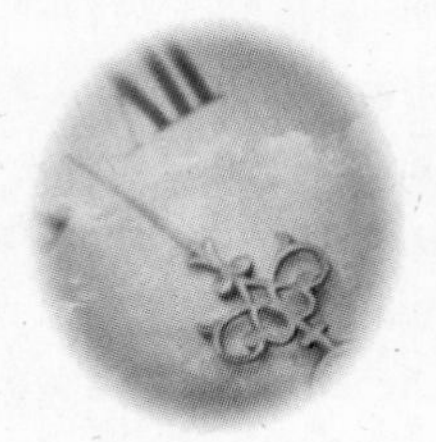

A Woman, Her Child, and the Dragon

Old-timers have a habit of repeating themselves, especially when they're recounting something in a conversation. The apostle John did a little of that in Revelation, but I don't attribute that to age. Instead, I believe that John had so much to tell from the visions the Lord gave him that he repeated some things because his audience couldn't possibly retain it all when this letter to the churches was read aloud to them. Not surprisingly, he moved back and forth in the account, adding details here and there, sometimes describing the same events from different perspectives. This happens in Revelation 11 through 14. In particular, I believe Revelation 12 is a flashback to events that happened *before* the return of Christ in Revelation 11.

What a Woman!

In Revelation 12:1, John saw "a great sign" in heaven, the first of seven great signs he would experience in the Revelation. In this vision, he saw "a woman clothed with the sun, and the moon under her feet." She wears "a crown of twelve stars" on her head. This is a very poetic picture of a woman, but to make things interesting, the woman was not only pregnant but in labor.

The obvious questions are, who is this woman? What does this mean?

The three most common answers are that the woman symbolizes (1) Mary, the mother of Jesus, (2) the church, and (3) Israel, namely those who in the last days will believe in Jesus as the Messiah. The idea that this woman represents Israel stems from an association with Joseph's dream, in which he saw the "sun and the moon and eleven stars" bowing down to him (Genesis 37:9–11), indicating that his father, mother, and eleven brothers would eventually bow to him—which is exactly what happened.

In the Old Testament, the imagery of a woman crying out in labor was often applied to Israel's giving birth to God's people and His plans for them, events regarding their role in history (Isaiah 26:17–18; Hosea 13:13; Micah 4:10; Matthew 24:8). There is good reason to consider all three of these suggestions as valid, since Israel gave birth to Mary, Mary gave birth to Jesus, and the Lord's church grew as His followers increased in number.

ENTER THE DRAGON

Meanwhile, this vision of the woman in labor is overshadowed by another vision, a frightening, gut-wrenching series of events in heaven and on earth: "Behold, a great red dragon having seven heads and ten horns, and on his heads were seven diadems. And his tail swept away a third of the stars of heaven and threw them to the earth. And the Dragon stood before the woman who was about to give birth, so that when she gave birth he might devour her child" (12:3–4).

The dragon's red color implies his murderous intent. Later, this dragon is identified as "the serpent of old who is called the devil and Satan" (12:9). The appearance of the Dragon, like the appearance of the woman, is significant. The Dragon has seven heads, indicating power, intelligence, and worldly wisdom. It has ten horns, implying power over the kingdoms of the world. It is huge, because its tail swept away one-third of the stars of heaven, and they fell to the earth in what many scholars believe is a reference to the rebellion of Lucifer in heaven, who was cast out and took one-third of the angels with him, thus becoming demonic entities (Isaiah 14:12–15; Ezekiel 28:12–17). Ironically, Lucifer and his cohorts wanted to be like God, but in their rebellion they became as unlike God as possible.

In Revelation 12, John saw the Dragon standing in front of the woman, who we now understand to be the mother of Jesus. The Dragon, however, is poised to devour the Child as soon as he's born. Down through history Satan has sought to destroy this child. Even after the Christ child was born, Satan made every effort to terminate Him. John expanded this thought, seeing the Enemy perpetually trying to destroy Jesus and the followers of Jesus.

When I read about the Dragon positioning itself to devour the newborn, I am convinced that a sort of satanic animosity toward children still poisons our world through the atrocities of abortion. Satan still seethes with anger against the Child in Revelation 12, and that animosity spills onto as many children as the evil one can destroy. You see Satan's manipulation behind a number of biblical intrigues. He prompted Cain to kill his brother Abel, the first murder in history (Genesis 4:8; 1 John 3:12). Moreover, Satan inspired Pharaoh to kill the newborn males of Hebrew families in an attempt to exterminate their coming deliverer, who was Moses (Exodus 1–2). The devil encouraged Saul to kill David, God's chosen heir to the throne (1 Samuel 18:10–11). The Enemy caused Haman to plot against the Jews during the time of Queen Esther. Most significantly, Satan used Herod the Great, a devious Roman puppet, at the time of Jesus' birth to call for all baby boys less than two years old to be put to death in an attempt to snuff out the life of Jesus.

Satan has no qualms about killing babies, especially when those lives hold the great potential that God wants to do in and through His people. Although all these plans were hatched by Satan, God holds accountable the people involved. For example, in the Old Testament, God pronounced His judgment against the country of Ammon, saying, "I will not turn away its punishment, because they ripped open the women with child in Gilead, that they might enlarge their territory. But I will kindle a fire in the wall of Rabbah, and it shall devour [Ammon's] palaces, amid shouting in the day of battle, and a tempest in the day of the whirlwind" (Amos 1:13–14, NKJV).

Why is the Dragon obsessed with destroying this child in Revelation 12? John understood. According to prophecy, a male child would be born who would rule the nations (Psalm 66:7; Isaiah 66:7; Revelation 12:5). So when

Satan discovered the woman pregnant with a special child, he intensified his efforts to thwart God's plan to save the people who would love Him, trust Him, and obey Him.

The Dragon's effort did not go unnoticed in heaven. When the child is born, He immediately is rescued from the Dragon and snatched up to heaven, to God, and to His throne. Interestingly, the word that John used to describe the child's being caught up to heaven is the same word that the apostle Paul used in describing how Christians will one day be "caught up together" to meet Jesus at His return (1 Thessalonians 4:17). It is also the same word Paul used when he described being caught up to experience a bit of heaven (2 Corinthians 12:2).

After the Child is saved, John saw the woman flee into the wilderness, an unspecified location of protection, prepared for her by God, where she is nourished for 1,260 days—a period the readers of Revelation are familiar with—three and a half years. Since the Antichrist makes a deal with Israel, there does not seem to be a need for their protection during the first three and a half years of the Tribulation. So the similar reference here may coincide with God's protection of His people during the second three and a half years of the Tribulation, when persecutions break loose on earth. Despite the Dragon's vehement anger and devilish attempts at destruction, God will take care of His people, Christians and Jews. God may possibly protect His people during the final three and a half years of tribulation in a similar manner as He did the children of Israel during the plagues that He sent on Egypt when Moses was negotiating the release of God's people.

Regardless of how it happens, God will protect the woman and the Child from the attacks of Satan and his cohorts, but the woman and her offspring will have to flee to the wilderness for a while. That is not unusual or without precedent in the history of God's people. Something similar happened in 167 BC, when Antiochus Epiphanes came to Jerusalem and, in a prefiguring of the Antichrist, desecrated God's temple by sacrificing pigs on the altars and persecuting the Jews. For three and a half years (there's that same time period again), Antiochus mocked everything sacred and did all he could to exterminate the people of God. During that time, it was illegal in Israel to worship God. But God intervened and spared His people, although many suffered horribly and were forced to flee their homes and seek refuge in the desert.

The desecration of the temple by Antiochus Epiphanes is what the prophet Daniel called the "abomination of desolation" (Daniel 9:27, 11:31, 12:11), and he accurately predicted it from the viewpoint of the sixth century BC—hundreds of years before Antiochus was born. Moreover, Daniel's words seem to have a dual meaning, implying that a future Antiochus, to be known as the Antichrist, will repeat the heinous acts of the original.

Similarly, Mary and Joseph, the parents of Jesus, were forced to flee to Egypt with the infant Jesus to escape Herod's extermination of newborn males (Matthew 2:7–22). Satan was behind this attempt to murder the Messiah, and he was quite willing to murder innumerable babies in order to kill the one.

Jesus also warned that such a need to flee to the wilderness would take place again. He told His disciples that when they saw the terrors coming, they "must flee to the mountains" (Mark 13:14–20). Later, when Rome invaded and destroyed Jerusalem in AD 70, that is precisely what many people did while the enemy wreaked havoc upon the city. For a while, the Dragon was free to do his worst. And he did.

That is the backdrop for the vision and the message pertaining to the woman, the Child, and the Dragon, but suddenly, in Revelation 12:7, the scene in John's vision shifts to the heavenly realm, and a war breaks out in heaven.

War in Heaven

We don't really know when this war takes place. Some scholars believe it goes back to Lucifer's rebellion. Others say this scene describes the Crucifixion. Still others believe it will happen at the midpoint of the Tribulation, when the Antichrist breaks his agreement with Israel.

It seems that even though Satan and his cohorts were cast out of heaven, they still have some access to God. We know that the devil had conversations with God during their confrontation over Job (Job 1:6, 2:1).

In the book of Revelation, Satan and his thugs come calling. This time, they are met by the angel Michael, whose name means "who is like God." Interestingly, this is the same archangel seen in Daniel 10:10–13 and Jude 9, doing battle with the satanic forces on behalf of God's people. He is one of only two angels that are named in the Bible, although myriads of other angels are mentioned. The other named angel is Gabriel (Daniel 8:15–26; 9:21–27; Luke 1:11–18).

As John described this vision of the war in heaven, in Revelation 12:9 he provided four descriptive titles for the Enemy. First, he referred to the "great dragon," which emphasizes the Enemy's ferocity and terror. Second, John saw him as the "serpent of old," the beguiling snake of Genesis 3, who seduced Adam and Eve into mistrusting God's intentions for them and eventually sinning against Him. Then John also straightforwardly called the Enemy "the devil," taken from the word *diabolos*, which means "the accuser." Finally, John simply names him Satan, which means "adversary." Jesus also referred to Satan as "the evil one" (Matthew 6:13) as well as acknowledging him as "the prince of this world" (John 12:31). That's who he is, too, the one "who deceives the whole world" and leads people astray.

This is a far different image of Satan than the caricature of a red figure with horns, a tail, and a pitchfork. No doubt, Satan prefers that we not take him seriously, since that makes his work of deception, sabotage, and subterfuge that much easier. The Bible is clear, however, that we are to be wary of him, since he and his demonic assistants often masquerade as angels of light (2 Corinthians 11:14–15; Ephesians 6:12; 1 Peter 5:8–9).

Certainly, we face a formidable foe, but the devil and his demons are no match for God and His angels. In fact, during the war in heaven that John described, Satan and his cohorts are bounced out of heaven (Revelation 12:8–9). While that was good news in heaven, Satan's ouster did not bode well for the people on earth. The Dragon went wild, persecuting God's people (v. 13). He had been accusing the brethren night and day before the throne of God, but now a loud voice in heaven announced, "The salvation, and the power, and the kingdom of our God and the authority of His Christ have come, for the accuser of our brethren has been thrown down" (v. 10). Although Satan has been accusing Christians, heaping guilt on them for past sins, tempting them to doubt their own worth and their salvation, placing every sort of evil obstacle before them, trying to rob, kill, and destroy them, God's people proved victorious!

The Secret Keys to Victory

John realized the three secrets to this victory, and he shared them with us. He reminded his readers, "They overcame him because of the blood of the Lamb and because of the word of their testimony, and they did not love their life even when faced with death" (Revelation 12:11). These three principles will be vital for the survival of God's people in the difficult days ahead. We need to learn how to appropriate the blood of Jesus and use it to conquer the demonic forces coming against us. Because of what Jesus did on the cross, shedding His blood and paying the price for our sins, we can be forgiven. No matter how badly we have sinned against God, other people, or ourselves, if our sins have been washed in the blood of the Lamb, accepting the atonement of Christ on our behalf, we are forgiven now and forever, and no accusation of Satan's will stand against us in heaven. Since I was a little boy, I remember my Grandma Irwin telling us that whenever we were afraid we could plead the blood of Jesus, and the devil could not get through the blood.

The second key to victory was the word of their testimony. There is something incredibly powerful about a bona fide Christian testimony in which a person can say, "I once was lost, but now I'm found. I once was blind, but now I see! I am not all that I want to be, nor am I all that I am going to be, but thank God, I'm not what I used to be!"

The third principle is one that causes many comfortable Christians to flinch. John said, "They did not love their life even when faced with death." It wasn't that those early Christians didn't love life. Their power came from the fact they loved Jesus more than they loved themselves. Their love for the Lamb of God was greater than their love for their own lives. Why are so many Christians today afraid to die? You know you will be with the Lord in the same moment you leave this life. Others are afraid to suffer for Christ. I understand, and I don't relish the idea of pain, suffering, and martyrdom, but in these days, we need to recognize those as part of the genuine Christian life. Jesus said that the world hated Him, so they will also hate you likewise. Why should we expect otherwise?

No one knows if a situation will demand martyrdom. If you read about some of the great saints of the faith, many of them wondered if they had the strength to lay down their lives for Christ. The truth is that some didn't. But many others discovered that, in the hour of decision, in the time of their greatest trial, by maintaining their love of Jesus and the word of their testimony, they found that God gave them the strength they needed to do whatever He called them to do—even if it meant giving up this earthly existence. Remember, Jesus promised that no one will give up anything for Him that our heavenly Father will not repay. If you find your life on the line, God will give you the grace and the faith you need to bear whatever is required, and He will also reward your testimony, both in this life and in heaven to come.

OPPOSITE RESPONSES

John noticed that Satan's ouster from heaven evoked two responses: rejoicing in heaven and woe on earth. Satan knows that he doesn't have much time left, that "he has only a short time" (Revelation 12:12), so he unleashes every evil he can. First, the Dragon attacks the woman (v. 13), namely, Satan launches vicious, heinous attacks against the people of God—including Israel and the church (any Christians who are alive on earth at the time).

I believe Satan harbors a particular hatred of Israel. We've seen abundant evidence of this in history, for example, the Jewish Holocaust and present-day Iranian president Mahmoud Ahmadinejad's declarations to wipe the state of Israel off the map. But these are nothing compared to the animosity that Satan will pour out against God's people. The good news, however, is that the Enemy will not be able to destroy God's people, because God will help them to escape—perhaps supernaturally—and will lead them to a safe place during the three and a half years when the world is in such tribulation and turmoil.

Somehow God's people will be protected in "the wilderness" (12:14), perhaps a literal wilderness, or maybe a more figurative wilderness where the Antichrist's fury cannot touch them.

The woman—representing God's people—will escape on the wings of an eagle. Because John saw an eagle involved in the rescue of God's people, some apocalypse watchers have suggested that aircraft will be involved in the rescue mission. Others have seen the eagle as a symbol of the United States, coming to aid Israel and the persecuted Christians. I am dubious of this interpretation, because in recent years the United States has pressured Israel into decisions detrimental to its survival as a nation. Increasingly, Israeli leaders have been treated rudely by American presidents and diplomats. Perhaps, not surprisingly, with each rebuff of Israel by America, some disaster has befallen the United States.[27]

Recently, John Kilpatrick and I discussed diplomatic relations between the two countries and the anti-Israel stance of many American leaders. For example, on August 29, 2005, President George W. Bush and other leaders pressed Israel to give up sovereignty of the Gaza Strip, forcing eight thousand Israelis to leave their homes. One week later, Hurricane Katrina stormed across Florida and then settled on New Orleans, flooding the region and forcing evacuations. The percentage of evacuations in the United States was almost identical per capita to the forced Israeli evacuations. That might be a coincidence, but if you track the number of similar coincidences, you will be shocked.

Shocking But True!

At least ten major catastrophic events have occurred in America recently, and the timing of each seems eerily correlated to instances when U.S. leaders have publicly insulted Israel, spoken against Jerusalem, or exerted pressure on the Israelis to relinquish part of their land. Consider the following events:

1. On October 30, 1991, as President George H. W. Bush opened the Madrid Conference to consider "land for peace" negotiations, pressuring Israel to return land in exchange for a more peaceful Middle East, a perfect storm developed in the North Atlantic, creating the largest waves ever recorded in

that region. The storm traveled a thousand miles from east to west, instead of the normal west to east pattern, and crashed intó the New England coast. Thirty-five-foot waves smashed into the Kennebunkport, Maine, home of President Bush, causing significant property damage.

2. On August 23, 1992, shortly after the Madrid Conference relocated to Washington, DC, and peace talks resumed (with worldwide pressure on Israel to surrender land for peace), Hurricane Andrew, the worst natural disaster ever to hit the United States, came ashore in south Florida, producing an estimated $30 billion in damage and leaving 180,000 people homeless.

3. On January 16, 1994, President Bill Clinton met with Syrian president Hafezel al-Assad in Geneva to discuss a peace agreement with Israel that included the Israelis surrendering the Golan Heights. Within twenty-four hours a powerful 6.9 earthquake rocked Southern California. That quake, centered in Northridge, became the second most destructive natural disaster to hit the United States next to Hurricane Andrew.

4. On January 21, 1998, Israeli prime minister Benjamin Netanyahu met with President Clinton at the White House and was coldly received because he refused to relinquish more of Israel's land. In a rebuff of the prime minister, Clinton and Secretary of State Madeleine Albright refused to meet with Netanyahu over lunch. Later that day, the Monica Lewinsky scandal rocked the Clinton administration.

5. On September 28, 1998, President Clinton met with PLO chairman Yasser Arafat and Prime Minister Netanyahu at the White House to finalize an agreement in which Israel would surrender 13 percent of Yesha (Judah and Samaria) to the Palestinians. That same day, Hurricane George slammed into the U.S. Gulf Coast, causing $1 billion in damages. When Arafat departed the country, the storm began to dissipate.

6. On October 15, 1998, Arafat and Netanyahu met at the Wye River plantation in Maryland. Their talks were scheduled to last five days, with the focus on the land exchange. The talks were concluded on October 23. On October 17, heavy rain and tornadoes ravaged southern Texas, subsiding on October 22. The floods caused more than $1 billion in damage.

7. On November 30, 1998, Arafat returned to Washington to meet with President Clinton to raise money for a Palestinian state, with Jerusalem as the capital. Forty-two other nations participated in the meeting; the nations agreed to give the Palestinians $3 billion in aid. On the same day, the Dow Jones Industrial Average dropped 216 points, and the next day the European market had its third worst day in history, producing a devastating impact on market capitalization in both the United States and Europe.

8. On December 12, 1998, as President Bill Clinton arrived in the Palestinian-controlled section of Israel to discuss the land-for-peace process, the House of Representatives passed four articles of impeachment against him.

9. On May 3, 1999, Arafat was scheduled to declare a Palestinian state, with Jerusalem as the capital. On that day, a powerful tornado system swept across Oklahoma and Kansas. The Palestinian declaration was postponed until December 1999 at the request of President Clinton, whose letter to Arafat encouraged him in his "aspirations for his own land." He added that the Palestinians had a right to "determine their own future on their own land" and that they deserved to "live free today, tomorrow and forever."

10. During the week of October 11, 1999, as Jewish settlers in fifteen West Bank settlements were evicted from the covenant land in Israel, the Dow-Jones Industrial Average lost 5.7 percent of its value, the worst week in the Dow's history since October 1989. On October 15, the Dow lost 266 points, and a hurricane slammed into North Carolina. The next day, a 7.1 earthquake rocked the Southwest in the fifth most powerful earthquake of the twentieth century. The earthquake did little damage but was felt in three states.[27]

These are merely a few of the incidents in which the United States has suffered repercussions by willfully denigrating or dismissing Israel. I don't mean to imply that the state of Israel never makes a mistake when dealing with the myriad issues surrounding its everyday political decisions, but when our nation attempts to interfere with God's plans for Israel's existence, we are asking for trouble. Consider the actions of the Obama administration.

On March 23, 2010, Israeli prime minister Netanyahu was not welcomed at the front door of the White House but humiliatingly brought through a side door. None of the White House press corps was invited to chronicle the meeting and no friendly photos taken. Instead, Netanyahu was harshly addressed by President Barack Obama and then abandoned while the president had dinner with his family. Regarding peace in the Middle East and Israeli concessions, President Obama told Netanyahu, "I'm still around. Let me know if there is anything new." The prime minister flew home, and within forty-eight hours huge storms caused massive flooding in the United States. New England received another flooding from March 21–31, 2010, when three storms flooded the upper Midwest and Northeast in the second half of the month.

On April 19, 2010, speaking before the United Nations, President Obama stated that the United States would no longer automatically side with Israel at the UN. This was the first time that any U.S. president had ever made such a public statement. Within twenty-four hours of the Obama statement, an explosion occurred on the British Petroleum Deepwater Horizon oil rig in the Gulf of Mexico, killing eleven people and creating a multibillion dollar environmental catastrophe, an enormous economic setback for the area, and a moratorium on offshore oil drilling, making the United States even more vulnerable to the fickle whims of Middle Eastern oil lords.

John Kilpatrick pointed out that the issue specifically concerns Jerusalem, not simply Israel at large. The city of Jerusalem is, as scripture says, "the cup of trembling" (Isaiah 51:22, NKJV), that is, whoever mishandles Jerusalem will be cut into splinters. Clearly, how we regard and treat Jerusalem seems to be especially important to God. Pastor Kilpatrick said that he shuddered on April 19, 2011, when he heard President Obama embrace the Palestinian demand that Israel return to the 1967 borders, which Israel has declared would be tantamount to committing suicide. This was a radical departure for the U.S. foreign policy. Such a plan would essentially give back land that God had declared nearly four thousand years ago to be part of the inheritance of His people. Pastor Kilpatrick told his congregation the following Sunday, "Any time we mishandle Israel, it costs us. I'm in fear of what is about to happen."

On May 22, 2011, about 5:30 PM, the deadliest single tornado since 1953 tore through Joplin, Missouri, destroying almost half of the city and killing 183 people.

Kilpatrick said, "When you are dealing with the church, you are dealing with grace, but when you oppress Israel, you encounter the Law, and that Law remains an eye for an eye and a tooth for a tooth." He then shared a word of warning he deduced from a 2008 vision, shortly after the U.S. economy collapsed into a recession and potential depression. He was hanging over a river, running through a collapsing building, as the earth experienced a horrendous upheaval. Suddenly he was tumbling, being whipped so violently that his teeth were clattering. In the vision, he saw an old map with two names written on it: Indianola and Europa. He was unfamiliar with them, so he later researched them and found five U.S. towns known as Indianola. Two had been destroyed by hurricanes, one remained in Texas, another was in Mississippi, and another in Illinois. Europa was a town in Missouri.

He drew a line on a map from Indianola, Mississippi, to Indianola, Illinois, and found that the line went right through Europa, Missouri. Here is the shocker: the territory below this line runs along the New Madrid fault, a fault line now experiencing increasing seismic activity. Interestingly, three of the most powerful earthquakes ever to shake the United States occurred, not in Los Angeles, but in and around the town of New Madrid, Missouri, during the winter of 1811–12. The quakes were estimated to have been 8.0 earthquakes by seismologists, and one was as high as 8.8 on the Richter scale. The 1906 San Francisco earthquake was a 7.8; the 1994 Northridge, California, quake was a magnitude 6.7.

The December 16, 1811, New Madrid quakes shook the earth so violently that church bells rang in Boston, a thousand miles away! While most houses within a 250-mile radius were damaged, though some were destroyed, relatively few lives were lost due to the small population living in the area at the time. If such a quake should occur there today, the devastation in cities such as St. Louis, Memphis, Louisville, and Nashville would be horrendous.

John Kilpatrick believes the Lord has the seismic activity of the New Madrid fault line on hold. He is convinced that if the United States mishandles its relations with Israel in the days ahead, the New Madrid fault will split open, literally dividing the United States into two or more pieces. Prophetic teacher Rick Joyner concurs with Kilpatrick's assessment, adding that if that happens, a wide body of water would separate the two sections of North America.

Kilpatrick cautions, "Regardless of who is elected, the president of the United States needs some people around him who can say, 'Please be careful when you are handling Israel.'"

I do not see the eagle in Revelation 12:14 as representing the United States. More likely, the eagle's assistance to the people of God is simply an image of God's provision for and protection of His people. Eagle's wings are frequently used in the Old Testament to indicate God's strong arms of protection and support (Exodus 19:4; Deuteronomy 32:9–12; Psalm 91:4; Isaiah 40:28–31).

In Revelation 12:15–16, John saw a second attempt by Satan to destroy God's people. This time, the serpent spews forth a flood of water, which might be a literal flood of water, but there is also another possibility. Water is often used in the Bible to symbolize people—the more water, the more people. Here, this satanic flood may be a flood of military attacks, since the prophet Jeremiah pictures an army as a great flood of water (Jeremiah 46:8, 47:2). Still others believe this flood will be a torrent of arrogant and blasphemous—and potentially deadly—words spoken against God's people, just as Hitler and his henchmen influenced public opinion against the Jews to the point that German children who didn't even know what it meant to be a Jew hated them for merely existing. We're seeing a similar warping of public opinion against Christians today in many Islamic countries and, to some extent, in America. I expect that, under the influence of the Dragon, the Antichrist system, antipathy for Christians and Jews will intensify in the days ahead.

Regardless of whether this flood involves a literal flood of water or a flood of vitriolic words, the flood of the Enemy against God's people will fail. In some unusual way, the earth itself will help the woman (the people of God) by opening and swallowing the Dragon's flood. It may be an earthquake at just the right time to swallow the Dragon's efforts, similar to the way the Egyptians were swallowed by the Red Sea as they pursued Moses and the Israelites (Exodus 15:11–13).

Furious, no doubt, at his inability once again to destroy the woman, Satan will make war against her offspring: the followers of Jesus Christ. Any followers of the Lamb—either Christians or Jews who keep the commandments of God and hold to the testimony of Jesus—will come under horrendous attack.

It is important to note that this atrocious attack the aging apostle saw taking place hundreds of years before it happened did not affect pagans. John saw persecution against believers only. The Dragon and his followers will make war with these believers; the word here is the same as the one used in the Beast's earlier attack against the two witnesses (11:7), and it is the same word used to describe an attack against "the saints" (13:7). Clearly, there will be Christians alive on earth at this time, and Satan will launch a ferocious attack against them as an act of revenge. Satan knows that he has been cast down, and so, in one last terrible convulsion, he and his demonic forces will wreak havoc on the earth.

Remember, there is a way to overcome the Enemy: "They overcame him because of the blood of the Lamb and because of the word of their testimony, and they did not love their life even when faced with death" (12:11). Satan can kill our bodies, but he cannot touch our souls. Yes, the Dragon is roaring, but the Child is in a safe place. Jesus will soon return in power and glory. Granted, for a while, things are going to look bleak for God's people as the Antichrist makes war against God's saints—true believers like you and me. If you didn't know better, you might think the Dragon's going to win.

But you know better!

17

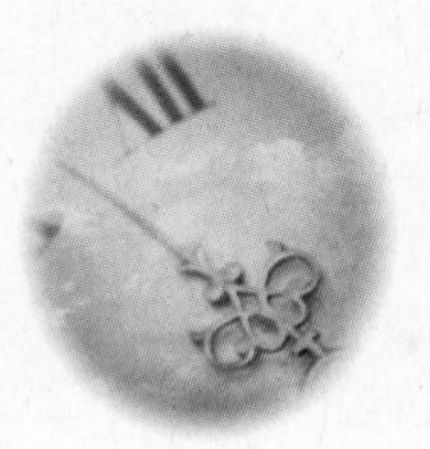

THE ANTICHRIST RISES

Satan attempts to counterfeit all the good things God has provided, so we should not be surprised that just as there is a Trinity of Father, Son, and Holy Spirit, the Enemy has a trinity as well. The players in this evil threesome are Satan (the Dragon), the Beast (the Antichrist), and a second beast (the False Prophet). This second beast is a public relations man of sorts who causes the world to worship the Beast and Satan. They are intent on ruling the world, and for a time, it looks as if the devil and his demon-possessed puppets will succeed. But then the Child shows up—Jesus Christ returns—and the devil and his motley crew receive everything they deserve.

You will be rewarded and will reign forever with Jesus in a new heaven and a new earth. That's where we are going, but the going gets extremely rough between now and then.

John saw the Antichrist, a world leader who rises to power because of his great oratory skills and his winsome charisma. He will promise people everything they want to hear, but he will ultimately lead them into bondage and death.

That title Antichrist means "against Christ" or "instead of Christ." It was used only four times in the New Testament, all by the apostle John, yet ironically, he did not use the title at all in the book of Revelation. Instead, in Revelation, John referred to the Antichrist as "the beast" (13:1).

THE GHASTLY BEAST

The Antichrist is variously described as a "stern-faced king," a "master of intrigue" (Daniel 8:23, NIV), a "despicable person" (Daniel 11:21), a "worthless shepherd" (Zechariah 11:16–17), and the "lawless one" (2 Thessalonians 2:8–9). He is not a nice person, but millions of people will see him as a messianic figure.

Although the apostle John called him a beast, the Antichrist is definitely a human being, a created being. He is not equal with God, nor is he equal to Jesus. He is not an angel. In fact, he is not a demon, although he may be the most thoroughly demon-possessed person the world has ever seen or ever will see.

With his winsome personality, persuasive oratory, and skillful negotiating, he will be the world's ultimate problem solver. He will rise to power on a platform of peace and prosperity, especially concerning peace in the Middle East, and for the first three and a half years of his rule, people will think he can do no wrong. But midway through the seven-year period, this world dictator will show himself for who he really is—the Antichrist—empowered by Satan himself. The Antichrist will be far worse than any dictator the world has ever known. He will be a personification of evil.

The apostle John saw the Antichrist—the Beast—"coming up out of the sea" (13:1). We know from our study of Revelation that water is a symbol of people, the more water, the more people. So if the Antichrist rises out of the sea, he will rise from a sea of humanity (17:15). Some scholars believe he may be Jewish, while others believe he may be a Gentile.

Coincidentally, one of my Master's Commission students researched this subject at length. He discovered some interesting correlations among Christians, Muslims, and Jews during these end days:

1. Christians believe the Antichrist will come and rule the world. It will be a time of chaos and catastrophes, according to the Word of God, and the Antichrist will make war against God's people.
2. Muslims believe their Imam Mahdi, the Shiites 12th Imam (their savior), will appear and redeem Islam. They believe a "big war" will pre-

cede Mahdi, who will kill all infidels (those who oppose Mahdi) and raise the flag of Islam worldwide.

3. Jews believe their Messiah is coming as a great military leader. They, too, believe there will be war and suffering (Ezekiel 38:16) following along the same timeline as that of the Antichrist.

All three anticipate war, chaos, and suffering on epic levels prior to the arrival of key figures in their faiths. Is it possible they could be the same war either partially or in totality?

John's description of this beast is horrifying, but as we've seen before, these descriptions have symbolic meanings. For instance, the Beast will have seven heads and ten horns; the heads most likely represent seven world empires and the horns indicate power. Seven usually means completeness in the Bible, so this evil beast will literally rule the world. The ten horns represent ten lesser rulers who will be associated with him, out of which the Antichrist will emerge. The ten crowns—diadems—represent absolute power. According to Daniel 7:24, the Antichrist will subdue three of these kings, so he can rule unchallenged. Whatever else this description of the Beast entails, it indicates a person with tremendous international power.

On the Beast's head are "blasphemous names." In John's time, the Roman emperors had taken such titles as *Dominus* and *Kurios,* both meaning "Lord" in Latin and Greek, respectively. During the reign of Nero, coins bore his image along with the inscription, "The Savior of the World." John said that this will happen again under the Antichrist.

It appears that the Beast will head up a one-world government, possibly comprised of the territories that were once part of the ancient Roman Empire. This leads some scholars to believe that the European Economic Union, which was formed out of the former European Common Market, will morph into a United States of Europe. Indeed, much of Europe has united. If you travel in the euro zone, you no longer use a specific nation's money. Today, most European countries do business with the euro, and although it is in fiscal trouble, this currency still is more valuable than American dollars.

In truth, the Bible does not specifically say which ten kingdoms will be involved. My friend John Shorey suggested that the ten crowns may represent ten regions of the world rather than specific nations. Others have suggested that the ten crowns may involve ten Islamic nations surrounding Jerusalem. Despite the dogmatic claims of some prophetic teachers, we don't know for sure yet where these powers will arise, but you can be certain that if John saw it in his vision and recorded it in Scripture, God's Word will come true.

This beast will initially come on the scene as a peacemaker, focusing his attention on the Middle East powder keg that has threatened the stability of the world for over sixty years. Because of his uncanny skills, the world will clamor after him and fawn over him. More than anything, he will be a smooth talker. He will proffer a settlement of the Middle East problem and negotiate a peace agreement between Israel and its neighbors (Daniel 9:27). World leaders have tried to bring peace to the Middle East, but the Antichrist will succeed. He may even go so far as to encourage that a new temple be built on Mount Zion, alongside the Dome of the Rock, Islam's second most sacred mosque.

Before long, however, the Antichrist, while giving an impression of inclusiveness regarding religion, will begin to speak against God (Daniel 7:7–8, 25; Revelation 13:5–6). After three and half years, he will break the agreement with Israel, desecrate the Jewish temple, and set himself up as god in that same temple! (Daniel 9:27; 2 Thessalonians 2:1–12)

Keep in mind that Satan is behind the Antichrist's rise to power and his subsequent actions (Revelation 13:2). As the Beast consolidates his power, the world will reel in shock as one of the Antichrist's "heads" receives a fatal wound yet somehow lives. John doesn't give a detailed description of this wound, but he mentions it three times and informs us that it was inflicted by a sword (13:14), although it might also be a bullet.

The Fatally Wounded Head

Many teachers of Bible prophecy believe that the Antichrist himself will suffer a fatal head wound, but if you look at the scripture carefully, you can easily get a different impression: "One of the heads of the beast seemed to have had a fatal wound, but the fatal wound had been healed" (13:3, NIV). Remember, John saw the Beast rising out of the sea, which probably means rising from many peoples. But John used the term "beast" in several ways in Revelation, sometimes talking about the Antichrist and at other times talking about the Antichrist *system,* the one-world government system that is against God. Here, I believe the latter is the more correct understanding, that is, this beast is the Antichrist system. This one-world government will have ten horns, seven heads, and ten diadems (13:1). Revelation 17:12–13 tells us that the ten horns are ten kings who will receive power with the Beast for a relatively short time, and their sole purpose is to give their power to the Beast. The seven heads, according to Revelation 17:9–10, are seven mountains on which the harlot rides and seven kings: "Five have fallen, one is, the other has not yet come; and when he comes, he must remain a little while."

The Bible says, "One of the heads"—that is, one of the Antichrist system's leaders—will receive a wound, not necessarily a wound in the head. He could be wounded in any part of his body. So when you see a world leader wounded, don't discount the event because the wound is not to his head. Remember, John said, "I saw one of his heads as if it had been slain, and his fatal wound was healed" (13:3); he could mean that any one of the individual leaders aligned with the Antichrist system will suffer a fatal wound and be healed. Regardless, the miraculous recovery from this wound will pave the way to the Antichrist's ascendency in the public arena.

There's another intriguing thought to consider about the Antichrist. While most prophecy teachers have deduced that the Antichrist will spring from the revived Roman Empire or the ten Islamic nations that surround Israel, John Shorey's suggestion that the ten heads may be regions poses another possibility. If the leader of the United States is one of the "heads" of the Antichrist system prior to the fatal head wound, it would be possible for the U.S. president to eventually become the leader of Babylon, the Antichrist system.[28]

Regardless, the response of the world to this miraculous healing is very significant. Ironically, the world will worship, not the Lord, but Satan as a result of the wounded head being healed. Worship is the one thing Satan has always wanted, and on that day he will surely have it. In Revelation 13:4, John told us, "They worshipped the beast, saying 'Who is like the beast, and who is able to wage war with him?' "

A similar phrase was used to honor God after the Israelites escaped Pharaoh's army and the Egyptians were destroyed in the Red Sea. The song of deliverance included statements such as, "Who is like You, majestic in holiness, awesome in praises, working wonders?" (Exodus 15:11). Satan seems to take special pleasure in hijacking God's glory, and the devil is the ultimate counterfeiter.

The Antichrist will speak powerful, blasphemous words, just as the prophet Daniel predicted (Daniel 7:8, 20, 25). Through his speech, the Antichrist will blaspheme God, His name, His tabernacle (which is in heaven), and His people who dwell in heaven with Him (Revelation 13:6). These blasphemies will go on for forty-two months (three and a half years).

Before long, however, the world's acquiescence at the Antichrist's words will no longer satisfy his ego. Consequently, he will launch a war against God's people, the saints, the true believers (13:7–8). For a while the Antichrist is going to appear victorious, defeating even God's people (v. 7). I believe many sincere believers in Jesus will be persecuted for their faith at that time. Many will die as a result of the Antichrist's war. But if there is an outcry from the world at his abuse, it will be quickly muffled, since he will have authority over the entire world.

We know for sure that John wanted us to pay close attention to this part of his vision. He made the statement, "If anyone has an ear, let him hear" (13:9), similar to the admonitions of Jesus in the earlier letters to the churches. John then offered an unusual observation: "If you are to be a prisoner, then you will be a prisoner. If you are to be killed with the sword, then you will be killed with the sword. This means that God's holy people must have patience and faith" (13:10, NCV).

John was not a negative-thinking fatalist; he was being a realist. He was telling us that it is useless to fight against the Beast with human weapons. Whatever God has ordained or destined for us as individuals, that is what is going to happen to us. Our choices will reap their inevitable results, similar to reaping what we sow. But John was also encouraging believers, letting us know that these Christians in the last days are not spiritual wimps. They have endurance, perseverance, steadfastness, and loyalty, which is not a passive acceptance of their plight but an attitude of taking the worst the devil and the world can dish out and turning that into glory for God. That is the kind of patience and faith John saw in these believers. No wonder the Antichrist wants to exterminate them.

Beast Number Two: The False Prophet

Next, John saw "another beast coming up out of the earth; and he had two horns like a lamb and he spoke as a dragon" (Revelation 13:11). This beast is known as the False Prophet because he functions as the Antichrist's public relations man. He works to organize the structure through which the Antichrist will gain control and maintain it. This beast does not come out of the sea, as the Antichrist did, but "out of the earth," leading some scholars to speculate that he may come out of Israel itself. We don't know for sure, and the Bible doesn't tell us.

John said that this second beast has two horns, like a lamb. The fact that he has horns but no crown implies that his power is not so much by force but by deception. Most likely his power will come from a quasi-religious political base.

This beast speaks like a dragon (13:11), and we know who that is: the serpent, the devil, the deceiver. His role will be to seduce people into accepting, following, obeying, and ultimately worshipping the Antichrist. As the Holy Spirit always bears witness of Jesus, this False Prophet will use his silver tongue to point people to the Antichrist.

This second beast works for the Antichrist; he is not as powerful as the first beast, but don't take him lightly, because he is no flunky. His goal is to cause people to worship the Antichrist, and he will use whatever is necessary to do it. Eight times in Revelation the phrase *he causes* or *he makes* is used in reference to the False Prophet. He is no paper tiger.

He will also use deceptive signs, and he will be able to perform miracles in his efforts to win people's allegiance to his boss (13:12–15). This is one reason why I so adamantly caution Christians not to be so enamored with miracles. Some Christians run from church to church, town after town, in search of the next big spiritual flash. Yes, our God does indeed do miracles. But be careful. Not every miracle comes from God! In ancient times, false prophets were able to perform miracles, whether real or through some form of chicanery, and in our time, we've seen our share of charlatans. Now, John warned us that the False Prophet is going to wow people with miracles and "great signs," even making fire come down out of heaven, as the prophet Elijah did and as the two witnesses to come will do in Jerusalem. Many people will be deceived by the False Prophet. This is the spirit of devils working miracles (16:14).

Although he may look and sound like a lamb, the Antichrist's beastly cohort is devious. He will establish a false religion, bringing all the world's religions together and forming an umbrella religion designed to worship the Antichrist (13:14–15), an eclectic, inclusive, tolerant religion. The only religious beliefs that will not be tolerated will be biblical Christianity. Can you not see that this is beginning to happen in the U.S. and throughout the world?

The False Prophet's public spectacles will deceive many people. He will encourage them to make an image of the Antichrist, and they will set up an idol to the Beast who had the head wound and came back to life. When will this happen? Probably midway through the seven-year Tribulation. Where will it occur? I believe it will occur in Jerusalem, but possibly this image will be seen in your home. Whether by television, the Internet, or some other means, the False Prophet will somehow cause the image to speak! He gives breath to the image, and this image will talk, deceive, and destroy, all by the power of Satan. Moreover, this image will have the power to have anyone killed if that person will not worship the Antichrist.

With the help of the False Prophet, the Antichrist will devise an economic system whereby people are given a mark either on their hand or their foreheads (13:16–17). Many well-meaning Christians have portrayed this mark as an ugly demarcation on a person, but that is highly unlikely to catch on in our beauty-conscious society. What form the mark of the Beast will take is uncertain, but it will probably be innocuous, such as an eye or hand scanner, or even inserted below the skin, observable only with scanners or other devices. With modern biometric devices already on the scene, and new technologies appearing every day, the possibilities are endless. Nowadays, we have the wherewithal to place computer chips in our pets, and many children's advocates want traceable identification to be implanted in children to help prevent child abductions and other pernicious evils. Besides having personal information about the child, the chip would function as a personal global positioning system. But the evil of the mark of Revelation 13:16 will far exceed any evil such implantation might prevent.

Who Would Be So Foolish?

Why would people accept the mark of the Beast? As the apostle John informed us, they won't be able to buy or sell without it. They won't be able to do business without the mark, the name of the Beast, or the number of his name (Revelation 13:16–17). This means that people will not be able to trade on the stock market without the Antichrist's mark. That's true, but that's not all. You won't be able to buy groceries either. Nor will you be able to sell your products or services. Imagine going to an automobile dealer and being refused service because you don't have the mark. Or think of how you will procure electricity or water or medical services.

For some time the world has been moving toward a cashless society. Soon, we are told, even checks will be a part of our economic history as more and more transactions will be done electronically. You know how this works; you probably pay many of your monthly bills now without ever taking a dollar out of your wallet or writing a check. Your computer is set to make the transaction for you in the right amount and on the proper date. It's easy and convenient. After all, you could lose cash or misplace the checks. Even credit cards will soon be history. With increasing threats of identity theft, the world will be ready and willing to accept some way of maintaining control. All of your personal information, from your bank accounts to your medical records, will be computerized and stored online, perhaps in the cyberspace "cloud."

Many U.S. businesses must file monthly payroll taxes electronically. They no longer have a choice to take the payment to a local bank. Clearly, the technology for controlling your financial life exists right now. The mechanisms by which a totalitarian Antichrist could demand worship or deprive you of all financial functions are already in place. In John's time, if a Christian did not acknowledge the current Roman leader, he could be killed or, as John himself was, imprisoned in a labor camp. Outspoken Christians might not have been physically beaten, but they may have been ostracized from employment, denied opportunities to purchase seed to grow crops, or disallowed from doing business in the community. Since nobody would deal with someone branded as a rebellious person, he or she could not buy or sell. John said it will be similar for those who refuse to worship the Beast and for those who refuse to show their allegiance by receiving the mark of the Beast. The mark of the Beast will be obtained by those who are willing to say that there is another gospel and another way of salvation besides Jesus Christ.

John gave us some information about this notorious mark: "Let him who has understanding calculate the number of the beast, for the number is that of a man; and his number is six hundred and sixty-six" (13:18).

While John thought his readers would have no trouble discerning the meaning of this number, to this day, nobody really knows what the number means. Consequently, it has become the most analyzed number of the Bible. The comparisons between the numbers six, as the number of man—man was created on the sixth day—and seven, the number of completion and perfection in the book of Revelation, have been extrapolated into all sorts of interpretations.

An intriguing fact in ancient times was that letters were often given numerical values. For example, we might say the number one equals the letter A. Two equates to a B. As such, every word could be given a numerical value, and there has been no limit to the number of attempts to ascribe a name for the

Antichrist. Social security cards, picture identification cards, computer files, and passport chips have all been linked to the Antichrist as well. While we don't know for sure how this number will work into the Antichrist's program, we can be sure of this much: if you are alive, do *not,* under any circumstances, acknowledge the Antichrist's authority in your life by accepting this mark in any form!

18

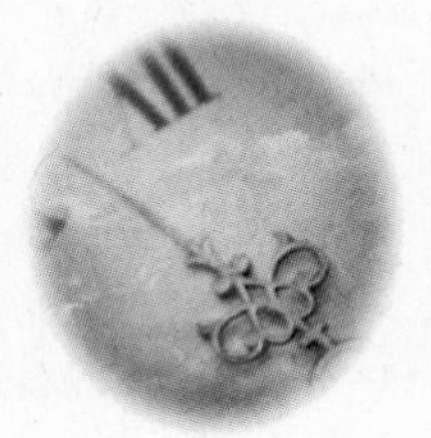

We Win! We Really Do!

Psalm 94:3 raises a baffling question: "How long will the wicked triumph?" Sometimes it seems as though the good guys always finish last, that we are wasting our time by serving God. Looking around, it seems to us that people who hate God, curse God, or simply ignore God are doing perfectly fine. Those who cheat, rob, commit adultery, or sin with impunity seem to prosper while so many dedicated believers suffer. How long will this go on?

As we've seen in Revelation 13, it certainly seems that the Dragon, the Antichrist, and his cohorts are winning the day. But that is not the end of the story. In stark contrast, John saw the next chapter in the vision that is meant to encourage those of us who follow, worship, and obey the Lamb of God (14:4). The first thing he saw was the Lamb standing on Mount Zion, and with Him are 144,000 believers who have "His name and the name of His Father written on their foreheads" (14:1). Imagine this sight! These saints of God are the same people we first encountered in Revelation 7:3. Some scholars believe these are Jewish believers saved during the Tribulation, while others feel that these Christians symbolize all who will be saved during this time. Regardless, they are standing with the Lamb—Jesus—on Mount Zion, either literally or figuratively in heaven, in what is known as the Holy City, the New Jerusalem. These Christians have been sealed; they have God's mark upon their foreheads, indicating they are His possession and under His protection.

At the same time, John "heard a voice from heaven, like the sound of many waters and like the sound of loud thunder, and the voice which I heard was like the sound of harpists playing on their harps" (14:2). The scripture doesn't say who the voice belongs to, but it seems to be that of Jesus since the same description (the sound like many waters) is applied to Him in Revelation 1:15. The voice also sounded like harpists joyfully celebrating, so perhaps this voice indicates both the majesty and the gentle grace of God.

John also heard the saints singing a new song, one that no one could learn but the 144,000. These believers had suffered through the Tribulation and had persevered; they had remained loyal and faithful to God. So now their song of sorrow has become a new song of victorious salvation. John pointed out six interesting details about them.

First, he said they were redeemed out of the earth; they were purchased from the earth. These believers were living in the nitty-gritty world; they were not part of some religious extremist group who had relocated to a mountain somewhere to await the coming of the Lord. No, they were in the world, but not of the world.

Second, John noted that they were celibate, virgins, that they were not defiled with women. Marriage and sexuality are not evil, but it could be that these believers were unmarried and had never experienced sexual relations. Perhaps their celibacy was more spiritual than physical, more symbolic than literal in that these believers had not followed after and given themselves to a false lover, namely, the Antichrist. Throughout the Bible, fornication and adultery are always connected to spiritual idolatry, so that may be what John intended for us to understand here.

Third, they follow the Lamb wherever He goes (14:4). In the original language "following" is in the present tense, indicating a continuous action. "I am following Jesus right now without ceasing" may be the best translation of that scripture.

Fourth, John reminded us that these believers have been purchased as firstfruits; they are the pick of the litter, the very finest, the initial batch of what is sure to be a marvelous harvest. In Old Testament times, during the Feast of Firstfruits, the priest would wave a sheaf before the Lord as a symbol that meant the entire harvest belonged to God (Leviticus 23:9–14). Here in Revelation, John said that these 144,000 believers are the firstfruits of a great harvest to come. They are the vanguard, leading the way for the rest of us who have trusted Jesus Christ as our Savior and Lord.

Fifth, there was no lie in their mouth. These saints speak the truth and will not tolerate falsehood.

Sixth, John told us that they are blameless, without blemish (Revelation 14:5), referring again to a word with sacrificial overtones. In the Old Testament, the animal sacrificed for sins had to be without spot or blemish. Years later the apostle Paul wrote that God has chosen us to be holy, blameless, and spotless (Ephesians 1:4; Colossians 1:21–22). That same description is applied to the church (Ephesians 5:27), and Jesus Himself is said to be without blemish (1 Peter 1:19). Moreover, the Bible makes it clear that Jesus is returning to take His holy bride to heaven. In the meantime, how are we to live? Paul prayed that "He may establish your hearts without blame in holiness before our God and Father at the coming of our Lord Jesus with all His saints" (1 Thessalonians 3:13). In closing, Paul also prayed, "Now may the God of peace Himself sanctify you entirely; and may your spirit and soul and body be preserved complete, without blame at the coming of our Lord Jesus Christ. Faithful is He who calls you, and He also will bring it to pass" (1 Thessalonians 5:23–24).

Clearly there is a beauty of holiness about these saints in heaven, and there ought to be a similar quality to our lives. If holiness is such a big deal to God in heaven, shouldn't it matter more to us as we get ready to go to heaven? The Scriptures speak plainly to this fact: "Pursue peace with all people, and holiness, without which no one will see the Lord" (Hebrews 12:14, NKJV).

Angelic Messages

John then saw three angels flying high in the air, in midheaven, who sound out three distinctly different messages. The first angel carries good news: "Fear

God and give him praise, because the time has come for God to judge all people. So worship God who made the heavens, and the earth, and the sea, and the springs of water" (Revelation 14:7, NCV).

This message has two main thrusts: the good news of the gospel and judgment has come. These two ideas seem contradictory to many people today, but they have always gone together in the Bible. The gospel has that double-edged sword quality, and for those who accept it, there is life. To those who reject the gospel, there is judgment. At present, the angels are not yet preaching this message, but we have the privilege and responsibility of announcing the good news and warning people of the judgment to come.

The message is imperative: fear God, not the Antichrist. Give Him glory and don't be duped by the False Prophet's attempts to distract you from the truth. Worship Him, not the gods of this world, such as money, power, sex, prestige, or any other vain idols.

The second angel's message is bad news, especially for the devil's crowd: "Fallen, fallen is Babylon the great, she who has made all the nations drink of the wine of the passion of her immorality" (14:8).

Throughout Revelation, John referred to Rome as Babylon, partly because of Rome's debauchery, but especially because of the Roman Empire's emphasis on emperor worship. Referring to Rome as Babylon is as far as John could get from a compliment. Moreover, he was speaking of the world system of the Beast, including the political, economic, and spiritual deceit by which the Antichrist ascended to power and ruled in opposition to God. That system, built largely on the lust for power and money and false worship, is coming down, the angel says.

Again, John used Old Testament images to predict the future, drawing a picture in which God's wrath is portrayed as a cup of wine to be drunk (Isaiah 21:9; Jeremiah 51:7–8). The picture is of a prostitute seducing and persuading a man into immorality by getting him drunk so he no longer resists. John was saying that Rome is like that. The influence of the Beast has been like that. Those who drink that wine will also soon drink another: the wine of God's wrath.

The third angel's message is a strong warning to anyone who might be tempted to compromise their faith, acquiesce to the Beast's system, and accept the mark of the Beast on their forehead:

> If anyone worships the beast and his idol and gets the beast's mark on the forehead or on the hand, that one also will drink the wine of God's anger, which is prepared with all its strength in the cup of his anger. And that person will be put in pain with burning sulfur before the holy angels and the Lamb. And the smoke from their burning pain will rise forever and ever. There will be no rest, day or night, for those who worship the beast and his idol or who get the mark of his name. (Revelation 14:9–11, NCV)

This is a serious admonition for many reasons. Those people who give in to the Antichrist will drink the wrath of God at full strength. Usually, God's wrath is mixed with His mercy, but not here. His wrath will be unmixed, undiluted. Moreover, their punishment will be eternally agonizing, in pain with burning sulfur, the most terrible kind of punishment imaginable. This is unending torment that goes on and on. The word the angel used actually means "on into ages of ages."

Of interest, as well, this torment will be initiated in front of the holy angels in the presence of the Lamb. Many times in the past, the heathen, pagan, bloodthirsty crowd had looked down at those first-century Christians who were viciously tortured and tormented by their persecutors. Now, the tables will be turned.

While there is no rest for the wicked, John was reminded by a voice from heaven that there is eternal rest for God's saints. John recorded two things in Revelation 14:13: "Blessed are the dead who die in the Lord from now on!" and "[May they] rest from their labors, for their deeds follow with them." This does not imply that these people worked their way into heaven. The message is saying, "As they lived, so they died." They lived in and for Jesus, so they died in the Lord. Interestingly, this is the only place in Revelation where the Holy Spirit speaks aloud, other than at the close of the book (22:17), and the Spirit confirms that these believers now have rest from their labors and their deeds follow them. He is not referring just to their work on earth, but he is talking about the character of these believers.

GETTING READY TIME

John had a vision of the judgment to come, describing two pictures that would be familiar to his readers. First, however, he saw a person who captured his immediate attention: "Then I looked, and behold, a white cloud, and sitting on the cloud was one like a son of man, having a golden crown on His head and a sharp sickle in His hand" (Revelation 14:14). The vision is reminiscent of Daniel 7:13–14 and Revelation 1:13, so John must have seen Jesus there. Moreover, the white cloud is one of dazzling brilliance, which points to majesty and glory (1:7). The term "Son of Man" was a favorite title of Jesus when He was on earth. The crown is that of a conqueror, and the sickle is an instrument of divine justice. Knowing all that, John must have been no less in awe at seeing Jesus in this role.

Then comes an angel with an announcement from the temple that it is time to begin the harvest (14:15–16). Although it is God's judgment, Jesus is the one who swings the sickle to begin the harvest. Nowadays, most Christians think of harvesting in terms of evangelism, since Jesus told us that the fields are ripe unto harvest (John 4:34–38). But harvesting is also a picture of God's judgment in the Bible (Joel 3:9–14; Matthew 13:24–43). Here, when the field is harvested, that which is good is kept and that which is not good is thrown away and burned. This picture disproves the modern idea that everyone is going to heaven or that a loving God would not allow people to go to hell.

The next image that John saw gives us our first hint at Armageddon. John saw clusters of grapes gathered by the angels and then thrown into a winepress—the winepress of God's wrath—in which they were crushed (Revelation 14:17–20). The imagery and the magnitude of this judgment are shocking: "They were trampled in the winepress outside the city, and blood flowed out of the winepress as high as horses' bridles for a distance of about one hundred eighty miles" (14:20, NCV).

The winepress being outside the city is not accidental. Jesus was crucified outside Jerusalem's city gates. There He paid the price for our sins. On this day, however, when the grapes of God's wrath are pressed, sinners will pay a price for the sins they have committed outside the city gates. It will not be a pretty sight.

The blood will rise to the level of a horse's bridle, about four feet deep, for a distance of 180 miles, which interestingly, is almost the exact length of Israel, north to south.

Is this to be taken literally? Most Bible scholars think it is meant to be symbolic. Possibly it refers to the bloodshed of the infamous Battle of Armageddon, which will take place in the Jezreel Valley, about sixty miles north of Jerusalem. Clearly, this graphic image is meant to convey the enormity of the punishment, the completeness of the judgment, and the staggering number of people who will be slain.

19

THE BEGINNING OF THE END

Looking out at the calm, glassy sea at the end of the day, John noticed the sun dipping below the horizon, casting a warm, reddish orange hue over the water. Despite his difficult conditions on Patmos, the scene reminded the apostle that God was still in charge. The scene also prompted his memory regarding a marvelous portion of the vision of heaven he had enjoyed.

Revelation 15, the shortest chapter in the book, introduces the last series of seven judgments to be poured out on the earth. We've already seen the destruction and pain that followed the opening of the seven seals. The seven trumpets wreaked even more havoc upon the world, although at the seventh trumpet we rejoiced because the kingdoms of the world became the kingdoms of our God. Now, however, in what some scholars believe could be another flashback, John saw the preparation of seven angels with seven plagues, the seven bowls of God's wrath. While we get the feeling that what follows is going to be ominous, John saw another period of relative calm, with great joy in heaven on the part of the people who had made it through the Tribulation victoriously.

How these people won the victory over the Antichrist and his system, we are not told. Perhaps they simply refused to compromise and endured the consequences of their commitment, scraping out a meager existence in a world that would not allow them to buy or sell and where their faith was constantly tested. Possibly they gave up their lives rather than deny their Lord.

Today, we tend to equate spiritual victory with surviving and thriving, but the Bible sees success differently. Faithfulness unto death is the qualifier for true success. The real victory is not always to live in peace and safety. If your survival requires you to compromise your faith, that is defeat, not victory. Real victory is to face the worst the devil can throw at you and do so with the attitude and commitment to be faithful to Jesus, regardless of the costs.

These rejoicing saints were singing two marvelous songs: the song of Moses and the song of the Lamb. The song of Moses reminded God's people of His great deliverance, bringing them out of persecution and into the Promised Land. As it extolled God's greatness, it memorialized the crossing of the Red Sea and the subsequent destruction of Pharaoh's troops (Exodus 15:1–19). This was a song that every Jew knew and sang each Sabbath.

The song of the Lamb, ironically, was made up almost entirely of quotes from Old Testament scriptures, emphasizing the greatness of God, that He is worthy of praise, and that His judgments are righteous. That is an especially poignant reminder, since the wrath of God is about to be poured out on earth.

It is noteworthy that these overcomers in heaven used scriptures to praise the Lord for His goodness and greatness. That should be a lesson for us. When you aren't sure how to praise God, draw praise from this passage of scripture and others.

Moreover, although these believers had beaten the Antichrist, there is not a word in their celebration about their own abilities, their own achievements, their own willpower, or their own spiritual commitment. Nor is there a trace of complaint, whining about their troubles and the tribulation they went through for the sake of Jesus Christ. Instead, they express praise to where it belongs: to almighty God. Their song is about *His* greatness, what *He* has done. Indeed, heaven is a place where we will finally forget about ourselves and center our attention on God. In heaven, we will truly understand that nothing else matters except God. All of our own self-will and ideas of self-importance will seem so foolish when we experience the glory and greatness of God.

In another part of the vision, filled with allusions to the Old Testament, John saw the seven angels coming out of the temple of the tabernacle, sometimes referred to as the "tabernacle of the testimony" (Revelation 15:5), which was essentially the tabernacle that God instructed His people to assemble in the wilderness, on their journey from Egypt to the Promised Land. The ark of the covenant that contained the Ten Commandments was kept in the tabernacle. Today, many Christians don't seem concerned about the Old Testament, but apparently God still has concern for His Law, all the way to the end of time.

Each of the seven angels was dressed in a white robe with a golden sash, similar to what was worn by a high priest. This heavenly outfit may have looked similar to the way the young man at the tomb was dressed after Christ's resurrection (Matthew 28:3; Mark 16:5). It certainly connotes royalty,[29] since these angels are representing the Lord God Almighty and executing His judgments.

When one of the living beings gave out the seven bowls of God's wrath to the angels to deliver, the temple was filled with smoke, symbolizing God's glory (Revelation 15:8). From that point on, no one could enter the temple until the seven plagues were finished.

John shuddered at this symbolism: the wrath of God was about to be poured out on sinful human beings. This is a place you never want to be.

Judgment Day Is No Movie

Hollywood has been fascinated by stories about the end of the world, but the judgment about to fall upon the earth is far beyond anything the most creative scriptwriter could conceive. Simply reading about the seven bowls of God's wrath in Revelation 16 is enough to make even a courageous person quake in fear.

The seven bowls of God's wrath have a familiar ring. They are strikingly similar to the ten plagues that God poured out on Egypt (Exodus 7:20–12:29). These plagues included turning water into blood, the land infested with frogs and lice and flies, a blight on the livestock, boils on people's bodies, thunder and hail, locusts, darkness, and the killing of the first-born child of every family in Egypt. The terrors that follow the sounding of the seven trumpets were similar to these (Revelation 8:1–9:21; 11:15–19). At first glance, the seven bowls of God's wrath seem almost identical, but there is a major difference. The destruction associated with the ten plagues in Egypt and the seven trumpet judgments was limited in scope. Now, in Revelation 16, all the stops are out. God's wrath is poured out completely.

Following the command to "Go!" from the loud voice in the temple, "the first angel went and poured out his bowl on the earth; and it became a loathsome and malignant sore on the people who had the mark of the beast and who worshipped his image" (16:2). This was the same word that described the boils that people suffered during the Egyptian plagues. Notice, too, the target of God's wrath: those who had the Antichrist's mark and who worshipped his image.

In rapid-fire succession, the angels did as they were commanded, the second angel pouring out his bowl with the result that earth's seawater turned to blood and all sea life died (16:3). Few things are more pungent than the smell of dead fish, but from the largest whale to great white sharks to the tiniest plankton, everything in the sea dies.

The third angel followed suit, pouring out his bowl of wrath and destroying all freshwater rivers and springs. Can you imagine a world with no clean water? In regard to this horrific scene, the angel of the waters said to God, "You are right to decide to punish these evil people. They have poured out the blood of your holy people and your prophets . . . " (16:5–6, NCV).

The angel's reference to the "blood of your holy people" is to the persecutions that have already happened or will take place in the future. In any case, his observation was keen. Those who shed the blood of God's prophets—including church leaders and other witnesses—are given nothing but blood to drink.

John recorded affirmations of God's righteous judgments coming from the altar, which could have been the voice of an angel or the praying of the martyrs. The statement concurred with the angel, "True and righteous are Your judgments" (16:7).

The fourth angel poured out his bowl on the sun, causing scorching heat on the earth. All earthly life depends on light and energy from the sun. Have you ever had a bad sunburn? Have you ever walked through an arid area during the heat of the day? Have you ever felt your lips parched from thirst? Now, imagine such heat with nothing to drink.

Still, these judgments are not enough to bring sinful human beings to their knees. John told us that rather than repenting "they blasphemed the name of God who has the power over these plagues, and they did not repent so as to give Him glory" (16:9). It is not that these people are unaware of God's power. In fact, they acknowledge Him, but they insist on going their own way.

Turn Out the Lights, the Party's Over

The fifth angel poured out his bowl on the "throne of the beast" (Revelation 16:10), and his world went dark. This could be a geographic area, but more likely this concerns the entire area of the Antichrist's rule. Despite the darkness, the followers of the Beast remained defiant and refused to repent: "They gnawed their tongues because of pain, and they blasphemed the God of heaven because of their pains and their sores; and they did not repent of their deeds" (vv. 10–11).

When the sixth angel poured out his bowl, the Euphrates River dried up, "that the way would be prepared for the kings from the east" (16:12). The Euphrates flows eighteen hundred miles from the slopes of Mount Ararat in Turkey to Babylon and the Persian Gulf. It formed the eastern border of the land God originally promised to Israel. Ironically, it had been dammed before as part of a military endeavor. Cyrus of Persia defeated Babylon by damming the Euphrates and sending his troops right into the city over the dry riverbed. Certainly, we recall the Lord parting the waters of the Red Sea so His people could cross on dry ground, and He did the same when His people crossed the Jordan into the Promised Land. John said that something similar is going to happen in the days ahead.

As I mentioned earlier, these "kings from the east" might be Chinese or possibly the Islamic nations that surround Israel. In John's day, the Parthians lived east of Israel, and they were the most feared warriors in the world. Regardless of who these people are who will come from the east, they will be a formidable force, and they will launch a violent attack.

John saw three evil spirits coming out of the mouths of the Dragon, the Antichrist, and the False Prophet. These unclean spirits looked like frogs "for they are spirits of demons, performing signs, which go out to the kings of the whole world, to gather them together for the war of the great day of God, the Almighty" (16:14). These evil spirits call the nations of the world to the climactic battle. We think of this as the Battle of Armageddon, although those words are not used in the Bible. Instead the Bible gives us the location of the battle, a place in Israel known as Har-Magedon in Hebrew (16:16). The name is derived from two words: *har,* which means "the hill of," and *Megiddo,* which means "the place of slaughter." The site is approximately sixty miles north of Jerusalem. It looks out over the plains of Esdraelon and the Jezreel Valley, which is about fourteen miles wide and twenty miles long. Napoleon Bonaparte called this valley the "most natural battlefield of the whole earth."[30]

Historically, it has been a battlefield numerous times. On this plain Barak defeated Canaan (Judges 5:19), Gideon defeated the Midianites (Judges 7), Saul committed suicide there rather than be taken prisoner by the Philistines (1 Samuel 31), and Josiah perished in battle there against Pharaoh Neco (2 Kings 23:29–30). The Roman general Titus marched his armies through this valley en route to destroy Jerusalem, and the Crusaders followed this route as well when they captured Jerusalem. During World War I, British general Edmund Allenby used the valley to defeat the Turks. And John wrote that the valley is going to be used for war during the final battle: Armageddon.

Although it looks as though the satanic trinity instigates this final conflict, John made it clear that this battle is according to God's plan, not the Antichrist's. We also know how this battle is going to end. The armies of the world will converge on Israel, but instead of fighting each other, they will unite to fight against the Lord and His heavenly army. We know from Revelation 19 that the forces of the world will be no match for Jesus. Nevertheless, blood is going to flow, as we know from Revelation 14:20, as high as a horse's bridle over an area two hundred miles long after the unprecedented carnage.

Before the battle began, John heard a familiar voice, the voice of Jesus, saying, "Behold, I am coming like a thief. Blessed is the one who stays awake and keeps his clothes, so that he will not walk about naked and men will not see his shame" (16:15). This is one of those statements in the Bible that almost takes your breath away as you realize what Jesus says He will do. He had told His disciples that He was coming again in power and great glory; the apostle Paul reminded believers as well that "the day of the Lord will come just like a thief in the night," not to believers, but to unbelievers (1 Thessalonians 5:2). And now that day has come.

It's All Over

When the seventh angel pours out his bowl of God's wrath, John heard a loud voice from the throne of God, say, "It is done" (Revelation 16:17). The results of this last bowl are mind-boggling. Flashes of lightning and peals of thunder fill the earth. Some scholars postulate that even the air will be ruined as a result. There will be an earthquake unlike any other in history, so mighty that the "great city" (possibly Rome, but more likely Jerusalem) was split into three parts, and the "cities of the nations fell" (16:19). In an instant, every city in the world will crumble, but Babylon gets special attention, and not in a good way. "Babylon the great was remembered before God, to give her the cup of wine of His fierce wrath" (16:19). We'll see the details of the judgment on Babylon in the chapters ahead.

In the meantime "every island fled away, and the mountains were not found" (16:20), perhaps pulverized or sunk to the bottom of the ocean. This earthquake really is the big one!

Hailstones weighing a hundred pounds each will pelt the earth, and yet "men blasphemed God because of the plague of hail, because its plague was extremely severe" (16:20). No wonder that when the Lord returns He is going to create a new heaven and a new earth. This earth is going to be a mess! The death and calamities on earth will be unimaginable, but the continuing stubborn, sinful defiance against God will be beyond all comprehension.

Sinful society will shake its collective fist in the face of God, blaspheming His name, but the King of kings is about to have the last word.

20

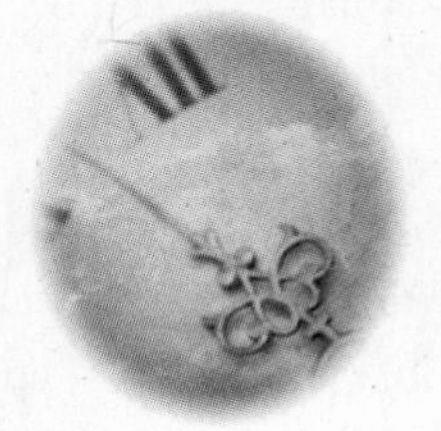

The Harlot

In the movie *Pretty Woman*, a modern-day twist on George Bernard Shaw's play *Pygmalion* and the musical *My Fair Lady*, a man befriends a prostitute and teaches her refinement, culture, and sophistication. In real life, men don't bring home prostitutes to meet Mom. To the contrary, prostitutes are used, abused, and dumped back on the streets to fend for themselves.

What is the church's false love today? I believe it is the love of money, because scripture says, "For the love of money is the root of all evil" (1 Timothy 6:10, KJV). Jesus said it too: "No one can serve two masters; for either he will hate the one and love the other, or he will be devoted to one and despise the other. You cannot serve God and mammon" (Matthew 6:24). The word *mammon* means "money," but it is more than dollars and cents. It includes any designation of material value. It is a comprehensive word for all kinds of possessions, earnings, and riches.

The harlot of Revelation 17 represents the world system based on the love of money and power—everything that takes the place God should hold in our hearts. It's because of the harlot—materialism—that the wrath of God is poured out. The harlot is what pulls us away from God.

It saddens me to see how quickly this generation has been taken captive by materialism. I've seen passionate youth put aside the chance to learn about the Word and serve God to make monthly car and credit card payments. Others, after finishing Bible school, wind up never working in ministry because they must pay off debt or find a high-paying job elsewhere.

HISTORY WILL REPEAT ITSELF

Keep in mind, for the Antichrist to rise to power and create the one-world government, there must be a global-wide crisis of epic proportion. The economic crash of 2008 was a warning, and I pray that it won't be the last warning before a total collapse comes. China, Japan, and even Russia are hard at work establishing a new standard for trade, replacing the once mighty American dollar. What will America do when it has to trade its dollar for the Japanese yen, the Russian ruble, and the European euro just to maintain its economy? When Japan or Russia or the Euro zone decide not to accept the dollar, the American economy will fade into third-world status.

Yet it is not enough for the United States to collapse to open the door for the Antichrist. The entire world must be caught up in a hopeless crisis. Since its introduction, the euro has been the second largest reserve currency in the world behind the American dollar. But in June 2012, the combined value of euros in circulation surpassed the dollar. Yet, euros are also unstable, weakining countries such as Ireland, Portugal, and Greece. The Greek economy is so precarious that many Greeks feared total collapse in May 2012 and withdrew almost 1 billion euros from their bank accounts.

When everything collapses, generations who have become dependent on a constant flow of money and personal debt will demand a new financial standard. Several Euro zone members are already doing so. If America and the rest of the world continue their downward economic spiral, it is only a matter of time before the world's financial leaders seek a new system—a one-world economic system.

THE GREAT HARLOT

In Revelation 17, John began to tell in incredible detail the step-by-step victory of Jesus Christ, the Lamb, over the devil, the Beast, and the False Prophet. In doing so, John saw several contrasts: the true church is a spotless virgin, but the false religious system of the Antichrist is characterized as a harlot who has abandoned truth and prostituted herself for personal gain. This woman is neither pretty nor fair. She is in bed with the Antichrist. John also saw the contrast between the cities of Babylon and the City of God. Babylon is a political and economic system that has attempted to control people's destinies, using money, power, and religion to do so. In contrast, the City of God is the New Jerusalem, our eternal home prepared for us by Jesus Christ, a place of peace and love. This is our ultimate destination. In the meantime, in the last days, our job is to stay true to Jesus, to be His witnesses, to keep ourselves pure from the false religious system, and to keep ourselves unspotted by Babylon's pollution spawned by the Antichrist's political and economic system.

I believe that Revelation 17 is a flashback to Revelation 14:8, where John filled us in on the destruction of Babylon: "And another angel followed, saying, 'Babylon is fallen, is fallen, that great city, because she has made all nations drink of the wine of the wrath of her fornication" (14:6 NKJV).

John saw the harlot's desolation and punishment (17:1–6). He saw a woman sitting on a "scarlet beast" (v. 3). Many Bible scholars believe the woman represents Rome, because she sits on many waters, which means she rules many people, and that was precisely the case when John was writing. Rome ruled the world. But this reference may not implicate the city of Rome so much as the power of the Antichrist system, because at some point, possibly in the near future, the Antichrist is going to rule the world in a similar way as Rome once did. What John saw indicated that, much like the way in which Rome had spread the seduction of power and immorality and luxury and lust all over the world, the Antichrist system would do likewise. The city was prosperous and powerful, but it was also idolatrous and dangerous.

Originally, Babylon was known as a city that sat on many waters. The Euphrates River ran through the center of the city known for its famous Hanging Gardens. Babylon also had a system of canals that spread in every direction from the Euphrates, thus the designation, the city that sat upon the waters. We also know that waters signify people in Revelation, so it makes sense that this harlot controlled many people.

The Beast on which the woman sat was a daunting image in itself. The Beast has seven heads and ten horns, most likely signifying power. This is the same beast that rose out of the sea in Revelation 12—the Antichrist himself! The woman was dressed in scarlet and purple and decked out with gold, precious stones, and pearls as though she were going out on the town for the evening. Scarlet and purple represent royalty, splendor, and luxury, but perhaps they also connote sin as well. The prophet Isaiah equated scarlet with sin: "Though your sins are as scarlet" (Isaiah 1:18).

The harlot was holding a golden cup in her hand—a direct reference to the prophet Jeremiah's words: "Babylon has been a golden cup in the hand of the LORD, intoxicating all the earth" (Jeremiah 51:7). But as you can see, the cup was in the Lord's hands. In Revelation 17, it is vile, filthy, and immoral. The harlot herself was drunk, not with wine, but with the blood of the saints, most likely a reference to Rome's deadly persecution of Christians. Rome did not merely persecute Christians as a matter of civic duty or as a police action against lawbreakers. No, Rome took delight in hounding Christians to death, slaughtering believers with impunity and without remorse. That's what John meant when he described the harlot as being drunk with the blood of the saints.

Interestingly, John saw that the woman's name involves "a mystery." In the New Testament, mystery is not the same as a police detective show on television or a mystery novel. In the New Testament, mysteries are hidden truths that only the spiritually initiated can understand. In this case, the mystery has to do with Babylon, which to the early Christians signified Rome because of its absolute power and evil. The Romans were the ones who had crucified Christ.

John, however, was not referring to the actual city of Babylon, because if everyone knew where Mystery Babylon was, then it wouldn't be a mystery. Rather, this was a government and a system that was opposed to God.

In John's vision, the woman was not just any harlot, but she was the "mother of harlots" (17:5). John asserted that this false religious system spawned other equally false religious systems. No wonder John "wondered greatly" (17:6).

Thankfully, the angel explained the vision to John, beginning with the Beast with seven heads and ten horns. The seven heads represent seven mountains, or rises in land, as well as seven kings. These seven mountains, or landmasses, seem to indicate Rome, a city built on seven hills. Although the consensus of scholars accepts this conclusion, I wonder if these landmasses represent the seven continents of the world, especially since the Antichrist system is worldwide.

The seven kings are more difficult to identify, with some Bible scholars convinced the kings are seven Roman emperors: Julius Caesar, Tiberius, Caligula, Claudius, Nero, Domitian, and culminating with the Antichrist. Other scholars believe these seven kings may represent seven successive world empires that oppose God.

Regardless, John was told a secret. Five of these kingdoms had passed off the scene already, one existed at the time John wrote Revelation, and one more was yet to come. Most scholars agree that the five empires that had already fallen are Egypt, Assyria, Babylon, Persia, and Greece. The one empire in existence at the time of John's writing was the Roman Empire, ruled by Domitian. The empire to come, to be ruled by the Beast, will embody the strength, wickedness, and brutality of the previous empires, but this last "revived Roman Empire" will be ruled by the Antichrist.

Besides the Beast's seven heads, it has ten horns, which represent ten kings or nations that will have power for only one hour, which is not a literal hour but indicates a short period of time. The function of these kings, the angel explains, will be twofold. One, they will enable the Beast to rise to power and gain worldwide recognition and control. Second, they will all yield their power to the Beast. I believe these leaders are alive and moving into power today!

We know that after the opening of the first seal (6:1–2), the Antichrist moves onto the world scene as a man of peace, which is easy to do if the world has plunged itself into the worst economic depression in history. The Antichrist will organize his empire, negotiate a treaty with Israel and encourage sacrifices to once again take place in a temple in Jerusalem. At the midpoint of his seven-year reign, he will break the treaty with Israel (Daniel 9:27) and begin to persecute the people of God.

He will become a world dictator, thanks to the help of the False Prophet who will control the world's political and economic systems. We are moving toward such a system every day with the constant emphasis on the global economy as well as a world government. I have a good friend who doesn't like to fly on a particular airline because the phrase "One World" is inscribed near every plane's door. The Antichrist will soon rise to the top of that one world system, ascending from the group of seven kings; he will be the eighth (Revelation 17:11).

Ultimately, the Dragon, the Beast, and the False Prophet will pick a fight with the wrong opponent: the Lamb of God. The Lamb and His called, chosen, and faithful ones will overcome them (17:16). In the midst of this war, the harlot will be made desolate by the same system that carried her (v. 16). Talk about two-timing lovers!

Satan and the Antichrist will actually use the false religious system to get what they want—absolute power—then their love affair with the false religion of materialism will turn to antipathy and sheer hatred. They will make the harlot "desolate and naked, and will eat her flesh and will burn her up with fire" (17:16). They will totally eliminate her. There is no loyalty with Satan and his minions.

Despite the appearance that the Antichrist is calling the shots, John recognized an important part of the story that often goes untold. He noted that God was orchestrating these events, causing the wicked to fulfill His purposes by giving their kingdom to the Beast until the plan of God was completed (17:17). No doubt the kings and countries involved will think they are accomplishing their own purposes, but, in fact, they will be doing exactly as God has planned for them to do. Likewise, unless they repent, God will allow His people to fall into the hands of their enemies. But although God is in charge, things are still going to get ugly. The Antichrist will pull both religious systems and political power under his dominion. He will not have to conquer the world to receive this power. The ten nations, or ten leaders, will agree to acquiesce to his authority, giving him this control.

Just to make sure that John didn't miss the point, the angel reminded him again that the harlot was to be identified as that "great city, which reigns over the kings of the earth" (17:18). While some see this city as Rome, others suggest this city may be a rebuilt Babylon. But I see it as the harlot system. Because of the colluding dynamic between money and power, I lean toward thinking this system may be centered in New York City, since it is often called the capital of world finance. Still others believe the woman represents not a literal city but the diabolical, diluted religious system of the Antichrist, resting on and supporting the perverted economic system perpetuated by Satan. As John saw in his next vision, the entire system is going to collapse in one day.

21

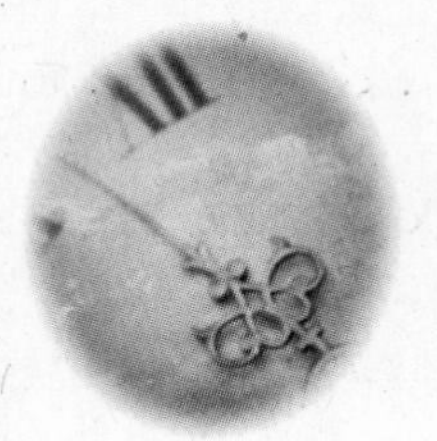

Gone in One Hour

Babylon was not only an ancient city, it is symbolic of humanity's stubborn rebellion against God. To John, the city may have signified Rome's unrelenting, merciless push toward emperor worship and all sorts of other weird religions. Most of all, Babylon represents the world systems put in place by the Beast, the Antichrist. These systems will encompass political and economic and religious entities. Politically, the emphasis will be on a one-world government with the Antichrist wielding absolute authority. Economically, it will be impossible to do business or purchase the basic necessities without acquiescing and accepting the mark of the Beast. Without this mark, a person will not be able to buy or sell goods. That is why it's important for Christians to prepare now for what the Bible tells us is coming. Stock up now, so you won't fall prey to the pressure of the Antichrist because your stomach is hungry.

Human beings can be resourceful in times of stress, so I can see those who have food and water doing a brisk underground business—for a while. I believe those Christians who have food and water and power generators will have opportunities to use these resources to help other people and possibly guide them to a relationship with Jesus. But I have no illusions; the Antichrist system will tolerate no rivals. Anybody who bucks the system will be considered a public enemy, and intense efforts will be launched to quash any rebellions.

You can be sure that life under the rule of the Antichrist, especially during the final three and a half years of the Tribulation, will be far worse than life under any of the brutal dictators of the twentieth century. Americans especially have difficulty comprehending this, because we take so many of our freedoms for granted.

Many Bible teachers believe John used the city of Babylon as a code word for Rome, and that is no doubt true. But beyond that, John was telling about a lifestyle, a system that the Antichrist espouses, develops, and perpetuates.

John had two great perspectives on the fall of Babylon, the destruction of the Antichrist system. First, he saw it from heaven's viewpoint and recorded the angels' comments about the fall (Revelation 18:1–8), and then he described the response of the people on earth at the time of the demise. Many of the people's attitudes will be shockingly crass. Just as on 9/11, while most of us watched the events in horror and reeled from the repugnant aftermath of the devastation, some people viewed 9/11 from a viciously selfish perspective, concerned about how this was going to affect them or their business.

That sort of response is evident in Revelation 18, where most people are lamenting the destruction of Babylon and its systems. They are not concerned about the people of the city or nation; they are simply worried about their own survival.

No Ordinary Angel

In Revelation 18 the vision begins with an angel making an announcement, but this is no ordinary angel. This messenger comes down from heaven, and he has great authority and power, so much so that the earth will be illuminated by his splendor and glory. This messenger sounds like Jesus, because when He comes, according to the Bible, He will light up the whole world! No one else can do this.

The message rings out: "Fallen, fallen is Babylon the great!" (18:2). The irony here is obvious. The Antichrist declares his own greatness with pride, arrogance, and pomposity, yet his worldwide system is easily destroyed by God, who is great and deserves all praise and worship.

The double-word phrase, *Fallen, fallen,* seems to imply a double dose of judgment on the Antichrist's systems. Indeed, God is going to pay back Babylon double for its sins (18:6).

Ironically, John wrote this passage as though it is already done, even though it is in our future. If God's Word says something is going to happen, God will always keep His Word. It may not happen in just the way we think it should, or according to our timetable, but you can be sure God will do what He has said He will do.

John could hardly believe how vile and decadent Babylon had become. It is a "dwelling place of demons," he reported, "and a prison of every unclean spirit, and a prison of every unclean and hateful bird" (18:2). The word John used here to describe Babylon is one we might use to portray a haunted house. If you can imagine demons haunting the ruins of a once-great building or a once-great city or a once-great nation, you have a picture of what the apostle was attempting to describe for us.

John said that judgment has come because of the Babylonian system. The Antichrist system has polluted the world with its sins of fornication and idolatry. Interestingly, John told us, "The kings of the earth have committed fornication with her, and the merchants of the earth are waxed rich through the abundance of her delicacies" (18:3 KJV).

All of this means that the religious, political, and financial systems have been colluding against God. The Beast's system intoxicated the world with riches and pleasures. It catered to those who were "lovers of pleasure rather than lovers of God" (2 Timothy 3:4). There is a serious word of warning here for us. How easy it is to become enamored with and fascinated by the things the sinful world offers. We know better, but how easily we are sucked into worldly ways. "All the nations have drunk of the wine of the passion of her immorality," John said in Revelation 18:3. Indeed, nowadays, we joke about someone who naively follows a shady political or spiritual leader. "They drank the Kool-Aid," we say, harkening back to the 1978 tragedy of the People's Temple and Jim Jones, when the people drank poisoned Kool-Aid and died at the behest of their demented spiritual leader.

In a very real way, the world will drink the Kool-Aid of the Antichrist's system and naively follow the Beast—for a while. But those of us who follow the Lamb know better. Worldly pleasures will never satisfy your soul, no matter how much money you have or what all it can buy for you. The Bible repeatedly warns us about the love of money and pleasures and possessions:

> But they that will be rich fall into temptation and a snare, and into many foolish and hurtful lusts, which drown men in destruction and perdition. For the love of money is the root of all evil: which while some coveted after, they have erred from the faith, and pierced themselves through with many sorrows. (1 Timothy 6:9–10, KJV)

Does God want us to be blessed to have nice things? I believe God desires to bless us with abundant life, wonderful possessions He has created, and marvelous experiences. Many of the heroes in the Bible were well off compared to their contemporaries, but if we think that is what our lives are meant to be, we are sadly mistaken. We are followers of Jesus Christ, and He did not even have a pillow on which to lay His head during His earthly ministry. Nor is having fun the most important priority when you are in the midst of a war, which we are! A spiritual battle rages with life, death, and eternity in heaven or hell in the balance, not just for us, but for everyone.

Come Out, My People

John reported that the first angel had barely begun describing the fall of Mystery Babylon when another voice from heaven summoned God's people out of Babylon: "Come out of her, my people, so that you will not participate in her sins and receive of her plagues" (Revelation 18:4). Throughout history, God has called true believers in Him to be separate from the systems of the world. Indeed, everything holy—and there is nothing in heaven that is not holy—has an element of separation about it, set apart from sin and from the world and set apart to God for His service and glory. This sort of separation has often been confused with legalism, aberrant behaviors or doctrines, but, in truth, being holy, separated to God, does not mean we are weird.

After all these years, Christians still don't seem to get that part of the story. God wants a people like Himself; we want to be people like the world. Thus the contradiction and the conflict with God if we don't bring our lives into conformity with His Word and His will for us. We want to be accepted and liked by the world more than we want to please God. That is a very dangerous position at any time in history, but particularly as we move into the end times. Keep in mind, Jesus said, "If they persecuted Me, they will also persecute you" (John 15:20).

This is God's final appeal to Christians to flee the harlot. Throughout the New Testament, Jesus and Paul both warned of false gospels and false christs and the dangers of interacting with them. Interestingly, in Luke, Jesus said "make friends for yourselves by means of the wealth of unrighteousness" (18:9). How could Jesus say to make friends of money when He constantly warned about the dangers of money? I believe He was instructing us to take care of those who need help, whether it be money, food, shelter, or other needs.

You must be ready for whatever is coming, not just for yourself, but for your family, your friends, and your neighbors, whether they know Jesus or not. It is the primary ministry of the church to reach out to hurting, hungry, underprivileged, and lost people. Perhaps this final call, "Come out of her, my people" is a notice to the church that the time of preparation is over. Now, the mission to take care of others and to spread the good news has entered its final phase.

Sadly, many churches have allowed their love for other things to take the place of God, and they are overlooking the true reasons why they exist. This final call to come out is so these churches, too, will turn away from their obsessions and return to God. He is calling for His people to come out of the world's systems before it is too late.

John gave us two reasons in Revelation 18 why God is calling His people out of Babylon, separating themselves from Satan's diabolical system. One, so they can avoid the pollution of their souls and avoid further participation in the sins of the world. Second, they must come out of Babylon so they will be spared the horrendous, terrible plagues that will soon fall upon Babylon. These plagues will bring famine, mourning, death, and fire (18:8). God is going to judge Babylon's sins that have been piled high (v. 5) and give them double the trouble they gave to His people (v. 6). The Antichrist's crowd is going to be on the receiving end of God's wrath, and you know what they say about payback.

THE LOVE OF MONEY ALWAYS LEADS TO A FALL

For what specific sins is God going to pay back Babylon? First, the world is guilty of the idolatry perpetrated by the Antichrist system. Second, Babylon is condemned for its pride. "She glorified herself" (Revelation 18:7). Babylon sees itself as a royal ruler who could never be dethroned. Beyond that, Babylon worshipped pleasure and luxury, usually at the expense of other people (v. 7).

The Antichrist system encourages people to satisfy their senses, live luxuriously, obsess over pleasure and possessions, and surrender to materialism and money. Do you know anyone like that? First John 2:15–17 warns us:

> Do not love the world nor the things in the world. If anyone loves the world, the love of the Father is not in him. For all that is in the world, the lust of the flesh and the lust of the eyes and the boastful pride of life, is not from the Father, but is from the world. The world is passing away, and also its lusts; but the one who does the will of God lives forever.

So how are we to live in this world? We must be wise. We must come out of the world and get the world out of us. We are called to love the people of this world, to minister to them, and to point them to Jesus. But we must be careful about getting too involved in secular practices and lifestyles. We are to be in the world, not of the world, yet minister to the world. Certainly, you should have good relationships with nonbelievers. How will they ever hear about Jesus if nobody tells them? Sometimes the best witness is a lifestyle that points irrevocably and consistently to Christ. But if most of your closest, long-term friendships are with non-Christians, you either need to get some new friends or brush up on your witnessing techniques.

Devastated in One Day

In Revelation 18:8 John's vision takes a frightening and fascinating turn. He recorded that "in one day" God's judgments are going to suddenly come. In one day, the Antichrist's entire political and economic system will collapse, burn to the ground, and be wholly consumed.

It's not all that difficult to see how quickly the world can change in one day. The day can start out so beautiful and in a moment suddenly become a nightmare. The blue sky was crystal clear above New York City and Washington, DC, on the morning of September 11, 2001. That changed abruptly, and black smoke filled the sky within minutes of the planes striking the World Trade Center and the Pentagon. The World Trade Center was a longtime symbol of commerce and materialism, but within minutes the Twin Towers collapsed to the ground. I believe 9/11 was a warning, and unless the United States turns from sin, something like 9/11 is going to happen again, only worse.

For those who have suffered greatly because of Babylon—and no doubt that is a large number—John reminded us that God remembers the iniquities of the oppressor (18:5) and will judge Babylon accordingly (v. 8).

In Revelation 18:9 the scene suddenly moves from heaven to earth. After we have seen how heaven regards the fall of Babylon, we are shown the same events on a human screen. The difference in perspective is staggering. John said that the "kings of the earth . . . will weep and lament over her when they see the smoke of her burning, standing at a distance because of the fear of her torment, saying, 'Woe, woe, the great city, Babylon, the strong city! For in one hour your judgment has come'" (18:9–10). Their lament is joined by the merchants (18:11–16) and the ship makers and the people who make their living by the sea (18:17–19). People around the world will weep. They will all mourn as they see Babylon going up in smoke and all its wealth and prosperity destroyed in one day! Politicians, businessmen, and laborers will see the vast destruction and mourn. They will "weep and lament" (18:9), not merely with whimpering and sobbing, but with loud lamentations, bawling over Babylon.

Here is the amazing aspect: all this mourning is not for Babylon. The people do not weep for Babylon; they are weeping and mourning for themselves! They are filled with nothing short of naked self-interest. The stock market has crashed. The merchants and tradesmen are devastated because of their loss of income. Their god was killed, destroyed! The startling ruin of the scarlet woman will unnerve the business community as it sees all its dreams go up in smoke. Everything they have toiled for over their lives will be gone, almost instantly. They lament the doom of the Antichrist's commercial system. Similarly, the seamen are crying because they have lost their favorite port. John said they won't even go back to the city. I believe this could be the result of nuclear fallout.

John gave us a long list of commodities bought and sold in Mystery Babylon: gold, silver, precious stones, costly garments, and chariots. The Greek word indicates these chariots have four wheels. I believe John saw Mystery Babylon in our modern times and did not know the word *automobile*, hence he used the Greek word for a "four-wheeled chariot." All of these things were readily available in Babylon, but now they are suddenly gone.

This description reminds me of New York City. Those who insist that Babylon represents the Roman Catholic Church and its influence, I believe, are off track. The entire world will not grieve over the loss of the Roman Catholic Church, but shake the world's money systems and materialistic way of life, and people will cry like never before. New York City is the center of multiple industries: fashion, diamonds and other precious stones, exotic foods, sensuous perfumes, media centers, theater, and music. The Big Apple also is the seat of the world monetary system. New York City is the nexus of the world—the ultimate center of the Antichrist system.

John relayed the message describing the total destruction of this bastion of worldly pleasure. While it is still known for its bright lights, music, art, merchandising, and bustling traffic, all commerce and entertainment will suddenly cease, similar to the way it did on 9/11. In lightning-fast manner, God will avenge the blood of His apostles, prophets, and saints, many of whom were persecuted by the harlot and the Antichrist.

Along with all the goodies and treats that will suddenly go away, John gave us another shocking revelation. Included alongside the many commodities of life that will be destroyed, John listed "slaves and human lives" (18:13). Slavery was rampant in Rome, and Babylon was a hotbed of prostitution (as are New York and other cities today). Certainly human trafficking has become rampant in America and around the world. But John may also have been implying that people living under the domination of the Beast have been living in slavery as well. People in many parts of the Middle East live in a type of slavery, enslaved by their rulers' power and lust for money. Other people in the United States are enslaved by debt or their own egos. Regardless, the Antichrist system's control over the bodies and souls of other human beings will come to an abrupt end on that day.

Rejoice over This?

In Revelation 18:20 a strange command follows: the people in heaven are instructed to rejoice over Mystery Babylon's destruction. That seems unusually harsh to some people. How can we possibly rejoice over such horrible events? What is the meaning of this?

This is about the holy, righteous justice of God. Remember, this is payback time. It is not the eternal punishment for sin that will be meted out at the last judgment, but it is definitely part of the earthly destruction that inevitably follows sin. That's why it is important to look at these events from God's perspective, not ours. The people in heaven are commanded to rejoice over God's justice finally being poured out. Keep in mind how patient, merciful, and longsuffering God has been with these people who have continually mocked Him and disregarded His Son. He could have snuffed them out at any point, but He allowed them time to repent, "not wishing for any to perish but for all to come to repentance" (2 Peter 3:9). These people who aligned themselves with the Antichrist system have had their last chance, and they will now get what they deserve.

Certainly, God's judgment on anybody should break our hearts. We must always remember, as the English reformer John Bradford said, "There, but for the grace of God, go I." Nor would I ever speak of these things without a tearful attitude, that some soul is going to be lost for eternity because of his or her stubborn rejection of God's gracious offer of salvation.

This punishment meted out here is not about personal revenge or getting even with someone. Far from it, the Lord says, "Vengeance is Mine, I will repay" (Romans 12:19; Deuteronomy 32:35; Psalm 94:1; 1 Thessalonians 4:6; Hebrews 10:30). We are simply to rejoice that justice is done.

John showed us the total obliteration of Babylon and the Beast's system in Revelation 18:21–24. The Beast himself will be punished in the chapters ahead, as will the False Prophet and Satan, but here it is all about the destruction of Babylon. An angel with a huge boulder like a millstone hurls it into the sea. It plunges to the bottom never to be seen again. The implication is that, in the same way, Babylon is going to be completely buried.

I believe Mystery Babylon could be New York City. There is no other city like it. If New York City were to be destroyed, the world economy would be wiped out. I am convinced that this will happen either by an asteroid or a nuclear bomb. The bomb is perhaps the one human invention that could so quickly lay waste to a city of such magnitude. It's possible that terrorists could set off this bomb, and I believe these terrorists with bombs are already in the United States and waiting for the right moment to strike.

John spoke of the city burned by fire (18:8), that many will stay far away from in fear as it is destroyed (18:10, 15), and they will never return to it anymore (vv. 21–23). Why would they stay so far away and not return?

In 1986 a meltdown of a nuclear reactor resulted in the complete evacuation of the Soviet city of Chernobyl. Today, radiation levels around that city remain at lethal levels, preventing anyone from living there. Those who monitor the radiation must wear protective clothing. I believe New York City will experience a similar level of radiation, whether it is the result of a nuclear explosion or an asteroid strike.

Gone in One Hour

On September 11, 2001, terrorists succeeded in bringing down the Twin Towers of the World Trade Center, the symbol of the world economic system. From the moment the first plane crashed into the first tower to the collapse of the last tower, one hour passed. When they fell, the amount of debris was not enough to account for half of one of the two towers. The buildings were practically vaporized as they fell. New York City may see a similar fate on a much larger scale. If this is the case, there won't be anything to go back to.

This event could be a natural occurrence, such as a meteor or asteroid strike. Scientists postulate that if a relatively small meteor or asteroid were to hit near the New Madrid fault line that lies beneath at least five states in middle America, the repercussions of the impact could cause all the fault lines on earth to suddenly shift, producing unprecedented devastation in densely populated areas of the United States as well as in other countries. Jesus said that one of the signs of His return would be earthquakes in many places (Matthew 24:7). Can you imagine hundreds of massive earthquakes all over the world going on at one time? While moving to less congested parts of the nation will not immunize anyone from the ripple effect brought on by the destruction of the pervasive Babylon system, it might provide a better opportunity to survive when the buildings and the powerbrokers begin to topple.

Deafening Silence

All of this was followed by the awful sounds of silence. "No more" is the theme. Babylon will not be seen anymore, nor will the many elements that made it great in the world's estimation. Interestingly, in the Old Testament, when the prophet Jeremiah warned Israel about the impending destruction of the nation at the hand of the Babylonians, he used the same sort of language (Jeremiah 25:8–10). Now, judgment has come to Babylon, the Antichrist's system. All luxuries and even some of life's basic necessities will be gone.

Two reasons are given for this. Babylon's sorcery and magic spells led the people of all nations astray. John used the term "sorcery" to describe the insidious influence of the system's "great men." The word derives from *pharmakeia,* which may imply drugs, poisons, or magic spells. I am convinced that the powerbrokers of Wall Street who control the world's economic systems, and who have worked their magic spells on society for a very long time, will suddenly come to nothing.

Second, to avenge the blood of the saints, the prophets, and the true believers killed as a result of the Antichrist's actions and opposition to God, judgment is now unleashed on Babylon. The Antichrist's spirit of greed, power, and corruption caused the death of the prophets and saints. God never takes martyrdom lightly. While it may seem that millions of people have been martyred in recent centuries, God takes each murder of His witnesses personally. He will avenge the blood of all those who ever died because of their witness. When you see a sinner prospering, and you wonder why God is letting that person get away with it, always remember, the final judgment is yet to come.

At this point, the Beast's religious, political, and economic systems have been destroyed in one hour, similar to what happened in New York on 9/11 on a similar scale. All that remains is for Jesus to return from heaven and personally meet, greet, and defeat the Beast and his armies. Then He will establish His righteous kingdom on earth.

You are going to be a part of His kingdom!

22

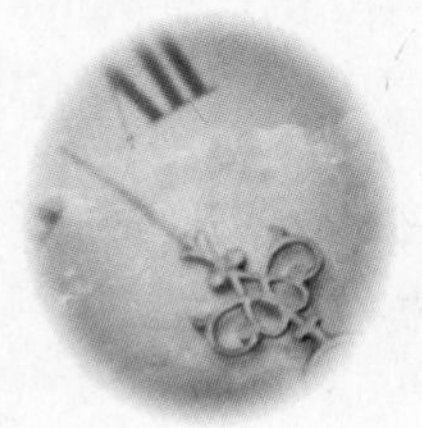

We're Going to a Wedding

John's spirit soared when he saw an outbreak of spontaneous rejoicing in heaven at the destruction of Mystery Babylon, the harlot. The power of the Antichrist system was totally dismantled. Watching in awe, John saw the conquering Christ defeat the hostile powers assembled against Him. In his vision, John also saw the False Prophet and the Beast thrown into the lake of fire, and he wondered aloud, "Lord, what about the Dragon?"

John felt the answer in his spirit.

"Soon."

The old saying "It's all over but the shouting" sums up the beginning of Revelation 19. John's vision was not quite over, but he was about to experience the most thunderous shouting ever heard as the celebration in heaven began. John was awestruck by the rejoicing in heaven after the destruction of Babylon. Multitudes of angels and martyrs joined in a mighty shout of "Hallelujah!"—"Praise the Lord!" They praised God for His marvelous plan of salvation, His glory, His power, and His judgments—especially His judgment on the great harlot (19:2).

The twenty-four elders and the four living creatures join in and applaud the justice of God. About that time, a voice is heard from the throne, commanding the great and the small to give praise to God. So a mighty shout of the redeemed goes up in heaven, and the sound like many waters and peals of thunder says, "Hallelujah! For the Lord our God, the Almighty, reigns. Let us rejoice and be glad and give the glory to Him, for the marriage of the Lamb has come and His bride has made herself ready" (19:6–7).

John used an interesting compound Greek word here to describe God. He referred to Him as *the Lord our God, the Almighty*, which means "the one who controls all things." This phrase is used only ten times in the New Testament, and nine of these are in Revelation. It means "He reigns!" In spite of the Dragon, the Beast, the False Prophet, and all the persecutions that God's people endured at the hands of the Antichrist's crowd, God is still the one in control. No wonder the population of heaven cannot seem to contain themselves. Hallelujah, the Lord God Almighty reigns!

THE WEDDING YOU DON'T WANT TO MISS!

John saw and heard the announcement of the marriage supper of the Lamb, the full and final uniting of Christ and His church. The relationship of God and His people throughout the Bible is often portrayed as a marriage (see Hosea 2:19–20; Isaiah 54:5–7; Jeremiah 3:14). In the New Testament, the bride, of course, is the church, the universal group of believers from every nation, every denomination, every century.

I think that is why God is so interested in the marriage relationship, because it is meant to be a symbol of our relationship with Him. The relationship between a husband and a wife is intended to be characterized by love, intimate communion, the sheer joy of loving and being loved unconditionally, and fidelity and faithfulness between the partners. These same qualities should describe our relationship to Christ as well, only on a much deeper level.

There are all sorts of theories regarding when this wedding will occur and how long the celebration will go on. Some think it will begin at the Rapture and carry on for a thousand years. Others think it may begin after that. All of these theories are guesses, because the Bible does not tell us the time of the wedding. Instead, it tells us who is involved! The Bridegroom at this celebration is Jesus. The bride is the church, individual believers, clothed in fine white linen, bright and clean, symbolizing the righteous acts of the saints (Revelation 19:7–8).

An angel instructed John, "Write, 'Blessed are those who are invited to the marriage supper of the Lamb'" (19:9). Whether this marriage supper is real or figurative, don't miss the point. An invitation is involved, and anyone who refuses or ignores this most important invitation will be excluded from the celebration—forever.

Overwhelmed by this marvelous wedding, John fell down at the feet of the angel to worship him, but the angel redirected John's worship, saying, "Do not do that; I am a fellow servant of yours and your brethren who hold the testimony of Jesus; worship God. For the testimony of Jesus is the spirit of prophecy" (19:10). As powerful and as magnificent as they may be, we are not to worship angels, but always to center our attention on Jesus and God. We don't worship angels, relics, or icons. We worship almighty God.

King of Kings, Lord of Lords

John saw one of the most dramatic scenes in the entire book of Revelation. He wrote about seeing Jesus again; only this time, Jesus is the conquering king, the warrior king, a royal commander, with a dazzling army behind Him. He is seated on a white horse—a far cry from the donkey on which He rode into Jerusalem on Palm Sunday. Roman generals rode white horses when they celebrated a great victory, and John's readers, no doubt, understood the implications.

He who sat upon the white horse is known as "Faithful and True." By *faithful,* John meant that He is absolutely trustworthy, He can be relied on; you can stake your life on Him. By *true*, John meant not only that He never lies, but that He is real, genuine, not a counterfeit Christ; He is the standard by which all else will be measured.

The Lord judges and makes war in righteousness, not like a capricious tyrant picking a fight out of selfish ambition or misguided motives. The King on the white horse only attacks to make things right.

John went on to describe the King (19:12–13). His eyes are a flame of fire, which stands for the consuming power of Jesus. He has many crowns on His head, and here the word for "crowns" is not *stephanos,* the crown given to one who wins a race, but *diadema,* the royal crown. Many monarchs wore more than one crown to show they were king of more than one area. Jesus wears many diadems to show that He is Lord of all.

He has a name written on Him that nobody knows, possibly "Lord" or "Yahweh," from the consonants YHWH for the name of God in Hebrew. We don't know what this name is, but one day we will.

Jesus also wears a robe dipped in blood. Some say this is not His blood but that of His enemies. Others see it as a reminder of His atonement for our sins, paid for with His own blood.

The King on the white horse is called "The Word of God" (19:13). This would remind John's readers of the opening to his gospel, "In the beginning was the Word, and the Word was with God, and the Word was God" (John 1:1). In Hebrew thought, words had power and energy for good or evil. That's why a father's blessing on a son was so important, because there was power in those words. We know, too, that by His Word, God created heaven and earth and everything in them. Here, the implication is that everything God is and has ever said is summed up in Jesus Christ.

This King leads an unusual army: "And the armies which are in heaven, clothed in fine linen, white and clean, were following Him on white horses" (Revelation 19:14). Whether these are angels or Christian saints in heaven, we don't know, but the sight of this formidable force must have astounded John. When he next looked and saw Jesus, he probably shook in his shoes (19:15–16). In that moment, every knee will bow to acknowledge the fact that the Child born in Bethlehem is the Master of the universe and Lord of all!

A KEY BATTLE

John did not attempt to give us a play-by-play description of the ensuing battle. Possibly, the sharp sword in Jesus' mouth implies that the battle will be won with just a word from the King of kings. Regardless of how it happens, John told us what is going to happen to the enemies of Jesus, and it is not a pretty sight.

An angel standing in the sun calls out for the birds to come together for a great feast. This is going to be a banquet of a different kind. The angel calls these birds together to eat the bodies of the kings and generals and famous people, their horses and riders, people small and great. Anybody who supported the Dragon and his cause will be fodder for this meal of the defeated foe.

John saw the Beast and the kings of the earth gathered together to make war against the rider on the white horse—King Jesus—and His army (Revelation 19:17–21). Some scholars believe this battle may be the same combat the prophet Ezekiel described centuries earlier, when the prophet predicted the forces from north of Israel would strike southward to take a spoil (Ezekiel 39:17–20). The countries north of Israel today are almost entirely Muslim, and then there is Russia, the bear looming over the region. Others see the attack described by Ezekiel, the Battle of Armageddon, and this climactic battle as three separate battles. We don't know for sure when these things will happen, but we can be sure they will occur in God's perfect timing.

We also know in advance the outcome of this final battle. The Beast and the False Prophet will be captured and "thrown alive into the lake of fire which burns with brimstone" (Revelation 19:20). But their armies, gathered together from all the earth, will be slaughtered on the battlefield. The birds called together by the angel will be waiting for them, to pick their bones clean, devouring the bodies of the dead armies until they are satisfied (19:21).

What's next on our King's agenda? Dealing with the Dragon and giving him what he deserves.

23

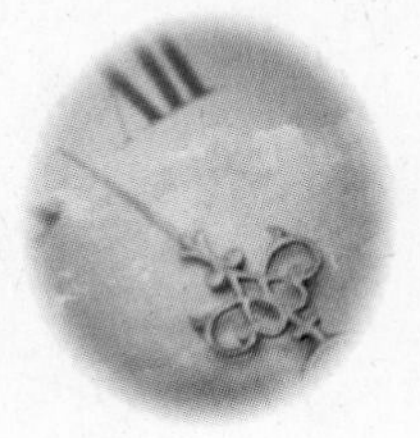

The Millennium at Last

John breathed a sigh of relief as he watched the Antichrist and the False Prophet being dumped unceremoniously into the sulfurous lake of fire. *Two beasts down, one dragon to go,* he thought. From the beginning, John knew that the Enemy was no match for Jesus. But seeing it all play out before his eyes both inspired and humbled John. What a privilege it was to know these things in advance. What blessed hope and assurance it brought to his heart to know that his faith in Jesus was not unfounded, that everything Jesus ever said He would do, He will do!

About that time, John saw another angel coming down from heaven, and this angel held the key to the abyss—"the bottomless pit"—and a great chain in his hand, with which he ties up another loose end. In case you have any doubt about to whom John was referring, he said specifically that the angel laid hold of "the dragon, the serpent of old, who is the devil and Satan" (Revelation 20:2). The angel bound Satan and threw him into the abyss for a thousand years so he could not deceive the nations any longer—at least not for a thousand years. The angel locked the abyss tightly, sealing it over Satan. Of course, this shutting up of Satan has been hotly debated ever since John wrote about it.

The Millennium

The first seven verses of Revelation 20 form the foundation for all the talk and teaching about the Millennium, a period of a thousand years before the end of the world as we know it, when Christ will reign on earth in a kingdom populated by His saints. This is the only passage in the Bible where the millennium is mentioned, although some scholars see a Millennium type of kingdom described in Daniel's prophecy (Daniel 2:44; 7:14, 27), in which the kingdom is said to be eternal and will never end. To say there has been a bit of disagreement over these passages is an understatement. Some Christians believe Jesus will come before the Millennium, some believe He will return after the Millennium, while others believe we are already in the Millennium. Confused? Don't feel bad. You are not alone.

Just about the time you think you have it figured out, someone will remind you of scriptures such as Psalm 90:4 ("For a thousand years in Your sight / Are like yesterday when it passes by, / Or as a watch in the night") or 2 Peter 3:8 ("With the Lord one day is like a thousand years, and a thousand years like one day"). Other scriptures tell us that God owns the cattle on a thousand hills, which is obviously meant to describe the all-inclusiveness of His domain rather than a thousand hills dotted with cattle. So did John intend for us to interpret this thousand years literally or symbolically? We don't know. And devout Christians disagree.

In the early church, from around AD 100 to the late 300s, the church fathers tended to take the idea of Christ's one-thousand-year rule quite literally. Then around AD 400, three centuries after John recorded his vision of the end times, some Christians began to look at the millennial reign as figurative and symbolic rather than literal.

One of the things that caused confusion was that some Christians taught that during the Millennium, God would reward believers with luxurious pleasures as well as with special rewards, including all sorts of gastronomical delights and even sexual pleasures. Does that sound familiar to you? If you are thinking that Islam offers these outlandish incentives for people who die while fighting for Allah, you are on the right track.

Not surprisingly, some of the early Christian leaders, men such as Origen and Augustine, concluded that the Millennium was a spiritual existence. Because they were highly respected Christian leaders, their opinions carried a great deal of weight, and the pendulum swung away from a literal interpretation of the Millennium kingdom.

Today, in some Christian circles, the thousand years is regarded as literal, while others view it as symbolic. It is still a matter of debate. Many who write and speak about the Millennium get their messages from each other.

We know that John mentioned the Millennium five times within a single paragraph, so it must be significant. But rather than focusing on conjecture—because that is what all these opinions about the Millennium are—let's look at what the Bible says and what we know.

Who Are These People?

John told us of "the first resurrection" (Revelation 20:4–5), a group of believers who died for their faith and are now rewarded. Obviously, not everybody—not even all the Christians who have died—will be included in this first resurrection. This is not a universal resurrection of Christians everywhere and from every generation. It is a resurrection and reward for two special groups of believers. The first are those who were martyred for their faith and loyalty to Christ. They were beheaded as a result of their faithfulness. Until a few years ago, we might have said, "That could never happen today." Sadly, we know better now. Several high-profile opponents of Islam have been publicly beheaded in recent years while the world watched and did nothing.

Will all of these saints who are rewarded have been beheaded? Possibly, but hopefully not. Perhaps this was John's way of emphasizing the violent way these Christians died as a result of their uncompromising faith. But don't rule out the possibility that these may, indeed, be literal beheadings rather than symbolic.

Also included in this resurrection will be those who refused to cave in to the Antichrist. They refused to worship the Beast or his image or to take the mark of the Beast. Obviously, there will be believers who resist the Antichrist, and these people will come alive again and reign with Jesus for one thousand years.

In some way these great Christians will have the privilege and responsibility of sitting in judgment, having some ruling authority during the Millennium (20:4), thus fulfilling prophecies and promises to that effect. Jesus told His disciples that when He returns they would sit on twelve thrones, judging the twelve tribes of Israel (Matthew 19:28; Luke 22:28–30). The apostle Paul encouraged the Christians at Corinth that part of their destiny is to judge the world (1 Corinthians 6:2). In Revelation 2:26, saints who overcome are said to have authority over the nations.

The idea here is that, for ages, the world has been turned upside down by sin, and finally things are being turned right side up. During their lifetimes many Christians are mocked, persecuted, and judged by nonbelievers. But in the world to come, many of those who thought they were the judges will find themselves being judged.

Loyal Christians will receive a tremendous honor. For one thing, they are assured that for these blessed and holy ones the "second death has no power" (20:6). Obviously, these people had already died, but this is not some strange vampire movie. These saints share in Christ's triumph over death. Even though some of them gave their lives on earth for Christ, they will not only live forever with Jesus in heaven, but they are rewarded here. They have no fear of hell, that is, the second death.

Moreover, part of their reward for their faithfulness will be that they will get to serve God and Christ as priests for a thousand years. The word John used here for "priest" actually means "bridge builder."[31] As priests, these saints have the opportunity to be especially close to God and Jesus for a thousand years, and they have the privilege of bringing others to Jesus. Of course, we have those two opportunities right now, to freely enter God's presence and to bring others to Jesus. But these martyrs and persecuted Christians who refused to compromise their faith in Christ will also receive a special reward: they will get to reign with Jesus for a thousand years.

What will that be like? Perhaps their reign will be as the prophet Isaiah described:

> And the wolf will dwell with the lamb,
> And the leopard will lie down with the young goat,
> And the calf and the young lion and the fatling together;
> And a little boy will lead them.
> Also the cow and the bear will graze,
> Their young will lie down together,
> And the lion will eat straw like the ox.
> The nursing child will play by the hole of the cobra,
> And the weaned child will put his hand on the viper's den.
> They will not hurt or destroy in all My holy mountain,
> For the earth will be full of the knowledge of the Lord
> As the waters cover the sea. (Isaiah 11:6–9)

Satan Released

Like a bad "B" movie, after a thousand years of bliss, Satan will be released from the abyss for a short period of time (Revelation 20:3, 7). Some believe this will be the final test for those living during the Millennium. Will the people born during the thousand years choose to follow God or Satan? With no evil to speak of during the Millennium, how will they know if they have chosen to live with Jesus? Although the Bible doesn't say, it is probably safe to assume the Millennium will be peaceful and calm, with the Antichrist and the False Prophet in the lake of fire and the devil in the abyss. With Jesus ruling the saints, life on earth should be good—perhaps almost like the Garden of Eden. Just as there was forbidden fruit in Eden, to give Adam and Eve a choice whether they would trust and obey God or their own desires, we may see something similar during the Millennium.

For whatever reason, apparently some of the Millennium people will choose to align themselves with Satan! So what does he do? Immediately upon his release, Satan foments another rebellion against God. He goes to the four corners of the earth to gather a huge army for a last war. Notice the similarities in verses 7–9 to what we've already described as the Battle of Armageddon.

Some Christians believe this battle will take place during the Tribulation, and that it may be the same battle described in Ezekiel 38–39 where Gog, the leader of the northern land of Magog, attacks Israel while they are dwelling in peace and prosperity. Some Bible scholars believe this may be Russia or possibly a group of Islamic allies moving into the Middle East.

Although we don't know much about this confrontation, we know who is victorious. The Messiah does not have to destroy the marauders with the sword of His mouth, as He did in Revelation 19:21. Instead, just as in Ezekiel 38:22, when the attackers surround Jerusalem, the "beloved city," fire comes down from heaven and consumes this demonic crowd in a single blast.

The devil gets his due. He is thrown into the lake of fire, just as Jesus predicted he would be (Matthew 25:41), where the Antichrist and the False Prophet are already stewing. Until now, except for the Millennium, Satan has been running free over the earth; he has had relatively easy access as the prince of the air, wreaking havoc in lives down through the ages. Satan, the deceiver, duped the Roman emperors and their subjects, as well as the kings and leaders of nations all over the world, deceiving billions of people. But not anymore.

Now they are gone—the Dragon, the Antichrist, the False Prophet, and the harlot and all who bought into their anti-God system, all who took the mark 666. All are gone. It is over. Except for death and Hades, we have seen the last of Satan's evil influence in the world. He is not the ruler of earth; he is not even the ruler of hell. He is merely another inmate. It may sound trite, but it is still good advice: when the devil reminds you about your past, remind him about his future. "And the devil who deceived them was thrown into the lake of fire and brimstone, where the beast and the false prophet are also; and they will be tormented day and night forever and ever" (Revelation 20:10). That is Satan's future and final destination.

The Final Judgment

Now comes the final judgment. John saw God seated on a great white throne. The very face of God causes all of creation to flee in terror (Revelation 20:11). Unbelievers are going to try to stand in their own righteousness before God to no avail. Imagine what is going to go through the minds of those who knew of Jesus, who saw Him grow up and die on Calvary, who heard of His resurrection or possibly saw Him alive after the Resurrection, yet they rejected His offer of salvation. What a horrifying moment that will be for them. There will be no hiding places. God sees where others fail to see. We can fool each other, but nobody fools God.

John told us that he saw both the great and the small standing before the throne of judgment (20:12). Our status in this life will not matter a bit when we stand before Almighty God in judgment. You may be rich or poor, famous or obscure; you may be a homeless alcoholic or a recent resident of the White House. On Judgment Day, the only thing that will matter is whether your name is written in the Book of Life. Otherwise, the judgment seat of God will be the great leveler.

John saw "books were opened; and another book was opened, which is the book of life; and the dead were judged from the things which were written in the books, according to their deeds" (20:12). These books will contain every thought, word, deed, and motive of every person who has not trusted Jesus as Savior.

It seems there will be degrees of punishment for sinners, based on the fact that their deeds are considered in their judgment. They will be judged from these books on the basis of three issues: (1) how they responded to the Word of God (John 12:48), which of course implies how they responded to Jesus Himself; (2) by their own words (Matthew 12:36–37); and (3) their works.

Death and Hades, the nether region, will be thrown into the lake of fire as well. John reminded us, "This is the second death, the lake of fire" (Revelation 20:14). Then comes one of the most terrifying and sobering thoughts in all the Bible: "If anyone's name was not found written in the book of life, he was thrown into the lake of fire" (v. 15).

Is hell a literal fire? I don't know—and I don't want to find out. I know that hell is real, and those who disregard hell are usually among the first to discard the cross of Jesus Christ and its implications.

On the other hand, the Book of Life is similar to a divine register. In ancient times, kings had a registry, a roll book, containing the names of all their subjects in good standing. The names in the Book of Life are the future citizens of heaven!

The most important question you can ever ask is, How can I get my name in the Book of Life? The only way to get your name in the Book of Life is to trust your life to Jesus Christ, accepting Him as your Savior, asking Him to forgive your sins and to save you. Otherwise, you can be certain that your future will not be bright. In fact, it will be total darkness, separated from God, isolated, alone, forever—with no second chances.

The Lord is coming soon to take us to where He is. Now that we have seen the worst that can happen, let's explore the best that not only can happen but will happen. It is time to go to heaven!

24

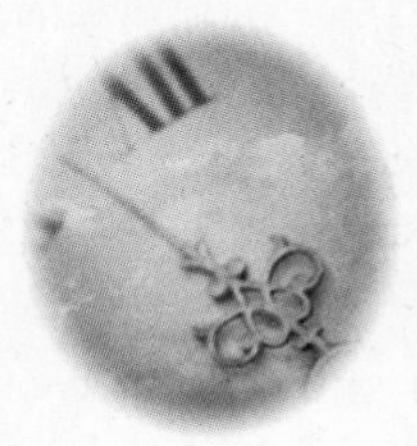

I'm Looking Forward to Heaven

"You're so heavenly minded you're no earthly good," was once a criticism of Christians. You don't hear that much nowadays. In fact, most Christians know little about heaven and have never heard a sermon about heaven. It is difficult to find a class on the subject even in most seminaries. Yet there remains a fascination in all of us about what heaven is really like.

In Revelation 21, the apostle John saw visions of the new heaven and the new earth; the first heaven and earth had disappeared after the tumultuous events of the first twenty chapters of Revelation. Some scholars say that everything John saw must be completely new because of the horrendous destruction foretold in 2 Peter 3:10, in which the earth is burned up. But the word for "new" that John used could also mean "new in character," not necessarily new in the sense that it had never existed before. It may be that God restores the earth to what it was originally in Genesis 1. That would truly be heaven on earth!

John observed that there were no longer any seas. That strikes us as odd, especially those of us who love the ocean, but in John's day, the sea was not considered a friendly place of recreation. Far from it, the sea was an enemy to be feared. The sea meant danger, storms, and separation. Even though fishermen traveled the seas, most of them feared doing so. There were no compasses in John's time. They were reluctant to launch out into the deep, so they steered their crafts as closely to shore as was safely possible.

John himself was writing from an island, living in isolation, cut off by the sea from everyone he knew. Imagine how it must have thrilled him when he saw no sea in the new heaven and earth.

THE NEW JERUSALEM

John saw the holy city, the New Jerusalem, coming down out of heaven. Like a bride beautifully adorned for her husband, it is a beautiful city, prepared by God for His people. At the time John was writing this, Jerusalem had been utterly destroyed. Moreover, Revelation 11:8 compares the city to Sodom and indicates that it will be decimated again. But John reported that God is going to make all things new, including the beautiful city of the faithful.

In heaven, we will praise and worship the Lord as never before. We will serve Him in new ways. Billy Graham believes that we will probably have meaningful work to do in heaven, something that satisfies us and pleases God. But the best part is that our heavenly Father will be with us. He will truly be Immanuel, that is, God with us (Isaiah 7:14; Matthew 1:23). John recorded:

> And I heard a loud voice from the throne, saying, "Behold, the tabernacle of God is among men, and He will dwell among them, and they shall be His people, and God Himself will be among them, and He shall wipe away every tear from their eyes; and there will no longer be any death; there will no longer be any mourning, or crying, or pain; the first things have passed away." (Revelation 21:3–4)

What an incredible message! What an astounding thought! All of our pain will be gone! There will be no more weeping! We will not attend another funeral! This will be one of the greatest moments in the history of mankind—when God wipes away all of our tears! We will be in the very presence of God, and He will be in our midst. The tabernacle, the dwelling place of God, will be among His people. Of course, if you don't enjoy being in God's presence now, that may not excite you a great deal. As the great preacher Billy Sunday used to say, "You can't get into heaven unless some of heaven gets into you first."

Some people think heaven will be boring, so they would rather go to hell. That would be a big mistake. Heaven is going to be incredible!

John then heard a voice from the throne saying, "Behold, I am making all things new" (21:5). Imagine what that new heaven and new earth will be like. Let God remove the blinders from your preconceived notions about heaven being a boring place where you sit around on a cloud, strumming your harp for a zillion years. No, in heaven you will be constantly amazed, continuously encountering new sights, sounds, and sensations that you experienced only in their most rudimentary forms here on earth. Paul said that man cannot imagine the things that He has prepared for those who love Him (1 Corinthians 2:9).

John heard the thundering voice from the throne as God commanded him:

> "Write, for these words are faithful and true." Then He said to me, "It is done. I am the Alpha and the Omega, the beginning and the end. I will give to the one who thirsts from the spring of the water of life without cost. He who overcomes will inherit these things, and I will be his God and he will be My son." (Revelation 21:5–7)

John's mind and heart must have been ready to burst with joy. "It is done!" The long journey is over. We are home at last. How it must have blessed John to be reminded of those words, "I am the Alpha and the Omega," the first and the last, the same words John had heard spoken by Jesus at the beginning of the vision (1:8). God was letting John know that He is the source, the beginning of all things, and the consummation, the ending of all things.

Sadly, not everybody will receive His rewards and be a part of God's forever family. Only those who overcome will inherit these things. We've seen that concept of overcoming throughout John's vision—overcoming the world, overcoming the flesh, overcoming the devil, overcoming because of the blood of the Lamb, the word of their testimony, and they did not love their lives more than Jesus.

What's the reward for those who overcome? Your heavenly Father says, "I will be his God and he will be My son." What a promise! Only a fool or an unbeliever would say, "Is that all?"

This is the same promise made to Abraham (Genesis 17:7), to David (2 Samuel 7:14), and about the Messiah (Psalm 89:27). Now it seems the promise is extended to you and me too!

THE BAD NEWS ABOUT THE GOOD NEWS

Unfortunately, not everybody will overcome. The word from the Lord is clear. The cowardly, not merely those who are afraid, but those who allow their fear to cause them to compromise their faith, will be punished. Those who loved comfort more than Christ, who cared for the acceptance of the crowd more than God, those who valued their own lives on earth above eternal values, and those who did not have the courage to take a stand for Christ will be excluded from the New Jerusalem. So will the unbelieving souls. Those who refused to believe in Jesus Christ and accept His offer of salvation will find themselves outside. Faith in any other god will not get a person into heaven.

The *abominable* (Revelation 21:8), which means "polluted and filthy," those whose values and lifestyles are tainted by the things of the world will be punished as well. In our world, we have the unbiblical idea that we can talk filthy, think filthy thoughts, watch filthy movies, television programs or Internet content, hold on to filthy attitudes, live filthy lifestyles, and still get into heaven. John reminded us that there will be no filth in heaven. Certainly, there will be a lot of formerly filthy sinners who have been washed by the blood of Jesus, but there will be no filthy hearts in God's eternal kingdom.

Murderers—especially those who persecuted and slaughtered Christians during the Tribulation—and fornicators, immoral people who compromised their beliefs in Jesus to satisfy their lusts rather than repent and seek forgiveness, are included in the group that God says will be eternally punished. Sorcerers, too, are included in that group. Those who indulge in witchcraft, wiccan activities, astrology, fortune-telling, and other forms of sorcery will have their place as well. But it is not in heaven.

Idolaters—those who worship idols of any kind, including creation itself, and certainly those who worship the Antichrist or other false gods—and all liars, those who attend church and those who don't, will have their place "in the lake that burns with fire and brimstone, which is the second death" (21:8).

Clearly, this list of people who will be excluded from God's new heaven and new earth includes many of the characteristics of the people who followed the Antichrist and the False Prophet. But make no mistake, we all have some of these traits in our lives, and they are equally damning. If you detect even a hint of these characteristics in yourself, use this time to repent immediately. We've already seen where the Dragon and the Beast and their crowd end up. You do not want to join them.

Your Future Home

John had the privilege of seeing some things that no one else has ever seen (with the possible exception of the apostle Paul):

> Then one of the seven angels who had the seven bowls full of the seven last plagues came and spoke with me, saying, "Come here, I shall show you the bride, the wife of the Lamb." And he carried me away in the Spirit to a great and high mountain, and showed me the holy city, Jerusalem, coming down out of heaven from God. (Revelation 21:9–10)

Ironically, the same angel who showed John the great harlot in 17:1 is now showing him the bride of Christ and all that is prepared for her. The angel gives John a more detailed picture of the New Jerusalem, the city of God. There's much about his description that we may not understand. That's okay. Just enjoy it! If you know Jesus, this is your future home, and it beats a retirement village in Florida anytime!

John saw the holy city coming down out of heaven from God, having the glory of God (21:10). He was impressed by the city's brilliance, like a crystal clear jasper or a diamond. The word John used to describe it is *phoster,* a word normally used to describe the luminance of the sun, the moon, and the stars. But John wrote later (v. 23) that the sun, the moon, and the stars are no longer needed, because Jesus is the light of the city. The city seems to have its own radiance, a reflection of the holiness of God.

The city has high walls and twelve angels guarding twelve gates, three on each side, implying that people would be coming from the four corners of the earth. The walls' foundation stones were inscribed with the names of the twelve apostles, which shows the honoring of both the Old Testament and the New Testament.

This New Jerusalem is huge! It is laid out as a square, which is not unusual since Nineveh and Babylon and other ancient cities were constructed similarly. But this city is a *cube!* The length, breadth, and height are all the same, approximately fifteen hundred miles in each direction, covering a territory as large as three-fourths the area of the United States! If you've ever wondered, Will there be enough room in heaven for everybody? John's answer would be an emphatic, "Yes!"

In the Old Testament, the Holy of Holies inside the temple was also a cube. So John may be saying that the holy city will be a place like the Holy of Holies, where God meets with His people.

You may be surprised that the walls surrounding the city are 216 feet thick, more than two-thirds the size of a football field. John described the walls in detail and noted that each of the gates is made of an enormous pearl and the streets of the city are pure gold, like transparent glass. While this description has been the material for hundreds of songs about heaven, it still defies comprehension!

WHAT IS *NOT* IN HEAVEN

Interestingly, there is no temple in heaven. Why? Because "the Lord God the Almighty and the Lamb are its temple" (Revelation 21:22). Possibly because the entire city of New Jerusalem is laid out as the Holy of Holies, the place where God dwells, there is no longer any need of a temple to symbolize His presence. Our heavenly Father and Jesus, the Lamb of God, will be right there with us!

Nor does the city have any need for the sun or the moon, because the glory of God has illumined it, and the Lamb is the light of that city! (vv. 5, 32). There will be no night in heaven, possibly symbolizing no sin and no need to fear. And the gates will never be closed, because the city will be secured by God, and He will have no enemies. The New Jerusalem will truly be the city that never sleeps! The sacred and secular will be one; there will be no separation of church and state.

It's important to know that nothing unclean will be in heaven, nothing profane or impure (21:27). No one who practices abominations, spiritual pollution; nothing shameful regarding body, mind, or spirit.

No one who practices lying will be in heaven. The Holy Spirit impressed that truth on John several times throughout these visions, so it cannot be ignored. Truth matters to God, and lies of any sort are an abomination to Him. In God's book, there is no such thing as a little white lie or a convenient truth. They are all repulsive, damning lies.

John concluded his description of this portion of heaven by reminding us that the only people in heaven will be those whose names are written in "the Lamb's book of life" (21:27). For those who have been forgiven and cleansed by the blood of the Lamb, heaven is their eternal home.

What does all this have to do with us? John's vision of heaven is a word of hope as well as a word of warning. Only the overcomers receive the reward. So don't give up! We're too close to heaven to turn back now!

25

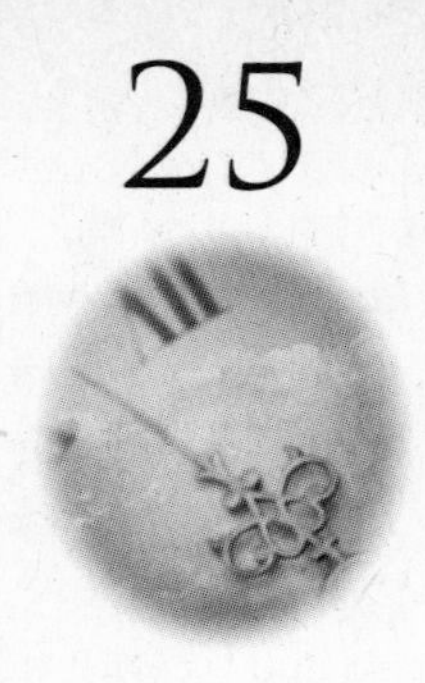

Even So, Lord Jesus, Come!

John's face was radiant, his spirit ebullient as he reviewed the end of the vision in his mind. Despite the difficult circumstances in which he was living, he could barely contain his joy at what God had in store for him in the future. He felt certain in his spirit that he would be released from banishment somehow—after all, he had an important document to deliver to the churches—but even if he didn't escape Patmos, he knew God would take care of him. Yes, his present situation was painful at times, but simply knowing that God was working all things for his good, and that the plan He put in motion back in Genesis was finally coming to its glorious conclusion gave John the boost of energy and spiritual stamina to withstand any pressure. *This, too, will pass,* he said to himself. *But God's Word will last forever.*

Some people have a fascination with a dying person's last words. Something about the final thoughts and phrases a person says leave indelible impressions. In John's vision of Jesus in heaven, the King's final words and John's response to them are enough to motivate us to keep trusting God and to keep living the way the Bible says. Before we get there, though, John had much more to tell us about heaven. In concluding the book of Revelation, he emphasized two main themes: (1) the reliability and truthfulness of the message he received and passed along to us, and (2) the time is short, because Jesus is returning soon. At least five times John mentioned that the Lord is coming quickly, implying, of course, that we need to be ready to meet Him on any day and at a moment's notice. Today, people turn to horoscopes, fortune-tellers, and all sorts of false sources of information, hoping to discover what is going to happen in their lives. Although we don't know all the details, God has given us advance information regarding where history is going, how it will end, and how He will create a new heaven and a new earth.

Revelation makes it clear that, in the future, for every person ever born, there is an unavoidable meeting with Jesus Christ. We will meet Him as our Savior, Lord, and conquering King, or we will meet Him as our ultimate Judge. Most people like Jesus as long as they can keep Him in the past. Even unbelievers don't mind talking about Jesus in the past tense, as a great teacher, but Jesus refuses to stay in the past. He wants to be in your present, and you can be absolutely sure He *is* in your future.

HEAVEN IS FOR REAL

In Revelation 21, John told us about the exterior of heaven. Then in Revelation 22 he took us inside our heavenly home, where the first thing we see is the "river of the water of life, clear as crystal, coming from the throne of God and of the Lamb" (v. 1). A similar image of life-giving water is used often in the Bible. To us, that seems a bit strange, although we can all identify with being thirsty. But to a person in the Middle East, where clean, pure water is a rarity and where parched, dry land is more plentiful than lush, well-watered landscapes, water was the difference between life and death.

Some Bible scholars have suggested that this river of the water of life in heaven is symbolic of the life-giving flow of the Holy Spirit, coming from God through the Lamb to us. Jesus once talked about the Holy Spirit producing "rivers of living water" (John 7:38–39) in believers, so such an idea may have some validity. But I personally believe this is a literal scene John witnessed.

John also saw "the tree of life," a reminder, no doubt, of the Tree of the Knowledge of Good and Evil that was in the Garden of Eden (Genesis 2:15–17). Later, the prophet Ezekiel described a similar Tree of Life (Ezekiel 47:12).

But the Tree of Life that John saw in his vision of heaven is different from these trees. This tree bears twelve kinds of fruit, yielding fruit every month. The text doesn't limit the fruit production to only one fruit each month, so it is possible that the fruit may vary as you have need of them, similar to the fruit of the Spirit (Galatians 5:22–23). But perhaps the most important point is that the tree is now accessible to everyone in heaven. The Tree of Life is no longer forbidden. Its leaves are for the healing of the nations, which can also mean it is for the health of the nations (Revelation 22:2). There will be no more physical or spiritual diseases in heaven.

Significantly, John realized that "there will no longer be any curse" (22:3). The curse brought onto human beings by sin began in Eden (Genesis 3:14–19) and carried all the way through to the last page of the Old Testament (Malachi 4:6), closing the old covenant with a curse. But on the cross, Jesus broke the power of the curse, and in heaven, the curse is nowhere to be found. Sin and its power have been destroyed forever! In prison I read every book I could about people who died, went to heaven, and came back. I was fascinated by one person who saw fruit fall off the tree of life and simply disappear before it hit the ground. There is no spoilage, rot, or decay in heaven. The curse of sin has indeed been lifted.

Regarding heaven, John told us, "The throne of God and of the Lamb will be in it, and His bond-servants will serve Him; they will see His face, and His name will be on their foreheads" (Revelation 22:3–4). God Himself will be in the midst of His people, and you will be able to see God's face! Do you realize that not even Moses was permitted to see God's face (Exodus 33:20, 23)? But His servants in heaven will.

John again seemed impressed to tell us there is no longer any night in heaven: "They will not have need of the light of a lamp nor the light of the sun, because the Lord God will illumine them; and they will reign forever and ever" (Revelation 22:5). Notice, too, that believers will reign with Christ. Those who rule also serve, and those who serve also rule.

At this point, it feels as though John's heart was so overwhelmed with the glorious things he saw, it is almost difficult to determine who is speaking in the scripture, but the apostle emphasized the validity of this vision. He began a rapid-fire report, "And he said to me, 'These words are faithful and true'; and the Lord, the God of the spirits of the prophets, sent His angel to show to His bond-servants the things which must soon take place" (v. 6).

John's point was that the same God who inspired the prophets to write also inspired these words as well. As such, they should be taken seriously, because God has provided insider information regarding things that are going to happen soon.

John then heard Jesus declare, "And behold, I am coming quickly. Blessed is he who heeds the words of the prophecy of this book" (22:7). It is as though Jesus is book-ending the vision, since one of the initial messages John heard was that the person who reads, heeds, and obeys these words will be blessed. The vision opens and closes with a similar promise of blessing. Jesus didn't say it would be easy to live for Him, especially through some of the darker days of tribulation, but He emphasizes that it will be worth it!

John added his own affirmation regarding the veracity of the visions he had shared:

> I, John, am the one who heard and saw these things. And when I heard and saw, I fell down to worship at the feet of the angel who showed me these things. But he said to me, "Do not do that. I am a fellow servant of yours and of your brethren the prophets and of those who heed the words of this book. Worship God." (22:8–9)

How different is the angel's attitude from that of some spiritual leaders today, who often encourage people to worship them. But the angel redirected John's enthusiasm and instructed him to present his worship where it belongs—to God.

THE TIME IS NEAR

I believe John felt the vision coming to a close, because the angel gave him some specific instructions that made John's heart pound: "Do not seal up the words of the prophecy of this book, for the time is near" (Revelation

22:10). This is an unusual ending, because the prophet Daniel was told just the opposite: "Seal up the book until the end of time. . . . These words are concealed and sealed up until the end time" (Daniel 12:4, 9). John, however, was instructed *not* to seal this message, because the time is near. The end of the world as we know it. The end of all things. The time is near for the coming of Jesus Christ.

The inevitable consequences of our faith and lifestyle are revealed here, and not even God attempts to change them at this point: "Let whoever is doing evil continue to do evil. Let whoever is unclean continue to be unclean. Let whoever is doing right continue to do right. Let whoever is holy continue to be holy" (Revelation 22:11, NCV). Clearly, right to the end of scripture, there will be some people who insist on living for themselves, and there will be those who want to live with Jesus. God Himself will not force a person to go to heaven if he or she insists on charting his or her own course.

At this point, Jesus moves to center stage in the vision for one last message. And what a message it is! "Behold, I am coming quickly, and My reward is with Me, to render to every man according to what he has done" (v. 12). We will be rewarded on the basis of how well we have served Him.

The message continues: "I am the Alpha and the Omega, the first and the last, the beginning and the end" (22:13). This is the fifth time in Revelation that this message has been repeated for us. We should understand at least three important principles from that. First, we need to grasp the idea of completeness. Jesus is everything you and I need, from A to Z, from the beginning to the end. Moreover, He has everything within Himself. He has need of nothing; He is our Source and our Resource.

Second, the fact that He is the Alpha and Omega indicates His eternal nature. Jesus did not just come on the scene in Bethlehem as a baby. The Christ child may have begun His earthly existence when He was conceived in Mary by the Holy Spirit, but Jesus has been with God from eternity, long before we knew how to measure time.

Third, Jesus is the absolute authority in our life. He is the first and final word on all of human history, from A to Z, and He is the last word on every one of us. As He said of Himself in Revelation 3:14, "The Amen, the faithful and true Witness, the Beginning of the creation of God, says this."

YOU'RE IN OR YOU'RE OUT

One last time He reminds us that not everyone will enter into that eternal kingdom with Him: "Blessed are those who wash their robes, so that they may have the right to the tree of life, and may enter by the gates into the city. Outside are the dogs and the sorcerers and the immoral persons and the murderers and the idolaters, and everyone who loves and practices lying" (Revelation 22:14–15). Those who have washed their robes, who have found forgiveness of their sins through the blood of Jesus, will be able to enter, but there will be those who are outside and not permitted in the New Jerusalem. They have chosen to live eternally with Satan the Dragon rather than accept Jesus as their Savior, and God will honor their choice, as tragic as it may be.

Jesus then authenticates and puts His stamp of approval on the message John was communicating. In doing so, He doesn't refer to Himself as "I, Jesus, the Lion of Judah," or even "the Lamb of God." Instead, He says, "I, Jesus, have sent My angel to testify to you these things for the churches. I am the root and the descendant of David, the bright morning star" (22:16). Both of these illustrations are from the Old Testament, reminding us again that this is one story that God has been telling from Genesis to Revelation.

THE PREEMINENT MESSAGE OF REVELATION

John then recorded a message that is one of the most poignant in the entire Bible. "The Spirit and the bride say, 'Come.' And let the one who hears say, 'Come.' And let the one who is thirsty come; let the one who wishes take the water of life without cost" (Revelation 22:17).

Oh, the wonderful love and grace of our God. To the very last page of your Bible, He says, "Come." And the bride of Christ—the church of Jesus Christ through every age—says "Come!" The offer is still open at this moment to anyone who is thirsty for God. The message rings all the way from Patmos to your house, "Come." Jesus knows you are thirsty. He knows every tear you have shed. He knows the pain you have suffered. And He says, "I came that they may have life, and have it abundantly" (John 10:10). Let him who wishes, take the water of life without cost. The price has already been paid by the One who bids you to come. All you have to do is come and drink.

This offer is reminiscent of the prophet Isaiah's words: "Ho! Every one who thirsts, come to the waters; and you who have no money come, buy and eat. / Come, buy wine and milk / Without money and without cost / Why do you spend money for what is not bread, / And your wages for what does not satisfy? Listen carefully to Me, and eat what is good, / And delight yourself in abundance" (Isaiah 55:1–2). The invitation is still open, the message is the same until the end of time. Come to the living waters, and Jesus will satisfy your soul.

If you are a Christian, don't miss your responsibility in this invitation. It says, "And let the one who hears say, 'Come.'" Remember, from the beginning of the vision, the blessing is for the person who hears the message and heeds it, keeps it, and obeys it. Now, part of that responsibility is to share the message with others, to be His witnesses in the world. We are not merely to say, "Yes, I want to go." We are to say to people who don't know Jesus, "I'm going. Why don't you come along too?" We will rarely convince them with persuasion; we must invite them to join us in love.

A Serious Word of Warning

Just before the close of the book, there is a solemn warning about distorting the message of the vision. Notice the math here: "I testify to everyone who hears the words of the prophecy of this book: if anyone adds to them, God will add to him the plagues which are written in this book; and if anyone takes away from the words of the book of this prophecy, God will take away his part from the tree of life and from the holy city, which are written in this book" (Revelation 22:18–19). Do you get the impression that God wants this message to be delivered intact, in its entirety? If anyone adds to this message in a deliberate attempt to confuse or mislead people, God will add to that person the plagues John described in this book. If a person purposely does not present this message in its fullness, picking and choosing some parts while ignoring other portions, God will subtract that person from His presence. The message is clear and emphatic: do not add to this prophecy and do not subtract anything from it.

OUR KING'S FINAL WORD

I can almost hear King Jesus, the King of kings, the Lord of lords, sounding out the final word of Revelation: "He who testifies to these things says, 'Yes, I am coming quickly'" (22:20). It is both a word of warning and a word of encouragement. Warning that we need to be ready to meet the Lord at any time, and encouragement that no matter how tough life gets, we know that our Lord and Savior, Jesus Christ, is coming back for us, that where He is, we may be also.

The old apostle picked up on Jesus' promise, because you can see the blessed hope in his eyes and hear the anticipation and the longing in his voice as he agrees, "Amen. Come, Lord Jesus" (22:20). Then, almost as though he is awaking from a dream, John addressed his readers one last time: "The grace of the Lord Jesus be with all. Amen" (v. 21).

Some people like to point out in John's farewell that the last word of the Bible is "grace." That is a sweet sentiment, and the grace of God is replete throughout the Bible, including Revelation, but if you look carefully, you will notice that the last word is "Amen." We know what that means. When I was a little boy, that's the word I loved to hear in church, "Amen." Why? Because it means, "It's all over. That's all, folks! It's time to go home. Let it be so." If I had been writing the ending of Revelation instead of John, I might have gotten emotional and excited and had Jesus bellow from the throne room with smoke and lights and all sorts of pyrotechnics, proclaiming one final exhortation, "Get ready! You've had thirty-nine books of the Old Testament and twenty-seven books of the New Testament showing you who I am. So get ready!"

But God did not choose to do it that way. He sent His beloved Son to die on a cross as an atonement for our sins so that we can live in the new home

He is building for us. His Son, who conquered death, made the straight and narrow way for us to follow to that new home. Revelation is not the story of the Antichrist and the end of all we know. It is not the final chapter in the story of our redemption. It is the first chapter of our eternal lives. This is the Revelation of our Lord and Savior Jesus Christ. And yes, He is coming soon!

As we celebrate our victory, we look forward to His soon return. Even so, come, Lord Jesus!

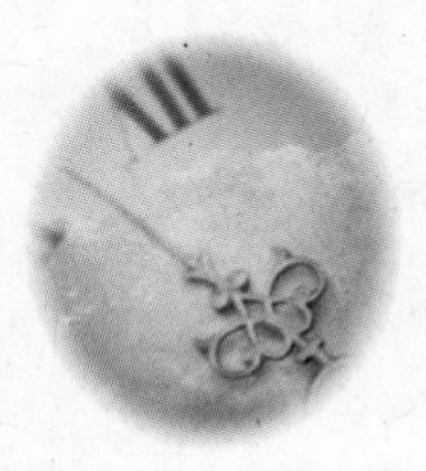

Epilogue: A Final Word

The night before I put the finishing touches on the manuscript for this book, preparing to send it to my publisher, I experienced a powerful dream. In the dream, I was in a town that looked like a movie set. I was seated on a huge movie-like crane, looking down from above. Large trucks filled with hay and straw, merchandise and material goods, rolled through town. It was business as usual for them. People were bustling, scurrying in every direction, as though in mass confusion. Some of them were wearing everyday work clothes while others were dressed to the hilt, decked out as though they were on their way to a lavish wedding.

Some people appeared oblivious to the fact that a wedding was about to occur. Ironically, some of those who believed that it was almost time for the wedding did not know when or where the wedding was to take place. They'd heard there would be a wedding, but they had no idea about the bride or the bridegroom and the beautiful love story that brought them together.

Some of the onlookers were getting impatient. Some were downright ornery and mean, almost as though they were at a church supper and the food wasn't ready. Many of them were getting upset at the bridegroom! But as I watched and listened to their conniptions and complaints, it became obvious that many of these people did not even know the bridegroom; they had merely shown up for the food and drink. Their attitude was, "Bride? Bridegroom? No,

I don't care about them. I'm just here for the party. I've been hearing about this wedding for a long time, so I want in on the action."

Near the close of His Second Coming discourse, Jesus told a story about ten virgins, five of whom were prudent and prepared to meet the bridegroom, and five who were foolish. They all were expecting the bridegroom to come at any time, but when He didn't come exactly on their timetable and according to their plan, they began to get drowsy. By midnight, they had all fallen asleep. Suddenly there was a shout, "Behold the bridegroom! Come out to meet him."

The virgins quickly began trimming their lamps, getting ready to receive the bridegroom they had been awaiting so long. It was then that the foolish virgins realized the folly of their mistaken priorities. They were out of oil. They begged the prudent virgins, "Give us some of your oil, for our lamps are going out."

But the prudent answered, "No, there will not be enough for us and you too; go instead to the dealers and buy some for yourselves."

So the foolish virgins ran to find a dealer who was open after midnight, where they could purchase some last-minute oil.

But they were too late.

While they were gone, the bridegroom came. The virgins who were ready, who had planned ahead and had diligently maintained their watchful attitude, went in with him to the wedding feast.

That would be bad enough, but once those who were prepared for the bridegroom's coming had gone in with him, the door was shut. When the other virgins returned, they said, "Lord, lord, open up for us."

But he answered, "Truly I say to you, I do not know you."

Jesus then drove home the point: "Be on the alert then, for you do not know the day nor the hour" (Matthew 25:1–13).

I believe that is the message of the hour. Be on the alert! Be prepared!

I woke up convinced that God was instructing me to be a clear voice, calling people to get ready for the wedding of the Lamb and His bride. People know that Jesus is supposed to return, and they may even be halfheartedly looking for Him, but they have not committed their lives to Him. Others have allowed their lamps to go out or are running around but going nowhere, dangerously short of oil because of a lack of diligence or perhaps they have been distracted by the things of the world. Regardless, they are not ready for Revelation to be fulfilled. Many people are majoring in minors, fussing about things that are unimportant, while ignoring the fact that the Bridegroom is coming for His bride; the wedding is about to take place!

Other people, even some who have attended church for years, are not ready for the consummation of Revelation. They think they are on their way to heaven merely because, at some point in their life, they made a casual commitment to Christ. They were told that God wanted them to be wealthy, and if they would simply give tacit approval to a tolerant, ultraloving God, they would be welcomed into heaven. They bought into the false message of "Come to Jesus and get food; come to Jesus and get healed; come to Jesus and get everything you want: wealth, ease, fame, power. Whatever you want, you can have it, because, after all, you were destined to be rich." They are focused on their own self-interest, their own pleasures, rather than being concerned about getting ready for the wedding and warning and helping others to prepare in advance. This self-interest flies in the face of Jesus, who pleaded with us not to love the world or the things of the world.

In Matthew 22 Jesus told a story about a king who gave a wedding feast for his son. He sent out servants to invite people to come, yet, shockingly, those who were invited refused to come. So the king sent out other slaves to tell those who were invited, "Behold, I have prepared a great feast and everything is ready. Come to the wedding feast."

But the people paid no attention and went on their way, one to his farm, another to his business. Worse yet, some of those who were invited to the wedding seized the king's servants, mistreated them, and killed them.

The king was enraged. He sent his army and destroyed those murderers and set their city on fire. He then told the servants, "The wedding is ready, but those who were invited were not worthy. Go therefore to the main highways, and as many as you find there, invite to the wedding feast." When the king found some at the wedding who were not prepared by being clothed in white garments, he cast them out (Matthew 22:1–14).

These are stirring stories, and they were not told by some wild-eyed fanatic. They were told by Jesus Christ, the Lamb of God, the King of kings, and Lord of lords. I believe He is giving us a final warning:

Get ready! I am coming soon.

One of the most frightening passages in the Bible is, "Enter by the narrow gate; for wide is the gate and broad is the way that leads to destruction, and there are many who go in by it. Because narrow is the gate and difficult is the way which leads to life, and there are few who find it" (Matthew 7:13–14, NKJV). I fear there are many on the broad way, even in our churches, and they do not know it. They are not focused on the Bridegroom; they are not prepared for the wedding.

In prison, whenever we went to the prison yard, there were grave restrictions on what we could do, including how long we could be out there. I still tremble in fear knowing that if I was in the yard a minute too long or disobeyed a rule, I could have been shot. When I was in the yard, I looked up above the spirals of razor wire on the compound walls, and I could see an image of heaven. I kept my eyes fixed on that heavenly city that God said He had prepared for everyone who loves Him, and peace came to my soul.

As soon as my feet touched the yard, I often thought of a song my dear pastor's wife, an amazing evangelist and singer, Fern Olson, used to sing: "I've Had a Vision of Jesus." I found that if I lived in that vision, and kept my eyes on Jesus, the reality of my present existence seemed tolerable.

I've had a vision of Jesus,
I've caught a glimpse of my Lord,
Down through the clouds He is coming,
Just as He said in His word;
See the bright light in the heavens,
Shining from east to the west,

I've had a vision of Jesus,
Bringing that glad day of rest.
As on the wings of an eagle,
We shall go soaring away,
Over the mountains and valleys,
Past all the cares of the day;
If we but live in the vision,
Just a short time it will be,
Soon the vision will have vanished,
Swallowed in reality.[32]

No matter what circumstances you find yourself in today, look above the situation and keep your eyes on Jesus. Now is the time to get ready. Keep your lamp trimmed and burning. Stay ready and keep watching. The Bridegroom is about to appear. The wedding will take place soon. I want to be there, and I know you do too!

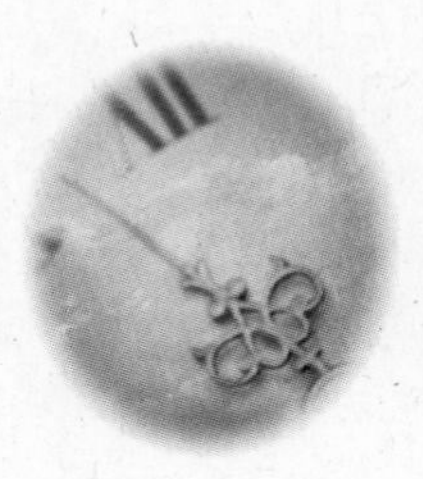

NOTES

1. John 20:31.
2. Revelation 22:20.
3. W. Graham Scroggie, *The Great Unveiling* (Grand Rapids: Zondervan, 1979), 43.
4. 2 Thessalonians 2:2–3, KJV.
5. 2 Thessalonians 2:4, KJV.
6. John 10:27.
7. See Revelation 1:10.
8. 1 Peter 5:13.
9. For more information, see jimbakkershow.com.
10. Jim Bakker, *The Prison Years* (Nashville: Thomas Nelson, 1996).
11. Tim Reid, "Banks foreclosing on churches in record numbers, www.reuters.com, March 9, 2012, http://www.reuters.com/article/2012/03/09/us-usa-housing-churches-idUSBRE82803120120309.
12. Matthew 7:14.
13. Matthew 24:8, NKJV.
14. See Warren Wiersbe, *Be Victorious: In Christ You Are an Overcomer*, 2nd ed. (Colorado Springs: David C. Cook, 2008), 32.

15. See William Barclay, *The Revelation of John*, Daily Study Bible Series, rev. ed., vol. 2 (Philadelphia: Westminster, 1976), 141.
16. *Jim Bakker Show*. #2045. Guest John Kilpatrick. Recorded April 15, 2012.
17. John Shorey, *The Window of the Lord's Return* (August 2010).
18. Shorey, *Window of the Lord's Return,* 114–116. See also www.tribulation.com.
19. Jim Suhr and Steve Karnowski, "U.S. Drought 2012: Current Drought Covers Widest Since 1956," *Huffington Post*, July 17, 2012, www.huffintonpost.com/2012/07/16/us-drought-2012-widest-since-1956_n_16769.
20. See Genesis 41:1–36, 53–57; 42:1–50:26.
21. President Reagan used the image in his 1984 acceptance of the Republican Party nomination and in his January 11, 1989, farewell speech to the nation. See http://www.reagan.utexas.edu/archives/speeches/1984/82384f.htm.
22. There are several population clocks online that incorporate estimates of growth. See, for example, www.worldometers.info/world-population.
23. "Supervolcano," BBC, 2005, www.bbc.co.uk/sn/tvradio/programmes/supervolcano.
24. Charles W. Petit, *U.S. News & World Report,* September 10, 2001, p. 73.
25. See www.templemountfaithful.org.
26. See Barclay, *Revelation of John,* 2:86.
27. See Mike Evans, *Cursed: The Conspiracy to Divide Jerusalem* (Phoenix: Time Worthy, 2010).
28. Shorey, *Window of the Lord's Return*, 113–116. See also www.tribulation-truth.com.
29. Barclay, *Revelation of John,* 2:159.
30. Wiersbe, *Be Victorious,* 117.
31. Barclay, *Revelation of John,* 2:247.
32. "I've Had a Vision of Jesus," words and music by Hattie B. Jones; © Gospel Publishing House, Springfield, MO, 1945, renewed, 1969.

About the Author

Jim Bakker has authored more than a dozen books and is considered to be one of today's experts on the book of Revelation. *The New Jim Bakker Show* is an hour-long daily broadcast seen on over 50 affiliates throughout the United States, over 600 cities in Canada, and in over 200 countries around the world through DIRECT TV and Dish Network. Jim resides in the Branson, Missouri, area.

Recommended Reading

The Prison Years

by
Jim Bakker

The Story of the Shocking Journey from PTL Power to Prison and Back

The media gleefully trumpeted every detail of Jim's dizzying descent from the pinnacle of the multimillion-dollar Heritage US and PTL Television Network to the depths of federal prison. He lost his freedom, his dignity, his confidence in his faith, and eventually, even his wife. In the humiliation, loneliness, and despair of prison, Jim realized that he had to face painful tings about himself that as a free man he had never seen.

In his own words, Jim Bakker tells his story—the glory days as a televangelist, the hostile takeover, the emotional breakdown. He shares how he got to prison, his experiences behind bards, and what God taught him there.

Jim Bakker was wrong about many things. Exactly what they were and how he came to confess them will surprise you and inspire you. This is his story.

1-888-988-1588 • PO Box 7330 Branson, MO 65615 • jimbakkershow.com

Recommended Reading

More Than I Could Ever Ask

by
Lori Graham Bakker

The Story of a Woman, Broken and Defeated, Who Found That Dreams Really Do Come True

Lori was the picture of the perfect church girl: beautiful, blonde, with dimples and eyes that danced with a smile. A series of bad choices found her marrying a handsome bad boy, experimenting with drugs, and finally crawling up on a table in an abortion clinic and assuming the most vulnerable position a woman can be in. How could she ever hear the voice of God again or feel His love in her life? How could she trust a man, give her heart again? Lori Bakker tells all in this candid testimony losing everything, but gaining not just her soul, but her soul mate. It is a story of God's incredible saving grace, not just for unbelievers, but also for believers who have gone astray. It is a story of love, redemption, romance and joy unspeakable.

1-888-988-1588 • PO Box 7330 Branson, MO 65615 • jimbakkershow.com

IF YOU ENJOYED THIS BOOK,
WILL YOU CONSIDER SHARING THE
MESSAGE WITH OTHERS?

- Mention the book in a Facebook post, Twitter update, Pinterest pin, or blog post.
- Recommend this book to those in your small group, book club, workplace, and classes
- Head over to Facebook.com/pastorjimbakker, "LIKE" the page, and post a comment as to what you enjoyed the most
- Tweet "I recommend reading #TimeHasCome by @jim_bakker / / @worthypub"
- Pick up a copy for someone you know who would be challenged and encouraged by this message
- Write a review on amazon.com or bn.com

You can subscribe to Worthy Publishing's newsletter at:
www.worthypublishing.com

Worthy Publishing
Facebook Page

Worthy Publishing
Website